THE
ZELDA
COMPLEX

HOW TO AVOID TOXIC RELATIONSHIPS

JOHN Q. BAUCOM, Ph.D.

Fairview Press
Minneapolis

Published by Fairview Press, 2450 Riverside Avenue South, Minneapolis, MN 55454.

Library of Congress Cataloging -in-Publication Data

Baucom, John Q.
    The Zelda complex: how to avoid toxic relationships / John Baucom.
        p.   cm,
    Includes index.
    ISBN 0-925190-75-6 (alk. paper)
    1. Interpersonal conflict. 2. Interpersonal conflict — Case studies. 3. Fitzgerald, Zelda, 1900-1948. 4. Fitzgerald, F. Scott (Francis Scott), 1896-1940. I. Title.
    BF637.I48B38   1995
    158'.2 — dc20   95-23635
                                                                                                              CIP

First Printing: January 1996

Printed in the U.S.A.
00 99 98 97 96   1 2 3 4 5 6 7

Publisher's note: Fairview Press publishes books and other materials related to the subjects of family and social issues. Its publications, including *The Zelda Complex*, do not necessarily reflect the philosophy of Fairview Hospital and Healthcare Services or their treatment programs.

To the memory of Zelda Sayre Fitzgerald —
and all the other Zeldas everywhere

ACKNOWLEDGMENTS

My greatest thanks to the various people who have contributed to this book. The first and foremost are Bud and LA. It is not a cliché to say that without them *The Zelda Complex* would not have been written.

Many others have helped in various ways, including contributions of editing, quotations, and metaphors. My personal thanks go to Roy Glenn, John Thornton, Leah O'Neal, Mary Bryant, Barry Wagner, Deana Hilbert, Carol Rogers, Lois Smith, Harrison Bierman, Katie McKnight, Jeremy Fox, Julie Smith, and Deborah Bihler.

Quotations from and excerpts of letters by F. Scott and Zelda Fitzgerald, unless otherwise noted, are reproduced from *The Romantic Egoists*, by Matthew J. Bruccoli, Scottie Fitzgerald Smith, and Joan P. Kerr.

Lyrics from "So Close" are from *Change of Seasons*, a Daryl Hall and John Oates album (Arista, 1990).

Contents

Chapter 1

A PRESCRIPTION FOR AFFLICTION
AN INTRODUCTION TO THE ZELDA COMPLEX

There's a restless look in your eye tonight
There's a secret hurt in my heart
And the dream that pulls us together girl is a dream
That's gonna tear us apart.
—Daryl Hall and George Green, "So Close"

I didn't discover the Zelda Complex.
I lived it.
I had observed it in others for years. After experiencing my own Zelda relationship, I began thinking about it in a different way. The end result was this book. Had I not lived it first—in all its melodramatic intensity—I never could have understood the Zelda Complex.

I had spent my entire adult life as a so-called expert on human behavior and interpersonal relationships. I had been a psychotherapist, college teacher, and speaker on a variety of topics dealing with human behavior. I was busy. Probably too busy. Most people would have described me as successful when I experienced the Zelda Complex firsthand. The truth was, I had become a workaholic. I was getting my emotional needs met by fixing other people's lives, and ignoring my own. I avoided my marriage, until my wife gave me a divorce and the custody of our two young boys, ages five and seven.

It was the first of four major wake-up calls I would experience over the next two years. I begged her to stay. But it was too late. I had already done the damage. And she left.

Out of necessity, I dealt with my pain quickly by busying myself. I buried myself in being a single parent and a self-employed businessman. I returned to my workaholic pattern, and in many ways probably became worse. I attempted to overcompensate for my children's loss of their mother by becoming a *dadaholic*. I worked, parented, and did almost nothing else.

My ex-wife had been my best friend, and later my wife. Our marriage had been extremely calm. At times, it was almost boring. Obviously, *calm* doesn't necessarily mean *healthy*, as I later discovered on a personal level. It mirrored most of my relationships up to that point in my life: They were calm, rational, and reciprocal. Then I met my own Zelda, and it was time for the second wake-up call.

In retrospect, as I later described to a friend, we were like two comets colliding. When she blasted into my life, I was at my lowest. Perhaps it was my emotional condition, or who she was, or some combination of the two. Whatever the ingredients, the result was toxic. I became intoxicated. She was everything I wasn't. She was fiery, passionate, and seductive. What she lacked in emotional stability, she made up for in undiluted sexuality. The relationship quickly became the only mood-altering drug I had ever used. It was filled with melodramatic intensity, punctuated by attempts at manipulation and excessive surges in adrenaline. Within days, I thought I was in love. Two weeks later, she moved into my house under the pretext of helping with the boys. Perhaps she was helpful for a brief period of time. Unfortunately, I was too busy to notice.

According to my Zelda, she had been in love with me for years. She had attended, by her estimate, more than a dozen speaking engagements or seminars I'd conducted. I had noticed her on several occasions, but thought nothing about it. She claimed it was the way I communicated and my emotional honesty that had attracted her. I was married at the time, so she didn't express her feelings outwardly. After discovering I was divorced, however, she began her pursuit. Initially it was phone calls and greeting cards. Then it was invitations to go out together. Shortly afterwards it was sexual overtures to which I was extremely vulnerable. She pretended to be compassionate, helpful, and nurturing toward the children. The energy expended by pretending, however, soon exhausted her, and the truth began to surface.

The relationship began to deteriorate. Like an addiction, it became a chronic, progressive, debilitating disorder. We rotated between arguing, feeling insecure, and then making up passionately. The resulting chaos left little time for anything else. Like illness is to a cancer patient, the sickness of this relationship had become the center of my life. I received numerous invitations to speak or conduct seminars, most of which I turned down. Immediately prior to my third wake-up call, I received another invitation to speak. For some reason I accepted this one and asked my Zelda to attend. It was either a grand mistake or a grand awakening, depending upon one's point of view.

I was speaking at a student assembly at Baylor School, a large prestigious high school in Chattanooga. I had prepared well for my topic but was not prepared for the response. Adolescents are an extremely difficult audience. The younger the audience, the more time I spend in preparation. Even so, the reception is usually lukewarm at best. This time the response was overwhelmingly positive from both students and faculty. I was mobbed on the podium after my presentation. When the crowd thinned, I finally saw the object of my obsession. She had been sitting in the back as promised. But while everyone else was smiling and complimentary, there she stood with her arms crossed and a scowl on her face.

"What's wrong?" I asked. "Did something happen?" I feared she'd had car trouble or something else had gone wrong. "Did you get here in time to listen to my entire speech?"

"I sure did." She nodded her head back and forth disapprovingly.

"So, what's the problem?" I asked. "What happened?"

"Oh nothing," she shook her head sarcastically. "You just didn't say anything about me. I thought you might talk about how wonderful I am, or at least mention how lucky you are to be with me now."

I paused, trying to formulate a response. Finally I stuttered, "Well . . . you see . . ." As I look back on it, I realize I was actually trying to defend myself as though I'd done something wrong. "See, I was here to talk to a bunch of high school kids, and . . . you know, they don't really care about *you* . . . or *us* . . . I mean . . . they don't really care about *our* relationship. And—"

"Well!" She turned dramatically to walk out. "You'll live to regret this." It wasn't the last time I'd hear that threat from her.

Marriage is the only adventure open to the cowardly.

—Voltaire

The next morning, I received a telephone call from Gordon Connell, a close friend of mine who coaches wrestling at McCallie School, a rival high school in the area. "Did you speak at Baylor yesterday?"

"Yeah." I laughed. "Don't worry. I'll be glad to speak to your students as well—"

"No," he interrupted me. "That's not why I called. Have you read the sports section in today's paper?"

"No," I responded curiously. "Not yet. Why?"

"A girl from Baylor's softball team quoted your speech in the paper. She said it made her believe in herself and helped her pitch a no-hitter yesterday. You know, they were incredible underdogs in that tournament. No one figured they had a chance." He continued to read the article to me.

I was admittedly excited as a result of the phone call from Gordon and hung up rather quickly. I drove to a nearby convenience market and purchased a copy of the newspaper. Then I rushed back to read the article to my Zelda. Frankly, I wanted her approval. I really wanted to demonstrate that my speech was meaningful to the students, despite my not mentioning how wonderful she was. I wanted her to tell me she was proud of me, or that she loved me. Or at least say she understood. At worst, I figured she would nod her head and say, "Great!"

I was wrong. Wake-up call number three was about to occur.

After listening to me read the article, she jumped up. "Damn you!" she screamed as she ran out of the room. I sat in my chair, stunned by her reaction. I had no idea what to do. I was more than puzzled; I had become almost emotionally immobilized. I eventually got up and sauntered into the office where my colleague Bud was working. I asked him if he had a few minutes to talk. "Sure," he responded, nodding his head. I described the entire series of events leading up to the conversation that morning. "You know," Bud squinted his eyes, "I've been watching you for some time with this gal. She reminds me of Zelda Fitzgerald. Do you remember reading about her in college? She was married to F. Scott Fitzgerald. Do you remember anything about the relationship?"

I nodded my head. "Yeah," I sighed, leaning back in the rocking chair. "I know a little bit about her. She had a lot of emotional problems after marrying Scott and ultimately was sent to a hospital or an asylum. I think she committed suicide or something like that. Why?"

"Well," he continued. "They had a relationship a lot like yours with this young lady. Zelda just couldn't handle Scott's success and it blew her away. I think that's what's going on here. You've got you a little Zelda here." Bud continued to offer his observations and interpretation. "She just can't handle your notoriety—even though that's what attracted her. She needs the recognition for herself. Don't you remember her saying she always wanted to be a star?"

"You're right," I replied, nodding my head. "I do remember. In fact she was nicknamed Star as a child." I gazed out the window, lost in thought.

Several hours later, I spoke to Kathy Pascal, a friend of mine and wife of a popular, local TV weatherman. We had a general discussion about how Kathy handled her spouse's notoriety. Then, almost as an afterthought, I asked her if she remembered the story of Zelda Fitzgerald.

"Oh, yeah!" Kathy replied quickly. "She was a very talented lady who was driven insane by her husband's drinking and womanizing." I laughed, noting the two vastly different perspectives, obviously coming from different genders. But it piqued my curiosity. The embryo for the concept of the Zelda Complex was born.

Less than an hour later, however, I stopped laughing. I was confronted by my staff. They had gotten together after my discussion with Bud, and decided to discuss some business problems with me. It wasn't unusual for us to have such a discussion. We have very open relationships in my office and discuss business and personal lives quite often. But the content of this discussion was different. They brought my Zelda relationship to the table. Over time, they suggested, this relationship had begun to adversely affect the business. I made several futile attempts to defend myself and rationalize my behavior. Finally, out of exasperation, they became more direct. Then LA played the staff's trump card.

"John, you simply aren't hearing us," she suggested calmly but sternly. "This relationship is destroying you, your boys, and the business. We care about you a lot. And we'll put up with almost anything. But we're not going to sit back and watch this happen. You can do whatever you want to with your personal life. But we've all made a decision. We're not going to sit back and watch this any longer. You're out of control. You need to get some help or you're going to destroy the business. It's that simple."

It was finally time to wake up.

Alas! The love of women! It is known to be a lovely and a fearful thing.
—Lord Byron, *Don Juan*

Several weeks later, I sat in my office across from a man visiting for his first counseling session. His story was uncomfortably familiar. As I listened, I thought to myself, Not only have I lived this but I've seen it in hundreds of others. I was beginning to see the true significance of the Zelda Complex. It was like watching a movie for the third time, and finally getting the point.

"I don't know," he leaned toward me. "I guess I'm crazy. One of us is, anyway. I was married to my wife for ten years. To me it was the best ten years of my life." He shook his head.

"Hell, I was ecstatic in the marriage. But she wanted a divorce, so I let her go. I let her have everything. We even went out to lunch together the day of the court hearing, and I paid for it! I was miserable, but I figured it was better to be friends than enemies. Now, it's like everything has changed. Everything was fine till I started getting serious about Sheri. Then my ex went psycho! She even broke into my house when she saw Sheri's car parked out front one night. We've been divorced for two years now! I ended up calling the police. Man! It was a big deal—me being a paramedic and everything. I guess if I really had to say it, I do still love her to a certain extent, but she's the one who wanted out. Now I want to get on with my life. I don't understand her reaction. It's so strange." He leaned back, looking at the floor.

I cleared my throat and gazed at the floor with him. "What happened that led up to the divorce?" I asked. "I mean, why did she decide she wanted out? It sounds like you were good friends and had a great marriage. You had lunch together after the court hearing. That's pretty unusual. If y'all were so friendly, why did she want out anyway?"

"It's a long story," he sighed. "And I'm not really sure I even understand it. I've thought about it a lot and it's beginning to make a little bit of sense to me. I don't know, maybe it will make more sense to you."

I laughed softly. If he only knew, I mumbled to myself.

"When we first got together everything was great," he continued. "We had a lot of financial problems and there was a lot of pressure, but other than that we were really happy. Then I got my job as a paramedic. Ever since I was a kid, I had wanted to be a paramedic. I used to watch the TV shows. I wanted to save people in real life like they did on television. Now, I had finally made it. I started making a little bit more money. I was promoted quickly. Things got even better financially. Then I got a second job driving a truck on my days off. You know how it is as a paramedic— twenty-four on and twenty-four off.

"Well, within a two-year period I had tripled my income. And people would stop me and ask how things were going. You know, we'd be out together and someone would want to know about this fire call or that emergency call, and I'd stop and talk to them. And I'd look over at her and there she'd be! Standing there with her arms crossed, tapping her foot, rolling her eyes, and saying stuff like, 'Well, I guess your wife's just too damn boring for anybody to ask about!' It was confusing at first. I didn't understand why it was such a big deal to her.

"Later, I realized that up to that point she had always been the center of attention. She was spoiled rotten by her parents. She was the only girl in a family with three older brothers. Then she married me. I was best friends with one of her brothers. She was five years younger than me, and I reckon I spoiled her a little bit too. She was real cute; people had always complimented her looks. I guess all of a sudden she just wasn't the center of attention anymore. And maybe she couldn't deal with it. So, she thought she wanted out. But maybe what she really wanted was to be the center of attention again! I don't really know."

His story, as well as mine, is far too common. Every day I hear about relationships destroyed by the same qualities that brought the two people together. Zelda's romantic tragedy with Scott was the archetype. It serves as a perfect model, because it encompasses so many of the symptoms discussed in this book. Their relationship is covered comprehensively in chapter 2. A brief synopsis is presented here to give you an idea of where the Zelda Complex got its name.

> *Speak of me as I am ... one that loved not wisely but too well.*
> —Shakespeare, *Othello*

Scott and Zelda met in a country club outside of Montgomery, Alabama, at a military base called Camp Sheridan. It was July 1918. Zelda was "gorgeous, precocious, and wild as a buck," as described by one elderly lady who claims to have met her. Scott was a twenty-two-year-old infantry officer. He was rather small and somewhat insecure. Even then, he was incredibly creative. At the time they met, Zelda was the spoiled, eighteen-year-old daughter of a Montgomery judge. They had an intense two-month courtship, filled with passion, rage, and jealousy. It was a pattern they repeated for the following twenty-odd years. The resulting marriage included, among other things: violent arguments;

suicide attempts; multiple affairs; bouts with alcoholism; arrests; fist fights; multiple psychiatric hospitalizations; periods of separation; incredible passion; several books; and one daughter.

Taken separately, each of them was individually brilliant. Scott's literary success has been well documented. But by some suggestions, Zelda was even more talented, though obviously less successful commercially. However, she was an accomplished dancer who was offered the lead in a Naples ballet in 1929. Her paintings are still on display in museums throughout the South. Her literary work was purportedly copied by Scott and used profusely in *The Beautiful and the Damned*, as well as in several other books of his. Some even describe *Tender is the Night* as nothing more than a description of his relationship with Zelda. Their literary competitiveness became an object of dissension between them and was at the root of many of their arguments.

Scott had forbidden Zelda to draw from their lives in her writings, but he borrowed extensively from their shared experiences in his own. Individually, they could have been creatively productive talents who continued vibrantly into their elderly years. Together, they became initially dangerous, and later extremely destructive. Ultimately the relationship was deadly. They couldn't stay away from each other, yet together they were like a combustible chemical mixture.

Sodium and water are two harmless substances. When we hear *sodium* most of us think of sodium chloride, or table salt. Chemically speaking, however, the element sodium is really a metal. By itself, it's harmless, and useful in many scientific applications. It combines with many other elements—such as chlorine—to provide compounds immensely beneficial to life.

When mixed with water, however, sodium is volatile and potentially dangerous. No catalyst is required. Simply drop a piece of sodium the size of a pencil eraser into a test tube of water and you get fireworks. In fact, sodium must be stored in kerosene to keep it away from moisture. Sodium and water separately are not bad. Together, however, they create a combustible and potentially dangerous reaction. A more serious example of this was the Oklahoma City disaster in April 1995. The simple combination of fertilizer and diesel fuel resulted in an explosion that took more than 165 lives. It was not only combustible, but deadly on a massive scale.

People can do the same thing. Two very healthy people can form a relationship that bears no resemblance to the sum of its parts. Zelda and Scott represented this very dramatically. The paramedic and his wife had the same reaction. So did I in my Zelda relationship. And probably so have you at one time or another. The Zelda Complex can happen to anyone, in virtually any kind of relationship. It obviously happens within romantic liaisons. But it can occur in other relationships as well. Siblings can experience the Zelda Complex. Business partners can. Social friends have been known to develop toxicity in their relationships. Teammates on professional sports teams have experienced problems with the Zelda Complex. I have worked with them, and corporations as well. The Zelda Complex can occur any time a particular mixture of personalities becomes combustible. The resulting explosion affects not only them, but others around them.

The Zelda Complex I experienced affected a number of people: my children, my business, and my extended family. Similarly, it had an adverse effect on my Zelda's job, her extended family, and several of her close friends. People in the community who knew us were also adversely affected. Many people who had confidence in me as a psychotherapist lost it as a result of the Zelda Complex I experienced. At the same time, people also lost confidence in the Clinton White House because of Zelda Complexes among high-level staff members and nominees. The Zelda Complex concerns more than romantic liaisons. It's everywhere. And it's about you.

> *The greatest griefs are those we cause ourselves.*
> —Sophocles, *Oedipus Rex*

We find the Zelda Complex throughout history, among Samson and Delilah, Romeo and Juliet, and certainly King Henry VIII and several of his wives. Any time two people come together and produce a combustible result, a Zelda Complex has occurred. I saw it repeatedly in clients who came to me for marriage counseling. I heard about it frequently from people who were depressed and seeking psychotherapy after divorce. And I replayed my own experience with the Zelda Complex thousands of times in my mind. Yet, try as I might, I could find no material in textbooks documenting such a phenomenon. The pattern seemed common. The phenomenon seemed real. For lack of a better term, I began calling it the Zelda Complex.

Formulating the Zelda Complex made sense of concepts that had puzzled me for a long time. For years I had been asked questions on radio talk shows I was unable to answer. For example, I often wondered why individuals got married and then spent the rest of their lives avoiding each other. While it's true that marriage brought added responsibilities that made it difficult to have private time together, many couples appeared to go out of their way to avoid one another. I had seen this pattern often. I called it intimacy avoidance, but later realized it marked the beginning stage of the Zelda Complex. Some couples don't advance beyond this stage, dancing in and out of it throughout their relationship. Others spend little time here and progress to later stages. Regardless, intimacy avoidance can take many forms. Most often, it resembles a dance. But it's a dance of shadows or images—a dance in which neither partner ever actually gets close to the other. People waste their entire lives dancing around, yet never touching their partner. As a result, they never know their partner. They only know the image. They never achieve true intimacy.

Zelda and Scott didn't either. They experienced passion. They lived life intensely. They went through intense highs and frightening lows. And all the while they ran from intimacy, and from each other. This pattern ultimately led to Scott's increasingly debilitating alcoholism and early death. Simultaneously, it put Zelda on her long journey toward incapacitating mental illness and ultimately permanent psychiatric hospitalization.

The Zelda Complex answered another question and identified a second pattern I saw among couples. Over the years as a therapist, I'd noticed people repeating unfinished business they began in their families of origin and carried with them into adulthood. Occasionally, this unfinished business was with one or both parents. It surfaced in marriages. Occasionally, I noticed it occurring with supervisors, employees, or other authority figures in the workplace. Some people even perpetuated sibling rivalry with co-workers, or chose spouses with whom they could compete. This pattern is Stage Two of the Zelda Complex. It often continues to the point of self-destruction and always ends unhappily.

The third pattern, Stage Three, concerned people who came into my office appearing to be in the throes of an identity crisis. Many times they were women, but not always. In general, these women were married to a spouse whom they considered more successful than they were. They may have been satisfied with their relationship at one point, but the inequity had become so great they were now in terrific pain. Being the wife of Mr. District Attorney, or so-and-so's mom was no longer fulfilling. One lady I saw was the wife of a workaholic husband who spent her days carpooling kids and her nights watching TV by herself. Another was a third-generation brick layer whose wife worked as a secretary in an insurance office and made more money than he did. Still another was a brilliant, underachieving college graduate who married a doctor "because she couldn't be one." Each of these individuals was tormented by their spouse's identity and their own perceived lack of achievement. This theme was also recurrent in the Fitzgeralds' relationship. Scott never felt he had "arrived" as a writer and Zelda never managed to carve out an identity of her own.

The Zelda Complex answered a fourth question. We all know people who have remained in abusive circumstances. Society is full of couples who remain together despite physical abuse, emotional cruelty, or general incompatibility. These people may be well educated, employed in high-level positions of responsibility, and appear to be pictures of success. Yet on weekends he gets intoxicated, on alcohol or rage. His girlfriend throws kitchen knives at him. He ends up chasing her down the interstate shooting at her car with his revolver. Behind him, all this time, his wife is chasing him. All the while, he remains married, visits his girlfriend when things have cooled down, and the pattern is repeated over again. Both of the Fitzgeralds contemplated divorce at one time during their relationship. Though they were emotionally and physically abusive toward each other, neither was able to stay away for very long. In fact, Scott seemed to be most creative when his relationship with Zelda was at its most chaotic. Unable to remain by themselves, they lived cycling through the various stages of the Zelda Complex.

Couples walk into my office every day. They appear to be two extremely rational people by themselves. It is only when they are together in a relationship that they become explosive. Once away from each other, through breakup or divorce, they are alone, individually happy, and rational once again. I saw this pattern many times, yet had no explanation for it. Sodium and water mixed together result in a combustible combination. So did Zelda and Scott. And so could you and your partners in life.

Wisdom consists in being able to distinguish among dangers and make a choice of the least harmful.
—Machiavelli, *The Prince*

By the time I entered my own Zelda Complex, I had been a therapist for more than eighteen years. I'd worked in psychiatric hospitals, alcohol and drug-treatment centers, and outpatient clinics. I had been in private practice, taught at a major university, and shared the speaker's podium with senators, stars, and the surgeon general. I never suspected I would be vulnerable to such a toxic relationship. Although I had observed the phenomenon in others, I didn't even know about the Zelda Complex. As I look back on my slow but methodical journey into the Zelda Complex, I began to wonder how many thousands of others take a similar path without any awareness. And I marvel at the seduction and the ultimate addiction of it all.

You have likely either observed or participated in such a relationship during your life. You may be in one currently or about to enter one. How do you know if you are? And if you are, what do you do about it? The Zelda Complex consists of twenty-five factors. Each factor can be looked at descriptively or prescriptively. It can describe the symptoms of the Zelda Complex. It also prescribes what to look for if you want to change the phenomenon. Your ultimate recovery from the Zelda Complex is an intensely personal process. Others can educate you. But only you have the ability to recover.

Acknowledging that you have the problem and understanding it is the beginning of your journey to health. As you read these factors the first time, simply make an attempt to understand them. At the end of this chapter, a test is included to help you evaluate how far along the path you have traveled.

Basic Factors

Factor One: One person cannot experience the Zelda Complex individually. It requires at least two people. The Zelda Complex can and does happen in intense romantic relationships. It also happens in families. Additionally, it can happen in organizations such as corporations, work groups and sports teams. It can happen with siblings, friends, or an institution such as a church or hospital. While it requires at least two people, the ultimate Zelda Complex will affect far more than those primarily involved.

Factor Two: For the Zelda Complex to occur, the two or more people involved must interact. It's not their mere presence that leads to the dysfunction. Interaction is necessary. The two people must communicate for the Zelda Complex to occur. The higher the expectations of the relationship, the greater the possibility of the Zelda Complex.

Factor Three: If two healthy people enter a relationship, the nature of the relationship can still result in an explosive reaction. These people can be perfectly healthy on their own, yet when joined together, for some undefined reason, they can become irrational, dangerous, and even deadly to each other. Obviously, the Zelda Complex can also occur between two people who are relatively unhealthy emotionally.

Factor Four: Typically, both participants of the Zelda Complex will gradually become psychologically symptomatic. Each partner will eventually act out in a marked and visible way, but the psychologically weaker of the two will usually act out first. In the Fitzgeralds' relationship, Zelda acted out before Scott. Ultimately, however, both became handicapped by the Complex. And in fact, Scott died first.

FACTORS INVOLVING FAMILY BACKGROUND

Factor Five: Zeldas have an intense need for approval. Occasionally this need stems from an extended family relationship. For example, a person who never experienced approval from his or her parents may continue to strive for it in some other relationship, usually with a loved one, an authority figure, or someone to whom they give control. Although both individuals experiencing the Zelda Complex may ultimately suffer psychological pain, it is usually the one who has the greatest need for approval who is most vulnerable. It is this vulnerability that weakens his or her position within the relationship. Partners may also alternate between positions. One may need approval more than the other at one phase of the relationship and then later shift roles. It is important to understand that both members of the Zelda Complex seek approval, yet the intensity with which they seek it will almost always vary.

Factor Six: At least one participant was usually spoiled or indulged as a child, and possibly as an adult as well. The resulting sense of entitlement leads this person to believe he or she is entitled to attention and happiness and should not necessarily have to earn it. Further, this person feels entitled to success, fame, and to be taken care of without paying the requisite price. In fact, the person with strong feelings of entitlement doesn't want to work for or earn anything. He or she simply feels it's owed, as a birthright. It is rare to find a strong sense of entitlement in both members of the Zelda Complex. When that is the case, however, the stage of toxicity will be reached much more quickly. Furthermore, the higher the sense of entitlement in the relationship, the less satisfying the relationship often turns out to be. The general rule is this: the more entitlement exists, the less successful the relationship. In marriage, a strong sense of entitlement yields many problems as well. A person who experiences a high degree of entitlement will rarely work on a marriage. He or she feel entitled to a good marriage, just as he or she feels entitled to happiness. If the marriage doesn't come easily, this person is more likely to seek stimulation elsewhere, or simply leave the marriage. When forced to accept responsibility, a person with strong feelings of entitlement can become depressed, and may exhibit self-destructive behavior, or even consider suicide.

Factor Seven: Zelda Complexes usually originate in families with long histories of mental illness, suicide, and alcoholism or drug abuse. It's often the case that Zeldas were parented by someone in a similar relationship. If not in the midst of a highly toxic relationship, their parents would at least have been in a very dissatisfying one. It's also likely that Zeldas come from families of excess. Sometimes this is an excess of money or privilege; other times, an excess of emotion. The combination of excess and disturbing behavior do not necessarily go together, but when they do, there is a much greater likelihood that tremendous difficulty will be realized in later relationships.

FACTORS OF ACHIEVEMENT

Factor Eight: People who experience the Zelda Complex are usually fiercely competent. They have achieved, but when judged by potential, they would most often be considered underachievers. They are capable, brilliant, and oftentimes gifted. But at least one member of the relationship has usually not achieved anywhere near his or her potential. This may also be true of both partners. Fascinatingly enough, in a Zelda Complex both people cannot achieve simultaneously. One partner will always be underachieving. Though Zeldas may contribute to their spouse's careers in various ways, achievement on their own is rare. This ultimately leads to jealousy or rivalry, and in some cases can perpetuate a degree of toxicity.

Factor Nine: The Zelda Complex requires participants who have above-average intelligence. It rarely occurs among the uninformed or ignorant.

Zeldas are usually highly intelligent, extremely creative people. This does not reduce their insecurity level, however. In fact, it often increases it. Zeldas are typically intelligent enough to realize something is lacking in their lives, but not astute enough to solve it. Many are very skilled in technical or academic areas, for example, but extremely weak when it comes to relationships. You will often find Zeldas among either one of two extremes: individuals completely cut off from their emotions, or intoxicated by them. There is usually very little balance. The result: an extremely intelligent person who is highly frustrated by an inability to solve his or her own problems.

Factor Ten: Zelda Complex relationships are usually extremely competitive. For whatever reason, Zelda Complex participants feel competitive toward each other. This competitiveness is often masked by superficial niceties or disguised under an intensely sexual relationship. And it often leads to a love-hate cycle within the relationship—a cycle that can develop into extreme hostility. Yet the couples remain dependent on each other. This hostile-dependent cycle can grow so pervasive that it eventually defines the relationship. At a minimum, the two Zelda participants will be extremely competitive. At the other extreme, however, the hostile-dependent cycle becomes overwhelming and ultimately controls the participants' lives.

Factor Eleven: In all Zelda Complexes there is a lack of appreciation. This usually results in one partner feeling unworthy. Occasionally one partner will divvy out the slightest amount of appreciation, whetting the other's appetite, but not satisfying his or her need to be appreciated. This intermittent reinforcement prevents the other partner from completely cutting off the relationship, but does not satisfy him or her, either. It creates a sickening pattern of control—a pattern of one partner continually coming back for more. And a pattern that often leads to serious abuse. This abuse can be physical, emotional, or verbal. Yet the abused partner will hold on, continuing to seek appreciation within the Zelda relationship.

Factor Twelve: The Zelda Complex is characterized by the inability of one partner to handle the perceived success of the other. This resembles jealousy, but goes beyond it. The emphasis here is on *perceived* success. It's not necessarily the case that one partner is visibly more successful. Rather, it is that one receives more attention than the other. This attention is interpreted as success, and the partner's inability to handle it is often what leads to initial conflict. This is often the central core conflict in the

Zelda Complex; occasionally it is the only one. When couples expand this factor, it becomes the focus of the relationship.

FACTORS INVOLVING ROLE PLAYING

Factor Thirteen: Zeldas usually identify with traditional gender roles. Men who experience the Zelda Complex typically fall on the masculine, or macho, side, whereas female members who experience the Zelda relationship are usually quite attractive and feminine. Both are usually successful professionally and would be perceived as socially attractive. In many ways, Zeldas are caricatures of traditionally defined male and female roles. Social appearance is very important; these people will invest a great deal of time in looking good within traditional definitions of how men and women are supposed to look.

Factor Fourteen: The Zelda Complex includes at least one member who boldly misrepresents him- or herself. This is more than pretending to be someone else, however. Zeldas can expend great energy pretending, or faking, their way into a relationship. They claim competence where there is none. They cite expertise, which ultimately leads to trouble. They pass themselves off as something and someone they're not. It takes incredible energy to pretend on such a level, however. Once the relationship is formalized and relaxed, the pathology surfaces. Unfortunately, Zeldas are blessed with such dramatic flair that when detected, it is woefully late for the relationship. Their partner has already fallen in love, but with a fabricated role, rather than a real person. What Zeldas do is far beyond the classic con. They are actors and actresses of academy-award-winning caliber. They put all their energy into playing a role rather than being authentic. When that energy is expended, they usually end up moving outside of the relationship and starting the cycle again.

Factor Fifteen: It may appear as though one participant in the Zelda Complex is the persecutor and the other a victim. At first this may be the case. In a fully developed Zelda Complex, however, participants eventually switch roles. They alternate between persecutor, victim, and even rescuer on a regular basis. There are no good guys or bad guys in the Zelda Complex. There are participants. Before the relationship ends, both partners will have played every role. To Zeldas, life is melodramatic. Each participant is willing to play the victim occasionally, simply for the dramatic virtue. Anything else would be boring.

Factor Sixteen: At least one participant in the Zelda Complex is extremely insecure. Zeldas cannot get enough of things; they depend on things rather than on people. They are not beyond using sex, emotional blackmail, or even pregnancy, to manipulate their partner. Zeldas trust things. They can control things. They can manipulate things. They can own things. They cannot do the same with people. Infants are the exception. As the child grows and develops a will of his or her own, Zeldas have increasing difficulty parenting. A car can be controlled. People, on the other hand, don't want to be controlled. They can repudiate the Zeldas' whims. True Zeldas do not trust people, but look instead to jewelry, cars, and homes to build a sense of security. On many occasions, they have far more difficulty leaving things behind, rather than leaving people.

FACTORS OF UNREALISTIC EXPECTATIONS

Factor Seventeen: Zeldas have tremendous difficulty defining love. They usually have extremely unrealistic and immature expectations of what love is going to do for them. They look to relationships as salvation for their misery. Zeldas expect to take from a relationship without offering much in return. As a result, they become extremely disappointed and usually act out when their immature and unrealistic expectations are not met. As children, Zeldas pout; as teenagers, they often have outbreaks of temper. As adults, they usually suffer from depression, have nervous breakdowns, and often experience long-term hospitalizations. These are all a result of feeling they are not getting what they deserve from love. The more unrealistic the expectations, the further the drop will be when those expectations are not met. Zeldas often grow up with storybook fantasies of how life should be. And because most of their expectations are unrealistic, they never seem to find happiness. Zeldas are looking outside of themselves for answers. They look to others. They look to drugs. And they look to things.

Factor Eighteen: In almost all cases of the Zelda Complex, one partner enters the relationship with somebody he or she would actually like to become. In a marriage or romantic relationship, Zeldas are often attracted to people they want to emulate. If it's a professional relationship, they may experience the Zelda Complex with someone they envy. Yet it goes beyond empathic envy. The Zelda Complex is an over-identification with another to the point of actually wanting to take on the qualities and characteristics of that person, sometimes to the point of wanting to consume the other person. Less dangerous is the belief a partner's success will convey upon one's self some sort of prominence or notoriety through osmosis. Sometimes it does. More often than not, however, it doesn't, and thus the relationship fails to satisfy the neediness Zeldas experience on a deeper level.

Factor Nineteen: The Zelda Complex will always involve some degree of intimacy avoidance. Zelda partners will often remain at a toxic level as a way of avoiding the risks of intimacy. This is not to say Zeldas don't want intimacy; normally they want it desperately. It's the risk associated with intimacy that they're dodging. They actually fear rejection, loss of love, and the pain associated with an open, honest relationship. Zeldas are not skilled at coping with pain. They associate tremendous pain with seeking intimacy. As a result, they avoid intimacy as a way of avoiding the pain.

Factor Twenty: Usually people in long-term Zelda Complexes are very dependent. They feel insufficient on their own, like they're never quite enough. They grow dependent on alcohol, people, drugs, and external stimulation. They are constantly looking for answers outside of themselves, and, as a result, can end up in very deep trouble when the things they depend on are not present. Often they look to their partner to "fill them up," looking at the relationship as a crutch. And when it ultimately fails them, as it always will, they look to something else. Zeldas are continuously searching for some easy, magical solution to their loneliness and diseased soul. But they never find it. As with those of their namesake, Zelda Fitzgerald, Zeldas' fantasies eventually go up in smoke.

HIGH-RISK FACTORS

Factor Twenty-One: High emotional energy characterizes the Zelda Complex. This energy may be pain or pleasure. But it is always intense. The Zelda Complex embodies passion in its purest form. Anger, laughter, sadness—they are all present, and each at its most intense. There is a constant element of toxic energy between Zelda participants. From their first meeting, there appears to be an almost biological or pheromonal reaction, on a visceral, palpable level. This primal response is not necessarily unhealthy or bad. In relationships that evolve into a Zelda Complex, however, this reaction fuels the combustibility and can become very dangerous.

Factor Twenty-Two: Most Zelda Complexes involve a high degree of sexual activity. People who enter Zelda relationships are considered extremely sexual people. Zeldas are highly sensuous and seductive people who, even in their repressed forms, emit sexuality. They dress, speak, and communicate sensuality. In their later years, when others have given up on sexual energy, Zeldas continue to maintain it. But it is not that they are just highly sexed, or have a lot of sexual relationships. It's far more than that. It's an aura and a persona they project. It is very attractive, and pleasant to be around. This sexual energy may be acted out in seductiveness or a high degree of sexual activity. Occasionally, it can be sublimated into creativity. It's not coincidental these two energies are similar, since most Zeldas are also highly creative.

Factor Twenty-Three: Within any Zelda Complex there will be a great deal of melodrama; these relationships are usually akin to soap operas. What Sigmund Freud referred to as "histrionics" is present in all Zelda Complexes. The unfortunate component of Zelda Complexes is that many go beyond melodrama. At the advanced stages of a Zelda Complex, humiliation fuels the toxicity of the relationship. Zeldas act out publicly, using melodrama as a way to manipulate their partners. They enjoy involving others in their squabbles. This can include family members, employers, and even authority figures such as police. Humiliation is the mettle of Zeldas. This can become extremely dangerous and is one of the factors present in almost all advanced stages of the Zelda Complex. I have never witnessed violence between members of a Zelda Complex that was not preceded by perceived humiliation. It is both a visible, and dangerous factor.

Factor Twenty-Four: These relationships contain an element of danger, and usually become dangerous for one or both partners. If not dealt with, this element can lead to psychopathology, illness, or even death. The Zelda Complex can result in people externalizing their anger by becoming violent, or internalizing it by such self-destructive measures as overdrinking, or becoming mentally ill or suicidally depressed. It's important to understand that danger means more than psychological danger. Zelda Complexes are physically dangerous as well. This is one of the most alarming aspects of the Complex. Eventually it controls the couple. At that point, the relationship is sincerely out of control and will lead to harm, usually physical harm. In almost all advanced forms of the Zelda Complex, physical violence of one nature or another will be present.

Factor Twenty-Five: For a Zelda Complex to occur, at least one member of the relationship must have a high degree of narcissism. In its classic form, narcissism is self-worship. It's a type of self-absorption that makes trusting and loving others virtually impossible. The narcissist in the Zelda Complex simply loves him- or herself to the degree that he or she simply doesn't want to share him- or herself with another. Narcissists use others simply as entertainment, not to be involved in a mutually loving relationship. Using a person as a plaything is the ultimate high to a Zelda.

I was a man divided — she wanted me to work too much for her and not enough for my dream. . . . I had spent all my resources till my health collapsed, and all I cared about was drink and forgetting."
— F. Scott Fitzgerald, from a letter to Scottie

Many Zelda relationships I have worked with exhibit only a few of the twenty-five factors. One couple, who will be introduced later in the book, exhibit many. This particular couple actually included three people, but the two individuals in this triangle relationship who most graphically represent factors of the Zelda Complex are Bob and Samantha. A brief conversation from Bob's childhood is presented here to illustrate how these factors come into play.

As children, male Zeldas attempt to control everything, including their bathroom visits. What Freud referred to as the anal-retentive personality oftentimes becomes the male Zelda partner. This personality type typically results from extremely rigid, unrealistically demanding parenting. One male Zelda described an experience that explains how this compulsion to control began.

"When I was a kid," Bob began, "I remember getting up in the morning and tiptoeing past the closet near my bed. I was convinced there was a pack of wolves that lived in the closet. I felt like I had to sneak past it so I wouldn't wake them up. 'Cause if I woke them up they would jump out and eat me alive. When I had to use the bathroom, I'd tiptoe past the closet and down the hall. Then I had to be extremely quiet when I was using the toilet, because if I made too much noise I'd wake up the wolves.

"I can remember sitting on the potty as a little kid and thinking I had to be quiet while I was having a bowel movement. I'd worry if the splashing into the toilet made too much noise. I just couldn't risk waking up the wolves. So I'd have to be very careful.

"I know all this sounds sick, but that's actually the way I grew up. We had to be real clean. It was so bad that if we went on vacation, my mom would make everyone go outside and she'd clean the house for two hours. Everything would be spit-shined and polished. Then, when we got home a week later—even though no one had been in the house—she would be the first one inside, and she would clean again for another couple of hours. Finally we would all be allowed to go in, but, of course, we had to take off our shoes. We couldn't go in the living room because we would mess up the nap on the carpet. We couldn't bring friends home because they would get the house dirty. I mean, it was just a crazy place to grow up.

"Of course as I got older, you know—What was I back then, when I thought the wolves lived in the closet? Six or seven years old? I realized the wolves I feared were my parents. They were just bizarre. I guess I adapted by trying—by becoming very perfectionistic and achievement oriented. I became a workaholic, you know? Just trying to make the wolves happy in my closet. I guess I was pretty lucky. I could have done worse."

But it's really not luck at all. Cut off from their emotions because of fearful childhood experiences, male Zeldas typically retreat into the world of work. They feel they have some sense of control over their professional destinies and commit most of their energy to that one area. For male Zeldas, control is the central theme of their existence. They seek to control their jobs, themselves, and even their spouses. Their inability to accomplish this results in a strong sense of frustration that never leaves them.

"The biggest thing was," Bob continued, "I had to always be on guard. I could never really relax. If I relaxed, the wolves in the closet could get me. I used to talk to them and tell them 'Nice wolf. Don't bother me. I'm just tiptoeing past the closet, being a good boy. I'm not doing anything wrong. You don't have to hurt me.' Eventually, I think the wolves moved inside of me and are still there." That proved to be far more true with Bob than I could have ever imagined.

When a male Zelda finally lets go of the need to control himself, it's like a dam breaking. They become almost irrational, showing intense emotions, no longer concerned about composure. These emotions flow out in their most raw form. Bob called it "emotional diarrhea." Considering Freud's terminology, I would say it's very appropriate.

Bob's female counterpart, Samantha, exemplified the female Zelda. Sam once described how she finagled her way onto Bob's sailing crew. "I'd always been so fascinated with the romantic aspects of sailboats. To me, they were the most romantic thing in the world. I love more than anything else the feel of a sailboat as it skims across the water.

"Well, I should admit," Sam began to explain in her own unique way, "I first met Bob in a business capacity. This was before I went to work for him. At the time, I was trying to sell him some property. He mentioned he had bought a sailboat that he was going to start sailing. I asked him if I could come as part of the crew since he said he needed another member. I told him I had sailed in the English Channel and in North Carolina.

"Well, sailing in the English Channel really amounted to making tea in the galley. And in North Carolina, it was sailing out to a sand bar to collect some sand dollars—but I didn't tell him that part. Anyway, it was arranged for me to meet him at his dock and go on the boat. And, I'll tell you, I found out right away it wasn't the same as making tea on the English Channel. This was work. 'Get this up. Get this down. Go here. Go there.' Hard work, period. So, the first day I went out, Bob says to me, 'Rig the boat. Get the sheets and rig the boat.' I looked around hopelessly. Sheets? I thought, If I were a sheet what would I be? Sheets—like on a bed?

"There was this one guy that sort of took me under his wing and helped me figure things out. 'Here's what you do with that,' he'd say. He showed me what to do. I loved it. So every week I showed up to sail. Sometimes there was no wind. Sometimes there was lots of wind. And little by little I figured it out. I came to know every position on the boat.

"But as I gained more experience and was able to do what was needed without help, I noticed I was getting verbally abused. I couldn't please Bob. There were times when he would say, 'Get the spinnaker up, or I'll cram it up your butt!' All this time I'm thinking, Why was he so upset? I was part of the crew. I was pulling my weight now. I was the only girl with six guys. They called me 'little guy' most of the time. He took a crew of six, and I always showed up. And it was as if he went out of his way to tease me. Sometimes the other guys joined in. In spite of my efforts, I was constantly being degraded and criticized in front of the other guys. I was always the one who was singled out as the reason for whatever failed. Even if it was three or four people up there doing a job that screwed up, it was always my fault somehow. When Bob would cuss and scream at me, I would have a hard time believing he was talking to me that way. But I would always show up the next week.

"It'll be different this week, I would think. He'll see. I'll try harder. It won't happen again. He'll see it's not my fault. One day he'll realize that, and I'll become so important to him. Then we'll sail together like other couples sail. We'll be partners. I tried week after week to make it different—to make it better and not mess up. And I knew one day he'd notice. It was almost as if the better I got, the more abusive he became.

"And the better I get at running the business, the more I'm abused. Right now, I'm the only one really generating any leads for the company at all. Yet the abuse continues. I gave him a lead for an opportunity to make some big money and he did a good job following up on it. He followed through and made some phone calls and pulled it off. But he never thanked me."

Bob and Sam were a perfect match. They were perfectly suited for each other. It was the exact prescription for affliction.

CHECKLIST

Instructions:

A. List one current relationship in which you are involved that may be a candidate for the Zelda Complex. This relationship does not have to be romantic in nature. But it does have to involve frequent contact on a fairly intense level. It can include sibling, adult, child/parent, peer, co-worker, or business relationships.

B. List a past relationship in which you believe the Zelda Complex may have come into play.

C. Answer the following questions for each relationship. Rate each relationship listed above on a scale from zero (does not apply to me at all) to five (applies a great deal of the time). Two spaces are provided. Use the first space for a current relationship and the second space for a past relationship. It may be easiest to rate your current relationship and then go back and examine the relationship from your past.

__ __1   I am happiest when I know my partner approves of me.
__ __2.   My parents paid most or all of my college education. Or, they gave me a car when I was sixteen.

__ __3. There is a history of depression, self-destructive behavior, or suicide on either side of my family.

__ __4. Either I or my partner have been told by others that one or both of us is not living up to our potential.

__ __5. One of us feels uncomfortable expressing our emotions, while the other sometimes seems overwhelmed by them.

__ __6. For some reason, I feel the need to compete in this relationship; this sometimes extends to recreation.

__ __7. Often I feel left out or passed over when my partner is recognized in public. Or, my partner has complained that I receive too much attention; he or she seems jealous of my accomplishments.

__ __8. Generally speaking, I probably fit the stereotype for my gender.

__ __9. When I have felt it necessary, I have exaggerated my skills or expertise to impress my partner. Or, my partner acts like an expert in areas in which little skill or formal training is evident.

__ __10. I feel as though I am always the one who takes most of the responsibility for an argument. Or, it seems as if my partner is always picking fights. If he or she would stay off my back we'd get along fine.

__ __11. I prefer babies to older children or teenagers.

__ __12. If a relationship requires a lot of caretaking to maintain it, then it must not be right, and it would be best to start over with someone else.

__ __13. One of the reasons I was attracted to my partner was because he or she was already successful in areas I would like to develop. Or, my partner has always wanted to be successful in areas I have achieved in, but so far hasn't made it.

__ __14. I don't have any one person with whom I am really honest. I share my feelings with several different people. Or, I don't feel comfortable sharing many of my feelings with my partner. I confide in at least one other person.

__ __15. I function best when my life has more than a moderate amount of stress and excitement.

__ __16. We have the best sex when we make up after an argument.

__ __17. I have created scenes in public in order to embarrass my partner. Or, my partner has embarrassed me in public more than once.

____ ____18. There are times when I feel our relationship is out of control.

____ ____19. I like to spend money on clothes. I have frequently bounced checks when buying clothes, makeup, or jewelry for myself. Or, my partner has done the same.

____ ____20. Deep down, inside, I consider myself a loser.

Scoring: Total your score. Scores less than twenty-five indicate a relatively low risk of the Zelda Complex for this relationship. Totals from twenty-five through fifty indicate the beginning stages of the Complex. Fifty through seventy-five suggest problematic behavior that is probably causing some problems in your relationship. Scores above seventy-five suggest a need for caution and serious reevaluation, and point to the fact that you may already be aware that something is seriously wrong but feel powerless to change things.

Chapter 2

DRAMA AND TRAUMA
THE HISTORY OF THE ARCHETYPE ZELDA COUPLE

They met on the dance floor in the old high school gym
He fell like a rock
She kinda liked him.
　　　　　—Daryl Hall and George Green, "So Close"

Zelda and Scott Fitzgerald cannot really be compared to any contemporary couple. There are elements of the Donald Trump-Ivana-Marla Maples triangle in the relationship. There could also be a comparison made of O.J. Simpson's obsessive relationship with Nicole. Others have suggested that the media focus surrounding Roseanne's marriages compares to the impact the Fitzgeralds had in their time. Actually, it's difficult to compare the Fitzgeralds with anyone in today's society. They socialized with Picasso. They were friends with Alice B. Tolkus, Gertrude Stein, and T. S. Elliot. Scott was extremely close to Ernest Hemingway and actually introduced him to his first publisher. In fact, Zelda and Hemingway had a running public feud that lasted beyond Scott's death. The Fitzgeralds were the talk of the time and among the most socially influential couple of their era.

Unfortunately, their life together was a romantic tragedy. In many ways it was an exaggeration. It was an overstatement of the most hyperbolic kind. Identifying with the Fitzgeralds is difficult. Their marriage was so extreme, their swings so dramatic, their place in society so socially influential, some have suggested it couldn't happen today.

But it does. It happens regularly. It happened to me.

And it could easily happen to you.

She's the wildest one of the Beggs, but she's a thoroughbred," people said.
Alabama knew everything they said about her—there were so many boys who want-
ed to "protect" her that she couldn't escape from knowing.
"Thoroughbred!" she thought, "meaning that I never let them down on the dramatic
possibilities of a scene—I give them a damned good show.
                                    —Zelda Fitzgerald, *Save Me the Waltz*

The Zelda Complex existed *in form* before Zelda; it existed in literature after her. It was identified and named subsequent to my own experience with it. But it can only be fully understood by learning about the
two people involved. Zelda was born in Montgomery, Alabama, on July
29, 1900. Her father was a forty-two-year-old judge, her mother a forty-
year-old housewife. Zelda was the youngest of six children and was
appropriately named after a gypsy queen from a novel her mother had
read.

Perhaps because of her mother's age, Zelda was totally indulged and
spoiled. Knowing this would probably be her last child, Mrs. Sayre
nursed Zelda until she was four years old. Her father, Judge Sayre, was
the disciplinarian, but quite busy and emotionally distant from Zelda.
Her sisters and brother were too old to be true playmates. As a result,
Zelda became her mother's toy. Mrs. Sayre gave in to Zelda and was
totally entertained by her. Zelda was the absolute center of attention, and
when not treated in the fashion to which she had grown accustomed,
Zelda distanced herself and pouted.

Girls her own age were not impressed by Zelda. They didn't give in to
her manipulations. Being attractive and charming didn't carry much
weight with female playmates, so Zelda did what came naturally. She
started focusing on boys at an early age. She got her way with boys—
especially the older ones. This perpetuated a pattern that began with a
doting mother and a distant father, and continued until Zelda's death.

Zelda's family reportedly had a history of emotional problems. Mrs.
Sayre's own mother, Zelda's grandmother, had apparently died from suicide. Zelda's older sister "became ill" when Zelda was still a child living at
home. This sister and her child moved back into the Sayre's home to live.
The illness was later described as a nervous breakdown. Her brother
later experienced "nervous prostration" and committed suicide. But such
things are rarely discussed in the Deep South even today. In pre–World
War I southern Alabama, it would have been considered almost blasphe-

mous to admit emotional problems or suicide. Thus, there were a lot of secrets in the Sayre family.

Several things contributed to Zelda's early boldness. She was considered quite beautiful. She learned to manipulate others and seemed to possess a certain command over her peers. She quickly learned, even as a young child, to use this to her advantage. Being the youngest of six children also had its advantages. She grew accustomed to being the center of attention.

Her financial background was also an important contributor. She was able to participate in ballet and got the finest dance training available. But more important than wealth and its trappings in Montgomery, Alabama, during that era, were proper family connections. Besides allowing Zelda access to high society, her father's position as a judge granted her a sort of social deference which precluded from experiencing the natural consequences of inappropriate behavior. All these things contributed to an artificially inflated sense of self-grandeur and entitlement.

Zelda was a precocious youngster. She was frequently in some kind of trouble. One day, when she was nine years old, she was bored and decided to create some stimulation. She called the fire department and reported a child was caught on the roof and couldn't get down. Then, with poise and self-confidence, she got a ladder and climbed out onto the roof. Pushing the ladder away, she sat patiently and awaited her rescue. This early experience was almost prophetic. Even to her death, Zelda continually searched, at a near frantic pace, for external stimulation. She looked to men and drugs, and even attempted to extract it from life itself. Zelda always seemed to be looking for that rooftop escape, followed by a dramatic, fire truck rescue. She lived in the realm of symbolism.

I've often wondered if Zelda's later fascination with pilots was also a symbolic connection with escape. One pilot crashed his plane while trying to gain her favor with his acrobatic skill. Another ended up conducting a semi-emergency landing on a road near her house as a way of entertaining her. Near the time of her death, Zelda continued to fantasize in her own writings about being rescued. This time it was her doctors who she hoped would perform the feat. They didn't. The firemen never arrived. Tragically, Zelda went up in flames, figuratively and literally.

I left Princeton in my junior year . . . and after a few months I went back to college. But I had lost certain offices, the chief one was the presidency of the Triangle Club, a

musical comedy idea, and also I dropped back a class. To me college would never be the same. There would be no badges of pride, no medals, after all. It seemed one March afternoon that I had lost every single thing that I had wanted.
—F. Scott Fitzgerald, from a letter to Scottie

Francis Scott Key Fitzgerald was born September 24, 1896. His background, like Zelda's, was steeped in tradition. He was a descendant of Francis Scott Key and Phillip Barton Key, a member of the Continental Congress. Another relative, Mary Surratt, was hung for conspiracy to assassinate President Lincoln. Scott's family was predominantly Irish-Catholic and he grew up in Buffalo, New York, and St. Paul, Minnesota. His father, Edward, was a stern, distant figure who apparently struggled with alcoholism. Edward had a near-aristocratic set of values and manners, which he passed on to Scott. When Edward later lost several jobs, these values led to a series of problems. One of those values was the male responsibility providing for his family gallantly. Edward was immobilized with depression and drinking problems after his job losses. As a result, Scott lost respect for his father. Sadly, Scott later followed in his father's footsteps.

Scott was closer to his mother, a dark, attractive woman, who coddled him. Scott was a small youngster who showed signs of creative giftedness at an early age. Yet, his formal scholastic achievement level was low. He excelled in drama and writing, but failed other subjects. At the time Scott was a child, athletic ability was firmly embedded in the traditional male role. Scott did his best, but struggled with his inability to compete. As a result, he retreated even further into the creative realm where he excelled. There were no limits to his young and fertile imagination, however limited his athletic prowess might be.

During his junior high school years, Scott began writing stories for the school magazine. He had long kept a diary, and wrote of his experience at a Catholic school in Hackensack—a school his parents sent him to out of concern about Scott's academics—that he was miserable, and found happiness only in going to New York City, attending theater, and drinking. A trend toward escapism had begun to emerge. Scott escaped into his own imagination, drama, and ultimately alcohol.

During this time, Scott lost more respect for his father. He viewed his father as a failure for not adequately supporting his family and wallowing in misery. He loved his mother deeply, but found her to be terminally unhappy as well. Though he once wrote they had little in common, they each seemed to share a common misery. Throughout his life, Scott seemed to be seeking an escape from his own unhappiness. At times, the pace of his escape approached dangerous. But little seemed to help. During his precollege years, Scott was grossly insecure and seemed to be desperately looking for help. He saw both parents as unable to help him, or themselves. And although Scott wanted to avoid their destiny, he didn't know how.

In September 1914, after barely passing his entrance exams, Scott entered Princeton. Once again he focused his creativity toward theater. He rapidly buried himself in an intellectual world where his talents were directed, polished, and refined. He acted in various productions and wrote lyrics for several plays. He became involved in the Princeton Triangle Club, a prominent drama troop, and seemed obsessed with their productions. He failed algebra, trigonometry, geometry, and hygiene, but excelled at creative writing. His contributions to the Triangle Club were limited because of his academic failures. Because of his poor grades, he wasn't allowed to act in some of the plays to which he contributed through his writing. Eventually, Scott left Princeton altogether, citing health reasons.

Christmas of that year, he returned home. There he met and fell in love with Ginevra King. Scott was obsessed with her and began a correspondence that spanned several years. She returned Scott's affection, but not his intensity. With little fanfare, she dumped him in 1917 for a naval aviator whom she quickly married. Even twenty years later, in a letter to his daughter, Scott lamented the loss of Ginevra. She may have been his only healthy romantic relationship. Perhaps Ginevra detected his problems. He later used her as a model for Isabella in his book *This Side of Paradise*.

Darling Heart, our fairy tale is almost ended, and we're going to marry and live happily ever afterward just like the princess in her tower who worried you so much.
— Zelda Sayre, from a letter to F. Scott Fitzgerald

Scott and Zelda led parallel lives in their early years. Both had doting mothers and detached or distant fathers. Each had an attraction to and flare for the dramatic. They were creatively talented and even gifted at early ages. Neither excelled in academics. Both seemed obsessed by romantic relationships. Zelda used hers as a means to an end. Scott seemed to search endlessly for the perfect mate whom he could almost literally make his. Both were desperately insecure, hopelessly romantic, and nearly irrational in their expectations of love. If psychopathology is any indicator, they were a perfect match.

Zelda was the quintessential flapper of the roaring twenties: she was beautiful, witty, indulged, capricious, and bound for glory. Glory appeared in the form of Scott. He was handsome, Princeton educated, and a young army officer. He was unlike anyone she had dated. He was unathletic, sensitive, and imaginative. Scott and Zelda could not have chosen better partners for the histrionic fireworks that followed. The timing was perfect as well. America was beginning to experience depression, repression, and prohibition. It was ultimately one of the most melodramatic events in our world's history that brought them together. Scott and Zelda would not have been possible without the "war to end all wars"—World War I.

In many ways, the relationship Scott and Zelda began during World War I was the mother of all obsessive relationships (with apologies to Saddam Hussein). They were the emotional grandparents of many who followed their path—maybe even Saddam. It's often easier to understand yourself by looking at or discussing others. (That's really the purpose of this biographical chapter.) Unfortunately, Scott and Zelda had no one to look to. Nor would they have looked had there been anyone. They were so wrapped up in their own lives, there was no room for anyone else.

Zelda once said she chose "to love first and live incidentally." Scott himself was in love with love, not necessarily in love with life. They leapt from one dramatic, intoxicating poignancy to the next. Like many people I see in therapy today, the Fitzgeralds were confirmed stress junkies. These individuals seem to fear boredom, and are willing to do anything—even to die—to avoid it.

Does this happen today? Absolutely! And with even more frequency than it did in the Fitzgeralds' era. By my observations, there are probably more Zelda Complexes than not. I also believe virtually everyone will go through at least one such relationship in his or her lifetime. This relationship may be one you experience in your family of origin. It may be a business relationship. More frequently, however, it will be a romantic relationship. These relationships normally occur amid drama. Crisis has a near magnetic quality with the Zelda Complex. My own Zelda Complex occurred soon after my divorce. Other than actual combat, it was the most traumatic event in my life. Most Zelda Complexes are born of melodrama.

The Fitzgeralds' relationship was a complicated equation. It included their individual upbringings and personalities. It was magnified by their extremely unrealistic expectations of what love should do for them. Both fantasized that the *right* relationship would make them complete as individuals. They assumed the answer to their problems was inside someone else, rather than within themselves. This was their mistake, and would be an equally disastrous assumption for anyone today. Their relationship was further complicated by each being highly narcissistic. These were people who thought of themselves exclusively.

The final factor in the Fitzgerald equation was probably the defining one. It was the drama of World War I that propelled them together. It was not unlike the late sixties and early seventies, when thousands of people got married who probably never should have done so. The drama of the Vietnam War, and the fear of not returning, led these couples to make decisions that later ended in tragedy. Many of these marriages ended in divorce; in most of them children were involved. The same thing occurred some twenty-five years later during the Gulf War. This was especially true in areas surrounding military bases such as Fayetteville, North Carolina, and Clarksville, Tennessee. The Fitzgeralds made a similar mistake.

My observations as a psychotherapist are consistent with this phenomenon. Marriages born of melodrama are dangerously unstable. They often fizzle out as soon as the intensity does. Or, the relationships become endless cycles of sensation seeking at any price. This sensation seeking is not only intoxicating but also addictive. To heighten the degree of intensity, people increase the risks involved to regain the sizzle. Either alternative is extremely unhealthy.

I've heard many excuses given for marriage. One person told me he entered his first marriage because he was afraid Jesus would return before he had an opportunity to experience sex. People often laugh when I tell this story, but it's more common than you might think. Most people, when asked why they married, pause for a moment and eventually respond, "I thought I was supposed to?" Often the inflection will rise at the end of this sentence as if it's a question. Other people respond, "because I loved him." This is usually given as a postmortem to divorce.

In most cases, it is a complex series of events that leads people to commit to each other. Rarely is it as purely mathematical as described above. Just as with the Fitzgeralds, it is commonly an algebraic equation rather than simple mathematics. At some point, however, there'll be a moment of pressure that propel the couple into the final decision. Such pressure may be self-induced, such as pregnancy or sex drive; at other times it can be the desire to escape family conflict or religious reasons that drive the decision. Still others marry for convenience or function. But there is always an element of trauma or drama that ultimately pushes them to make the commitment. With the Fitzgeralds, it was World War I.

In the summer of 1917, the U.S. entered one of the last "noble" wars. At the time, little was known about the real reasons the U.S. got involved. The government disseminated far more information than the press, but it was mostly propaganda, and served to pitch people to an emotional fervor. Scott and Zelda both saw the war at its romantic, narcissistic best. For Scott, it was an opportunity to be a knight in shining armor and slay the dragon; Zelda was provided an endless supply of men to manipulate. Scott, as a young infantry officer, would lead his troops into battle. His reward would be the decorations he wore on his chest. Zelda saw it as her duty to conquer young aviators, which she did with aplomb. She collected the insignia of each officer she conquered and kept them in a jewelry box by her table. It was always full.

The face of Montgomery, Alabama, changed profoundly as young aviators and soldiers entered their training at Camp Sheridan outside of the city. To Zelda, who had been relatively insulated, it was as if she had been liberated. Finally the doors to the wider universe were opened. Zelda seemed to resent the restrictions traditional Montgomery had placed on her. Her eyes and dreams were on the larger world now; in her self-absorbed interpretation, World War I represented liberation. At the beginning of her senior year in high school, September 1917, her mind was not on school. It was on aviators. Her grades, already low, dropped even further. She played hooky and was ultimately expelled. Judge Sayre manipulated to get Zelda readmitted, but her performance continued to sag. She was voted most attractive student in the senior class, but was far more interested in her growing cadre of men. By the time graduation ceremonies were held, she was extremely resentful of school and the restrictions it represented. She refused to sit on the stage with her classmates during the graduation ceremony.

One month after graduating, Zelda and Scott met at the Camp

Sheridan Country Club. She was a seductive and beautiful eighteen-year-old femme fatale, dancing ballet at the club. Scott was a lieutenant in the 67th Infantry stationed at Camp Sheridan. He asked a friend to introduce them and they danced. At eighteen, Zelda was already an accomplished tease. She seemed to enjoy the games that followed. One of the problems was, however, the games never stopped. Their dance began in July 1918. It ended only with their premature deaths.

> *I was sorry immediately I had married her but, being patient in those days, made the best of it and got to love her in another way.*
> —F. Scott Fitzgerald, from a letter to Scottie

Some observers described Scott as immediately smitten. Zelda was attracted by his old-world chivalry and sense of gallantry. But she toyed with Scott. He was different than her other beaux; he was small, cerebral, and romantically creative. She was used to large, athletic, adventuresome aviators. Scott's difference was not only part of the attraction, but apparently part of the addiction as well. She found him to be dashing and romantic. His correspondence matched hers in both intimate intensity and literary polish. To describe Scott as pursuing Zelda is to engage in an understatement of mammoth proportions. He was obsessed with her. She fit his romantic notion of a damsel in distress. He was overwhelmed by Zelda. And she continued to dance.

They met in July. According to his own journal entry, Scott fell in love with her on September 7, 1918. He wanted to marry her, but feared he could not be an adequate provider. He fantasized that after the war he would become a successful writer and sweep her off her feet. He had already submitted a manuscript to Scribner's entitled "The Romantic Egoist." It was first rejected August 19, and once again several months later. At times, Scott felt he was losing both at love and as a writer. But he didn't give up on either. He was persistent, yet cavalier. His romantic fantasy of rescuing the damsel and making her a princess would not die.

Zelda continued to replay the scenario that began when she was nine years old. She was the same impetuous child calling the fire department to rescue her, then climbing out on the roof and kicking the ladder away. Yet the stakes had now changed. The firemen were aviators and soldiers; the rooftop, love. Zelda fantasized her aviator prince whisking her away from Montgomery, taking her to her rightful throne in some romantic royal chamber. The only castles Scott could build were in the sand. The only planes he could fly were the windmills he built in his mind. He was robbed of the opportunity to build real castles when, in November 1918, the armistice was signed that ended World War I.

Like most men feel at some point in their life, Scott felt he had something to prove. He needed to prove it to himself, not to someone else. He hadn't gotten to do it as an athlete, though to his credit he had tried. Princeton had been a big disappointment to him. To Fitzgerald, the armistice was a cruel trick. It cheated him of his only other big opportunity, and was probably the beginning of his premature end. Had he proved his masculinity to his own satisfaction, maybe the self-destructive behavior that followed would not have been necessary. Up to this point, Scott's problem had been only minor. He hadn't been self-destructive. This drive began after the armistice.

Throughout time, the role of men has been to master the environment. The historical role of women, on the other hand, has been one of nurturing. At an earlier time, men were given the opportunity of mastery in a variety of ways. Hunters, farmers, and warriors proved their masculinity through mastery of their trade; it was a matter of growing up. By the time Scott was in his twenties, the options were fewer. Today, the options are fewer still.

The male aggressive drive is a complex interaction of biochemistry, socialization, and tradition, bred to be almost instinctual. When stripped of healthier outlets, this drive can manifest itself pathologically. Scott's life following the armistice was filled with such perversions. So are literally thousands of men today who have never had the opportunity to channel the need for mastery in a functional direction.

I have never observed a veteran of military combat who questioned his masculinity. I have seen many people who served in noncombatant roles during wartime who later had such problems. Through combat, the drives of those who served were directed; these men seemed to achieve a sense of peace. Similarly, and somewhat fascinating to me, I've seen relatively few combat veterans who hunt for sport, have problems with spousal abuse, or get into street fights. Because they're secure in their masculinity, there is no one else to impress. Scott never had this opportunity.

I'm not saying men must go to war to become emotionally secure. What I am trying to indicate is that many of Scott's problems were caused by his lack of security in his male role. Zelda seemed to sense this and used it mercilessly against him. This probably led to a great deal of the drinking, fighting, and acting out that followed. He was continually trying to prove his worth in her eyes. Many of Scott's escapades following their marriage were misdirected attempts at conquering Zelda. Unfortunately, they were unsuccessful. Scott's aggression ultimately exploded toward Zelda and imploded toward himself. His preoccupation with Zelda blocked his creative drive; all of his attention revolved around her. The relationship sickened over time.

In the summer of 1919, the Fitzgerald roller coaster took another dip. They had just broken their engagement and Scott had returned to New York City. He remained drunk for quite some time and then left for St. Paul to rewrite "The Romantic Egoist." He spent several months changing the book and gave it a new title. Back in Montgomery, Zelda was dating a variety of men. She had become somewhat enthralled with Francis Stubbs, an Auburn football star. She was drinking excessively, swimming in the nude, and rushing from one party to another. Scott had sent her an engagement ring in the mail; the ring, Zelda accepted. The commitment, she ignored.

Scott made several trips to Montgomery during this time. They fought, then made up, only to begin the cycle again. They corresponded regularly and Scott used entire passages from their letters in his reworked novel. Finally, in September, Scribner's gave him a contract on his new book, retitled *This Side of Paradise*. In October, Zelda once again agreed to marry Scott, but only after the book came out: March 26, 1920. They were married one week later, April 3, at high noon in New York City's St. Patrick's Cathedral. The chase stopped. The pretending stopped. Twenty years of near insanity followed.

I do want to marry you—even if you think I dread it—I wish you hadn't said that—I'm not afraid of anything—To be afraid a person has either to be a coward or very great and big. I am neither. Besides, I know you can take better care of me than I can.
— Zelda Sayre, from a letter to Scott, February 1920

It wasn't long before Zelda began to notice Scott's insecurity and fearfulness. Not only was she surprised and confused by this revelation, she found it repulsive. Zelda needed someone extremely stable to balance out her moodiness. She had thought that would be Scott. Meanwhile, he grew less and less confident. Both he and Zelda drank more. In his attempt to mask his insecurity Scott became a chronic liar. Apparently he realized that if Zelda was aware of his weakness, he would lose her. Zelda had been attracted to extremely masculine men in the past. Scott feared she would end up with someone more macho than he. Though more socially naive and inexperienced than Scott, Zelda herself was absolutely fearless. She was incapable of empathizing with him. Their arguments increased and at times grew physically violent.

There is evidence that Zelda was unfaithful to Scott early in the marriage, just as she had been during their engagement. Scott would react with furious jealousy, becoming almost frenetic. But Zelda continued to flirt. She seemed to enjoy watching Scott fret over her interest in other men. At one point during their engagement, Zelda had actually arranged to have four different men meet her at a train station in Atlanta. A confrontation and fight ensued, which she watched with glee. Zelda had orchestrated the entire event, as if for sport. And she did all of this while engaged to Scott.

By the fall of 1920, Zelda was considering divorce. Of the two, Zelda was initially the more dominant and controlling. She was probably psychologically stronger as well. It is evident they shifted roles regularly, taking turns victimizing each other. In the early years, no doubt, Scott was more dependent and needy. Zelda had her way with him and others. Yet over the years, a fascinating evolution occurred: as Scott grew more successful and secure, Zelda became the more needy partner.

Zelda had been the center of attention since birth. From her infancy onward, people revolved their lives around Zelda's whims. Apparently, by this time she had begun to define such treatment as her birthright. And probably in many ways it was. During the initial stages of their relationship, Scott seemed willing to accommodate Zelda. However, as he began to succeed, public attention was increasingly diverted toward him. Like many attractive women, Zelda was favored for her appearance. Beauty was her virtue. Yet it was genetic. It was not something she had earned; she was simply born with it. Throughout most of her life, Zelda remained attractive, stunning, really. She turned heads everywhere she went, and had grown accustomed to such attention. But things had changed. Now, when they went out, people focused on Scott.

By September 1920, *This Side of Paradise* had sold thirty-three thousand copies, and the Fitzgeralds were the talk of New York City. Scott quickly attained the status reserved today for actors, singers, or professional athletes. Financially he was doing better, although usually in debt to Scribner's. (Fitzgerald's writings actually earned far more after his death than during his life.) He constantly struggled for money. It wasn't earnings that brought him status, however. It was his incredible intuitive skill as a writer. Scott lived and wrote about the moral decay of his era. He was the voice of the Lost Generation; he was also its pulse. This brought respect from his peers, and celebrity. Zelda was Scott's wife—not the role she had auditioned for. She literally and figuratively became Mrs. Fitzgerald, the author's wife. The limelight was now exclusively on Scott. What had originally attracted Zelda to Scott now began to destroy her.

Within a six-month period, two other factors complicated the situation even further. On October 26, 1921, the Fitzgeralds' daughter, Scottie, was born. Zelda was now required to focus her own narcissistic energy on someone else. Before marrying Scott, Zelda had been the belle of southern society. She had gotten her way with family, friends, and, most of all, with men. Zelda was now a mother. She was expected to be respectable, and to care for her child. She was used to being taken care of. The attention she received had been reduced to shock from of the public at her increasingly violent fights with Scott. Even that reaction would be lessened, however.

In March 1922, Scott's next novel, *The Beautiful and the Damned*, was published. Again, he became the darling of high society. Zelda was growing increasingly dissatisfied with her roles of mother and wife. But to make matters worse, Zelda identified portions of her personal diary in Scott's novel. Apparently, Scott had stolen it and included entire sections in his book without consulting Zelda, or even acknowledging her contributions.

This was likely the point where the relationship's balance of power took a dramatic and destructive shift. During the first five years of their relationship, Zelda was absolutely empowered. She had been obnoxious, arrogant, and manipulative of Scott. She not only toyed with him, but seemed to revel in it. Basically, Zelda had been a spoiled brat. Scott's success in these early years balanced the relationship, and could have made it healthier, had they sought psychotherapy at this point. With their daughter's birth, the balance shifted even further. There is evidence that Zelda was maturing, developing, and learning to be less self-centered at this point. She was only twenty-two, still young. With time, she could have adapted.

But Scott's plagiarism of her writing raped Zelda creatively. It was a gross violation of her personal boundaries—a violation that would continue throughout their relationship. At this point, Zelda simply no longer had a life. The phenomenon that would eventually become F. Scott Fitzgerald had consumed her creative soul. She was no longer a person in her own right.

Zelda had enormous creative talent. She was a dancer of some accomplishment and would later be offered the lead part in a Naples ballet. She was a gifted artist, whose water colors were admired and are still on exhibit in museums throughout the South. Her writing was superb. Scott used her personal letters and diaries liberally. In fact, much of his original writing was actually Zelda's. When he plagiarized her work, Scott was symbolically labeling Zelda an extension of his imagination. In many ways, he murdered her soul by doing this. Zelda then began her struggle to put the pieces of her identity back together.

Show me a hero and I will write you a tragedy.
—F. Scott Fitzgerald, *Notebooks*

This struggle lasted some twenty-six years, and ended as tragically as it had begun. Her first publicly acknowledged suicide attempt occurred in 1924. She had conducted a very public affair with a French aviator while Scott was working on *The Great Gatsby*. They had been spending the summer on the French Riviera; Scott was supposed to be writing while Zelda vacationed. When Scott discovered the affair, Zelda overdosed on sleeping pills. It was the first of many suicide attempts that followed. Some of these attempts were quite obvious; the important ones were not.

In 1925, the Fitzgeralds met Ernest Hemingway. (Scott would later be responsible for Hemingway receiving his first big break as a writer.) But similar to Scott's early relationship with Zelda, Hemingway's personality was the stronger of the two. Scott was attracted to Hemingway's strong sense of masculinity. *The Great Gatsby* had been released one month before they met. And Scott's drinking increased during his early relationship with Hemingway. Zelda resented Hemingway, because of the drinking or the loss of control she was feeling. Regardless, a feud began between her and Hemingway that lasted until Zelda's death. In fact, Hemingway, along with several of Scott's other friends, blamed Zelda for Scott's early problems.

Zelda had a long history of combustibility. At age nine, she had her first encounter with firemen. In December 1919, an actual fire struck the Sayre home for the first time. Scott and Zelda were engaged at this point. Little mention of it is made, so it's difficult to determine the circumstances. However, fire is a recurring event in Zelda's life, and it is my opinion that she orchestrated this episode, just as she had when she was nine. She was crying for help; she was desperate for attention.

When she was twenty-seven, it happened again. On this occasion, Zelda was angry at Scott for what she perceived as his excessive interest in a young actress. In a jealous rage, she loaded some of his clothes into a bathtub and set fire to them. She also burned a $3500 watch Scott had given her as an engagement gift. It would not be her last pyromaniacal gesture. Perhaps it was a cry for help. Maybe she was, once again, the nine-year-old calling the fire department to come and rescue her. I consider it a gesture of despair. Zelda was crying desperately for someone to help her. She was indeed being swallowed up by her circumstances and didn't know how to get out. Regardless, the gesture didn't work. And ultimately the lack of acknowledgment such gestures brought would lead to her death. It would not be the last time Zelda tried symbolic signals. It had worked when she was nine; the firemen came to rescue her. She tried it on this occasion and, I believe, on four others. No one noticed.

Zelda's life was surrounded by symbolism. From her early upbringing in the Old South to the way she flirted and the fantasies she held about being rescued, the symbolism is rich. Her clothing was symbolic. Even the way she wore her hair symbolized the liberation from oppression that was common with ladies of her era. It's no coincidence that Zelda was the archetypal flapper of her age. In 1929, both she and America were about to enter a major depression. It would be devastating. America would recover from its depression. Unfortunately, Zelda never did.

> *For a long time I hated her mother for giving her nothing in the line of good habits—nothing but "getting by" and conceit. I never wanted to see again in this world women who were brought up as idlers.*
> —F. Scott Fitzgerald, from a letter to Scottie

The Zelda Complex can happen in any adult relationship. But there are two personality types far more likely to experience the Zelda Complex than others. Curiously enough, these personality types often do end up together and are the fodder for many marriage-counseling cases that end up in psychotherapists' offices.

The most typical Zelda personality, the female Zelda, is that of a woman who appears quite friendly on the outside. She has an excellent sales personality. Female Zeldas usually make extremely good first impressions and, in fact, will present an overwhelmingly favorable picture of themselves in the initial stage of any relationship. This bold misrepresentation, mentioned earlier and discussed elsewhere in this book in greater detail, applies not only to their words but to their appearance as well. The female Zelda will often boldly misrepresent her physical appearance through the use of make-up, hairdressers, and a good wardrobe. They constantly appear warm and charming. Beneath this facade is an individual who is usually miserable and insecure. Yet you would never guess it.

These are women who are extremely self-absorbed. They are self-indulgent to the point of narcissism. They are egocentric and expect the world to revolve around them. They do not have time to be considerate of others, because of their preoccupation with themselves. They usually have extravagant, materialistic needs, but rarely have the ability to satisfy their needs. They usually become dependent on men to take up the slack. Or they become good at appearing helpless, and adept at seeking security primarily through things rather than relationships.

As children, female Zeldas were usually given little healthy attention at home. They were unhappy children who came from families who provided wealth or the basic necessities of life, but ignored their emotional needs. As a result, they usually began looking for validation outside of the home at an early age. Consequently, female Zeldas often find themselves in unhappy relationships with unhappy men. Because of the lack of bonding during their early childhood, Zeldas are deeply convinced they are unlovable. They constantly seek experience to contradict this and are usually considered romantic escapists. They use melodrama to bring attention to themselves, and appear to have little or no control over their impulses. This includes a propensity to do things and say things purely to seek attention. Female Zeldas will often say things not only totally unnecessary, but also better left unsaid.

Deep within their hearts they feel like losers. They feel incapable of being treated fairly. As a result, a female Zelda often resorts to subterfuge and dishonesty to manipulate others, believing them to be the only way she can possibly win. This will often lead to legal and financial trouble that could have easily been avoided. In response to difficulty, female Zeldas usually suffer severe depression and emotional problems. Classic female Zeldas are needy of love and attention. They resort to melodramatic measures to get it. In relationships, most female Zeldas see it as their responsibility to take charge of emotion. And they experience emotion intensely, in a wide variety of ways.

Zeldas usually have been in a series of difficult or even disastrous relationships. Many have never experienced one they would describe as satisfying. They are often the object of sexual attention and flirtation from various men, and are frequently tempted to engage in extramarital affairs. They will usually jump from one relationship to another, and are occasionally rescued from bad liaisons by well-intentioned but misguided suitors. Female Zeldas attempt to return affection. They try to care for those they are involved with, but are simply incapable of caretaking. This is because deep within, female Zeldas see themselves as unlovable. They need constant confirmation of value, beauty, and worth. And they seek partners who cater to them. When the spouse finally runs out of gas, which he always does, she will be frightened by his withdrawal. Female Zeldas fear inattention above all else. Arguing is better than no attention at all, and they will provoke arguments simply to avoid the pain of apathy.

Female Zeldas attempt to take control in relationships. They often stage melodramatic, poignant scenes to get their way. Agitated to an impassioned emotional fervor, female Zeldas break things, or people, to make their point. They pack their bags and move out, only to return a few minutes later. They cry, scream loudly, and perpetually orchestrate emotional drama. Female Zeldas are usually takers who would sincerely like to be givers. They are lonely to a fault; they tirelessly search for love, but never find it. They are eternally angry, because they feel unloved and often unlovable. And without professional help, they are doomed to misery.

The classic male Zelda is a vastly different creature. In many ways, he is the exact opposite of his female counterparts. These men are usually emotionally remote and psychologically unavailable. What they lack in emotional honesty they make up for in other ways. Male Zeldas are usually rigid, inflexible, and overorganized. These men are controlling and constantly fearful that something will happen outside of their realm of influence. Male Zeldas are extreme conformists and respectful to a fault. This leads indirectly to a great deal of hostility, which is often expressed passive-aggressively. They are quite reliable, but at the same time a bit boring.

Male Zeldas have suppressed their impulses to the point that they are unaware such feelings exist. They are often horrified at their female partner's frivolity, but simultaneously attracted to it. To these men, an angry outburst, or even uncontrolled laughter, is so foreign they would have difficulty understanding it. They are typically aloof, and judgmental of anyone they consider overemotional.

The male Zelda is an extremely competent provider, but can't give of himself. He sees his responsibility as serving his family, which he defines as providing things. In this respect, he is usually a martyr who is shocked when his partner complains. "How can you be unhappy?" he will often ask. "Look at all I have done for you," he will say pointing to the cars, houses, clothes. The male Zelda feels he is keeping his part of the bargain when he has provided things. He has assumed responsibility for a damsel and sees her as his trophy; he has given her things and expects her to act like one of them.

In the evolution of a relationship, a male Zelda's suppressed emotions will surface. This can often be the result of alcohol-induced moments of weakness. He might demand some of the nurturing he has offered, and then, when it's not returned, resent it. He will become demanding and critical, which will be reciprocated and escalated by his partner. (Female Zeldas can rapidly become vile.) In turn, he will be shocked by the incredible venom his partner is capable of offering. In response, he withdraws, which results in his partner acting out more forcefully to regain his attention.

In spite of their differences, male and female Zeldas probably grew up similarly. They simply chose alternate ways of dealing with their emotions. The male member of the Zelda Complex had inadequate parenting. He usually never received approval as a child, and constantly strove to attain it. Yet he's not even aware of his behavior. As a child, he became perfectionistic and overadaptive to please critical parents. He turned off his feelings, consistently dismissing them as unreliable. The message he received as a child was never to trust feelings. It was a message he learned well.

She flirted because it was fun to flirt and wore a one-piece bathing suit because she had a good figure; she covered her face with powder because she didn't need it. . . . She had mostly masculine friends, but youth does not need friends — it only needs crowds, and the more masculine the crowds the more crowded for the Flapper."
— Zelda Fitzgerald, *Eulogy on the Flapper*

Between 1927 and 1929, the Fitzgeralds were busy traveling. Perhaps they were trying to escape boredom; maybe they were running from each other. Their marriage was alive in name only. In the fall of 1929, they were driving through the mountains and steep roads of southern France. Zelda reached over and grabbed the steering wheel of the car and tried to run them off the road. Had she succeeded, they would surely have dropped to their deaths. It was a genuine suicide attempt, the second attempt noted by biographers.

She was becoming more severely depressed and other people noticed. Zelda was gaining the reputation of being difficult in public and on multiple occasions created scenes. People were increasingly uncomfortable around her. Zelda began a series of psychiatric hospitalizations at this point. During these periods, she was generally uncooperative and appears to have been using her early hospitalizations as a means of refocusing attention back on herself. Eventually, she became frightened—a new emotion for Zelda—and claimed she was hearing voices. She was also experiencing delusions. In the spring of 1930, she was diagnosed schizophrenic. Zelda continued a revolving-door relationship with psychiatric hospitals over the next few years. Her father died in November 1931. Two months later, Zelda once again submitted herself for psychiatric hospitalization. While there, she completed her autobiographical novel, *Save Me the Waltz.*

Scott was furious at Zelda's literary efforts. He criticized her work mercilessly and tried to ban her from using material from their personal lives. He described their lives together as being his literary property, since he was the professional and she was the amateur. Scott was still struggling with his own insecurity. In actuality, Zelda had been the model for most of his heroines. She gave his characters style and life. Much of what he described in his books was about him and Zelda. Just as with *The Beautiful and the Damned,* much of his material was actually stolen from Zelda's diaries and letters. At least five short stories were published with his name attached but were admittedly not his. On the sixth story in that series, Zelda's name was dropped entirely, supposedly by mistake. It is unlikely a coincidence that after Zelda's series of hospitalizations began, Scott was able to write only one additional book, *Tender is the Night*. And that book, which was published in 1934, was actually begun in 1926 when Zelda was still healthy. Much of it was taken directly, almost verbatim, from Zelda's personal correspondence with Scott. Again, he neither admitted nor acknowledged her efforts.

By the early 1930s, Zelda was heavily involved in painting and writing. Her water colors were numerous and skilled. She also decorated lamp shades, paper dolls, and costumes for paper dolls. One paper doll was a rendition of Scott. In it, he actually wore a skirt. Additionally, he had wings extending from his shoulders, as if he were an angel. She was obviously deeply involved in escapist fantasy. Perhaps the wings symbolized her need to be flown away, as had her fixation with aviators during her adolescence in Montgomery. Zelda had never been pleased with Scott's lack of masculinity. At one point, she had publicly accused him of being homosexual. Yet still she begged him to rescue her.

Zelda's next encounter with fire occurred in 1933. A house they were living in near Baltimore burned, destroying manuscripts, paintings, and family heirlooms. The fire was officially attributed to faulty wiring, but in truth Zelda started the fire while burning some of Scott's clothes and papers. It occurred subsequent to one of the couple's most violent arguments about Zelda's literary efforts. Again, little attention has been given to this fire. In my opinion, however, it was another of Zelda's cries for help. But nobody heard this cry either. Her psychiatrist apparently missed it. Scott was too preoccupied with his own problems. The signal, however, rang loud and clear.

By late-1933, Scott's health problems worsened. It was likely a combination of stress and deterioration from chronic alcoholism and tuberculosis. He began *Crack Up Essays*, a penetrating view of deteriorating evolution, within himself and within Zelda. Scott apparently foresaw his own early demise. He remained busy, but not at all productive, from 1934 until his death. During much of that time, he and Zelda were separated. Scott continued his attempts to become involved with screen writing and had a small degree of success. His drinking continued, as did his cyclic bouts with depression. His tuberculosis and heart trouble became severe as a result of his heavy drinking. In November 1940, it appears he had an undiagnosed, mild heart attack. One month later, on December 21, he had a massive heart attack and was dead at age forty-four. He was buried in Rockville Union Cemetery, in Rockville, Maryland. Because of her psychiatric condition, Zelda was unable to attend.

After Scott's death, several of his manuscripts continued to be published, his unfinished novel, *The Last Tycoon*, among them. *Crack Up Essays* was published as well. Scott's productivity seemed to fade with Zelda's sanity. Fascinatingly enough, however, her literary productivity seemed to die with Scott. Zelda, free at last to write to her heart's content, refused to publish after Scott's death. She busied herself instead with painting, gardening, and religion. Her daughter was married February 13, 1943, but Zelda was unable to attend. She alternated between her mother's home in Montgomery and Highland Hospital in Ashville, North Carolina.

By the fall of 1947, it was obvious to people in Montgomery that Zelda's condition was deteriorating. She had begun to suffer from hallucinations and delusions. On several occasions, she was found having conversations with then-deceased Scott, whom she claimed was sitting beside her. In 1947, the social situation for the mentally ill in Montgomery was less than kind. As a result, Zelda decided to return to Highland Hospital in November of that year. As she was leaving, she reportedly told her mother not to worry, and that she was not afraid to die.

On March 10, 1948, Zelda had her fifth and final symbolic interaction with firemen. On that evening, a fire roared through the central building of Highland Hospital. An investigation indicated the fire began in the kitchen and later engulfed Zelda's quarters in flames. She died, along with eight other women. Apparently, firemen struggled to reach the women, but were prevented by the security locks at the hospital. Zelda was never rescued.

The fire was considered accidental, but I seriously doubt it. Zelda was involved in five fires during her lifetime. Coincidence? Not likely.

One week later, on St. Patrick's Day, 1948, Zelda was buried beside Scott. The fire had provided her what men alone were never able to. She was finally swept away, and at peace.

CHECKLIST

Instructions: The following statements are organized into two lists: those that characterize the female Zelda personality, and those that characterize the male Zelda. Complete the list that best fits you by putting a check mark next to each statement that applies.

If your Zelda relationship is with someone of the same gender, read both lists, and check each statement that most applies to you. Walt and David, brothers and business partners, are discussed in the next chapter. David's personality fit the female checklist, balancing out Walt, who was a male Zelda personality.

FEMALE ZELDA

_____1. I am a friendly person. My friends would classify me as an extrovert.

_____2. I rarely go out in public without makeup.

_____3. I have been told I would make a good salesperson. Or, I currently work in sales.

_____4. I consider it important to have my hair done professionally on a regular basis.

_____5. Looking good is vital to me, regardless of cost or pain.

_____6. One or both parents were emotionally unavailable to me in childhood. I was provided with things, but my parents' time and attention was mostly given elsewhere.

_____7. I can't imagine being without a romantic relationship.

_____8. I frequently say things I later regret.

_____9. When I was younger, I got into trouble to get my parents' attention.

_____10. I have moved out on my current partner several times and later returned.

_____11. Deep within, I consider myself unlovable.

_____12. I admire people who are unselfish, but I don't believe I am very skilled in that area.

_____13. I find flirting exciting.

_____14. I have been dishonest in situations where I felt it was the only way to win.

_____15. In order to feel really satisfied in a relationship, I need my partner to let me know frequently how wonderful I am.

Male Zelda

_____ 1. I am uncomfortable around other men who show their emotions.

_____ 2. I am most comfortable when I know ahead of time what is going to happen in any given situation.

_____ 3. I have been accused by family or peers of being overcontrolling.

_____ 4. I find myself attracted to or amused by people who appear to be fun-loving and relaxed with their feelings.

_____ 5. I consider my family unjustified in complaining about me not spending enough time with them. It takes all my efforts to provide for them.

_____ 6. In many areas, I am considered a perfectionist.

_____ 7. I believe decisions should be made using all the facts at hand. Feelings and hunches are seldom reliable.

_____ 8. Deep within, I consider myself unlovable.

_____ 9. One or both parents were emotionally unavailable to me in childhood.

_____ 10. I admire people who are unselfish, but I don't believe I am very skilled in that area.

_____ 11. I have used alcohol as a means of helping me feel more at ease in groups of people.

_____ 12. I sometimes feel my family doesn't appreciate my efforts to provide for them.

_____ 13. I am always punctual, even if it is extremely difficult.

_____ 14. I don't feel my partner pays as much attention to looking after my needs as I do hers (or his).

_____ 15. Though generally reserved, I am prone to angry outbursts.

Scoring: Total the check marks. Totals less than five indicate you do not have a problem with gender-based Zelda characteristics. Scores between five and ten indicate you have general Zelda characteristics for your gender which may be the cause of problems in your relationships. Totals above ten signify trouble. It would probably be helpful for you to discuss this questionnaire with someone else to get an objective opinion. It may also be helpful to discuss this questionnaire with a professional.

Chapter 3

TRUE INTIMACY
THE MISSING LINK IN ZELDA RELATIONSHIPS

And his heart beat like thunder as they moved 'cross the floor
But when the music was over she slipped out the door.
— Daryl Hall and George Green, "So Close"

Over time, I came to realize that in my own Zelda relationship I had grown almost addicted to the strong feelings emanating from my partner. Female Zeldas, by and large, are highly emotional. And to male Zeldas, who are taught to suppress their emotions, this can be seductively attractive. The difficulty arises, as described in chapter 1, because most Zeldas are so narcissistic they are unable to reciprocate. You can spend infinite time taking care of a Zelda, while ignoring your own needs. And most people will do so for a reason. It's believed to be an investment in the relationship. There is ultimately an expectation of returns, however, which is when the sparks flare.

While I was recovering from my own Zelda fixation, four different couples entered psychotherapy with me at approximately the same time. Though the couples differed in factual details, they were similar in spirit. Each was vastly different in personality. Yet the dynamics that brought them together as individuals, and into therapy, were similar.

Jack prided himself on his communication skills. He spent endless hours reading and could converse intelligently on almost any topic. He was willing and able to debate either side of any given question. Despite being able to discuss science, fact, and detail, however, he was uncomfortable discussing emotions. Sandra was attracted to Jack because of his practical turn of mind. She admired his ability to analyze a situation from both perspectives and thought she had found someone with whom she could discuss her most intimate desires. Jack was drawn to Sandra by her kindness, and the intense emotional energy she spent helping others around her. Of the four couples, Jack and Sandra were probably the most equally balanced. Yet, in the end, the attributes that brought them together ultimately caused severe problems in their relationship.

Walt and David had a similar balance. Though brothers and business partners, rather than spouses or lovers, they were locked in a relationship similar to that of the other couples I was working with at the time. Walt's personality was more sales oriented; he thrived on emotion. David, who was the technical and engineering side of the equation, was highly suspicious of Walt's moods. Their different styles had led them into a distant relationship since early childhood. They had competed in virtually all aspects of their lives, but were now thrust together in a business deal that would either make or destroy them. Similar to the other couples, however, if placed on a scale, they balanced each other out.

Gary and Katie also entered psychotherapy at approximately the same time as the others. In many ways, Gary was an extreme version of Jack, though more cerebral and aggressively detached. He dominated his wife, Katie, in a more vitriolic way. Their relationship was not a dance; it was rather a severe psychodrama. Gary was originally attracted to Katie for the same reason he was ultimately repulsed. Katie was an extremely emotional woman who gradually became intoxicated by her severe mood swings. They eventually inflicted damage, not only on her, but on her husband and children as well. She described Gary as not being able or willing to understand her. Yet he did a good job of moderating her emotional impulses with his "boring dryness."

Bob, introduced in chapter 1 as the boy who tiptoed past his closet where the wolves lived, kept his emotions contained. Because emotions are ultimately uncontrollable, his suppressed emotional responses eventually exploded in intense, angry outbursts. When he needed an emotional release he would turn to Samantha, a woman who was fairly emotional and reciprocated his intensity. Both Bob and Sam filled their engines from the emotional tank. When hung over from the emotional high created with Sam, however, Bob would return to his wife, Debbie, for stability and support. In this relationship, Debbie was the least emotional of the three. Bob, Sam, and Debbie found a triangular balance between them. The triangle worked quite well, until ultimately the intoxicants took over.

*One ought to hold on to one's heart; for if one lets it go,
one soon loses control of the head too.*

— Friedrich Nietzsche

Raw emotions and intimacy are two vastly different phenomena. Raw emotion is intense. Although frequently misidentified and confused to be the same thing, intensity and intimacy are vastly different. Emotional intensity is very seductive; men are almost magnetically drawn toward it. It's not the same thing as sex, however. Intense emotional energy can fuel sexuality and lead to sexual energy; it can also go elsewhere. The same energy source can lead to almost manic-depressive changes in emotional moods. It can create hyperactive moments of limitless energy, and several days later, a crash that finds the person balled in a fetal position under the bed. It can lead to excitement, drama, and joy. At the same time, it can result in emotional or psychological death. And it often can do both within a brief matter of days.

Men search for intimacy, but usually are not willing to pay the price for it. The typical obsessive-compulsive male will often end up with a partner as emotional as he is detached. The personality patterns mentioned in chapter 2 are almost parasitically drawn together in the Zelda Complex. Both partners are looking for ways to overcome their shortcomings. They seek to fill gaps. As Bob once described his relationship with Sam, "The rocks in her head filled the holes in mine." Each uses the other as a crutch to assist in the treacherous journey of life. Yet this is not intimacy, either.

Intimacy is at least as difficult to find as it is to define. It's an elusive concept and a rare commodity in a society ever more demanding of instant gratification. When one of my children was in kindergarten, he asked if we could go to McDonald's and get a Happy Meal; but he only wanted to go if there was a short line at the drive-through window. I grew alarmed at what I later discovered was his perception of excellence. To him, for something to be good, it had to be quick. The perfect meal was a Happy Meal—but only if he didn't have to wait long. This shake-and-bake culture seems to permeate society today.

Quality and quick are not synonymous. Yet we have grown to associate them as one in the same. In actuality, they may be diametrically opposed. The couples I have described were caught in this quick-fix mentality, just as my son was. Raw emotional energy is instantly gratifying. It causes an increased heart rate, heightened blood pressure, and hormonal changes in the brain—the "rush" can be addictive. But intimacy is not like that at all. It is deceptive in its subtlety, and can only be experienced by those who have the patience to persist. Few do, and that is one of the primary factors that has led to the soaring divorce rate, and the equally staggering, recent increase in family violence. Most often, domestic violence is a result of thwarted attempts to find intimacy. What they find instead is intense emotionality. It's important to understand that we have created this monster; now the monster is devouring us.

A study I read several months ago illustrates this. Interestingly enough, the purpose of the study was to identify the factors most predictive of which men would recover from heart attacks. Various factors were isolated in the study, but few were present in each male who recovered. One of the factors with the highest incidence of a positive recovery was animal ownership. This factor was later isolated more specifically as dog ownership. How owning a dog could help someone recover from cardiovascular problems confused researchers at first. What they soon discovered was quite significant. The men who had dogs ended up touching, rubbing, cuddling, and wrestling with their animals. Simply put: They touched the dog, and were touched in return. As a result, the men felt cared for and unconditionally accepted. The tactile stimulation received from rubbing a dog indirectly improved the patients' cardiovascular systems. The men recovered more quickly. In many ways, this was good news. But in my opinion, there is some bad news here as well.

Apparently, it's not as acceptable for a man to cuddle and touch people, as it is for a man to cuddle and touch his dog. Though scientifically the interpretation of the study is still open for debate, I think I understand it. It may be stretching the point to make the point, but the results speak for themselves. The men who did not have dogs failed to recover as quickly. There must be a reason for this—and it doesn't have to do with walking the dog. It is touching and being touched in return.

Considering this factor, it's no surprise to me that a man would find emotional intensity and stimulation—in any form—preferable to nothing at all. The male population is predominantly lonely. They are socialized to do many things well, but nurturing relationships is not among them. Emotionally and psychologically repressed, men look for a partner to take care of and elicit their emotion. When they do find someone who has wildly fluctuating mood swings, it's frightening, but inviting at the same time. Strong emotions add spice to their otherwise mundane, task-oriented lives.Frankly, it feels good. But it's still not intimacy.

Several years ago, Dr. James Pennebacker at Southern Methodist University conducted a study that sheds further light on the subject. He found that AIDS patients who had contracted AIDS through intravenous drug use or homosexual activity died far more quickly than those who had contracted it through blood transfusions or heterosexual activity. Puzzled at first by the results, Dr. Pennebacker ran various analyses until he isolated the important factors. What he discovered has influenced the course of thinking across the board when it comes to medical care.

Dr. Pennebacker found the difference was not in body chemistry, but in sociology. People who contracted AIDS through what would be considered more socially acceptable avenues were likely to behave quite differently in one important way: they were more likely to open up and talk about it. Dr. Pennebacker later found that talking about problems, whether AIDS, stress, or anything else, improved the healing process. He further found that it really didn't matter whom a person talked to. The primary qualification was that the listener be accepting of the person and nonjudgmental about what the speaker said. As a result of Dr. Pennebacker's research, *USA Today* speculated that psychotherapy might be "the cure for the common cold!" While the headlines exaggerated the researchers' results, the article did give some direction to the benefits of intimacy. At a minimum, Dr. Pennebacker found that intimacy is conducive to good health. Previous scientific implications labeled the effects of intimacy merely emotional and psychological. Yet Dr. Pennebacker's research defines intimacy as contributing to physical health as well. Intimacy, according to these studies, can contribute to the efficiency of the immune system. Intimacy just may be the "breakfast of champions."

Another researcher described intimacy as a perpetual process. It begins with two people feeling they have an understanding, an ease in being together, and an attraction. This attraction does not have to be physical or sexual; it could be an emotional attraction. They simply enjoy being together. Occasionally, this understanding may be caused by similar interests, or because the two people meet each other's mutual needs.

Ease of understanding is usually followed by a period of emotional discussion and self-disclosure. During this time, the people begin to reveal important emotional facts about themselves. This process leads to the next plateau of intimacy: deep companionship. At this point, the two people begin to see each other as outlets for many behaviors and activities. Marked predominantly by a period of viewing the other as a receptor for the expression of feelings, deep companionship is a powerful stage, leading to excitement and intensity between the two individuals.

The final stage of intimacy is a period of mutual interdependence. During this stage, the couple has a need to love each other. This period is often accompanied by a desire to confide in one another and encourage the other's achievements and ambitions. This is a best-friend developmental period, and a rewarding time for most. You will notice that nowhere in this explanation are the phrases "intense emotional addiction," "sexual attraction," or "intercourse"—those are all vastly different experiences and don't have to be present for intimacy to occur. Some might disagree. To say intimacy is misunderstood would be an understatement. It would be more accurate to say it's mysterious.

> *The richest love is that which submits to the arbitration of time.*
> —Lawrence Durrell

I suggest Scott and Zelda Fitzgerald died from their inability to find intimacy. They searched endlessly, an exhausting journey that led to early graves for both. Scott was forty-four years old when he died. He was the same age as Rush Limbaugh, Steven Seagal, Tony Danza, Kurt Russell, and Phil Collins—as of the date of publication. Zelda was forty-eight when she died—the age of Hillary Rodham Clinton, Carolyn Moseley Braun, Glenn Close, and Jacqueline Smith. They were both extremely talented people who died unnecessarily young. The medical reason for Scott's death was a heart attack, subsequent to prolonged alcohol use. Zelda died a slow and painful, psychological death, beginning in 1922 and ending in 1948. Her medical death was caused by fire; her psychological death, by her inability to find intimacy. Both deaths were avoidable.

In many ways, Scott and Zelda shadow boxed with intimacy. Their patterns involved an elaborate series of maneuvers by each of the Fitzgeralds. It was a sick way of remaining connected. They stalked intimacy. And it led to their demise, both creatively and medically. They wanted intimacy, but were equally frightened at the price it could extract from them. As a result, they both died unnecessarily young.

The Fitzgerald marriage was the embodiment of a mutually parasitic relationship. The term *parasitic* describes the process where one organism feeds off another. A fungus growing on a plant, as an example, is a parasitic relationship. Cancer growing within the human body is also parasitic. With the Fitzgeralds, the parasitism extended in both directions. Copies of their early correspondence revealed this dramatically. Confessions abounded, such as of "I can't imagine the sun rising without you in my life."

Scott used Zelda profusely in his books. He even plagiarized her diaries and letters. This lack of boundaries intensified their parasitism. Yet, at the same time, they were both productive within the toxic nature of their relationship. Scott's first three books were written and published during the height of his conflict with Zelda. During Zelda's prolonged series of hospitalizations, when things were probably more calm for Scott, it took him an astounding eight years to complete *Tender is the Night*.

Similarly, Zelda constantly struggled with the shackles Scott placed on her creativity. Their conflicts about Zelda's writing is well documented. Yet, when finally free of Scott—beginning at the time of their final separation in 1936 and lasting until her death in 1948, Zelda wrote nothing other than letters to her mother and daughter. In fact, her own autobiographical novel, *Save Me the Waltz*, was written during one of the most conflictive periods of their relationship. It is evident: Even their creativity was parasitic.

Together, they were toxic. One could only guess what would have happened to them had they not met. Zelda had begun her manipulative and narcissistic trends long before she met Scott. After meeting him, she simply became an exaggerated version of herself. Had she stayed in control, Zelda probably would have remained stable. Scott likely would have found some other damsel in distress, although it is doubtful that anyone other than Zelda could have stimulated the combustible reaction that eventually ignited Scott's creativity. Their personalities meshed perfectly to create an addiction for affliction, and they ended up with affliction rather than intimacy.

The Fitzgeralds were melodramatically romantic and likely had no understanding of true intimacy. They seemed totally unrealistic in their expectations. In their personal correspondence and novels, they demonstrated this repeatedly. They each wanted a relationship to fix them. The right romance, they thought, would make them complete. In reality, the opposite is true. The relationship doesn't cure you. You cure it.

In modern America, people look to intimacy as an elixir to solve their problems. Others see it as some magical salve to heal their open wounds. It is neither. Intimacy, in its purest form, is a by-product of two healthy people communicating in a vulnerable way and investing quality- and quantity-time together. It is not like prescription medication; it's something you can gain after you get well. It's a by-product of individual psychological and emotional health.

Scott and Zelda were not the first people to die in their quest for this ever-elusive quality. People have done it throughout history. But if it's so deadly, why would anyone want it at all? It's not intimacy itself that's toxic. It's the fear people associate with it. It's the fear of risking the openness necessary to obtain intimacy and then being destroyed. Destruction is the ultimate risk of intimacy. And it's the fear of destruction that usually ends up causing it.

> *You give but little when you give of your possessions.*
> *It is when you give of yourself that you truly give.*
>
> — Kahlil Gibran

I desperately tried to help Jack and Sandra during a marriage counseling session. They had come to an impasse about the subject of intimacy. Sandra wanted more intimacy, but she was having difficulty explaining what she meant. I suggested each of us close our eyes and imagine a picture that best represented our subjective definitions of intimacy. I paused while Sandra shut her eyes and Jack looked at the ceiling.

"Okay," I interrupted. "What picture did you see? What represents intimacy to you?"

"Sex," Jack nodded. "Two people. In bed. Wearing each other out. Just raw, undiluted, wild sex!" We laughed together at his characterization.

"Okay," I smiled. "That's a fascinating picture, by the way. But I saw something a little bit different. Actually, what I saw was two people walking in the woods holding hands. Nothing being said. Just walking. It's autumn. The leaves have fallen. It's about sixty-five degrees. The wind is calm. That, to me is intimacy." I turned to Sandra. "What about you? What picture did you see?"

She stared at both of us in disbelief, then shook her head incredulously. "Communication!" she exclaimed, throwing her hands in the air. "Two people communicating. Everybody knows that's what intimacy is. You're both crazy!" Intimacy is extremely difficult to define. If there are three people in a room, there will likely be three different definitions. People define it based on their own personal experience and culture. In modern society, the quest for intimacy has brought a corresponding and almost fearful misunderstanding of the word.

In this book, intimacy does have a particular meaning. Intimacy is defined as a strong attachment, or bond, between two people, characterized by trust, familiarity, and acceptance. In many ways, it's a relationship of emotional affinity or oneness. It's not at the same level of necessity as food or water; people can exist biologically without intimacy. It probably is, however, necessary for emotional health and happiness. There have been numerous studies that found a connection between lack of intimacy and such problems as depression and suicide. One major study found that the most significant factor influencing depression in senior citizens was the lack of a confidante. Not having someone to whom they could reveal their most private thoughts was found to be the leading cause of depression and mental illness in elderly people. There has also been a significant finding that this lack of intimacy led to suicide attempts among senior citizens and the adolescent population as well.

Most people only flirt with intimacy. Virtually all say they need it; few, however, report ever experiencing it. Fearing the of pain of rejection prevents these people from taking the necessary risks to find intimacy. To avoid these risks, some take extreme measures. Men may seek prostitutes, as an example, thinking they will find it there; prostitutes won't reject you unless you refuse to pay them. Many women gain weight for a similar reason. If you're so unattractive men won't flirt with you, there is no opportunity to be rejected. Massage parlors, strippers, pornography, and similar avenues provide stimulation without risk of rejection. Whatever their merits, none of these provide intimacy. What they do provide is a barrier from intimacy. This is not to say people never take risks. They do. But for some, the pain of rejection is so great they would rather flirt with intimacy than experience it.

You come closest to the shadows of intimacy in times filled with ritualistic symbolism. These are occasions filled with emotional significance. Among these are such rituals as birth, death, and the initial phase of falling in love. During these snapshots of openness, you are often awed by the significance of the other person's presence or passing, although this, too, ultimately becomes a sequence of bobbing and weaving.

Humanity surfaces eventually, and we begin issuing numerous qualifiers: "If only . . ." or "If you'd only . . . ," followed by a litany manufactured of conditions.

Certainly, Zelda did this in her early relationship with Scott. Later on, Scott's conditions for Zelda included limiting her writing. You have probably issued or received similar conditions at one time or another. And though you may have never visited a prostitute or a massage parlor, you have probably avoided intimacy. Bob described it to me in more colorful personal terms.

"I'm like the dog chasing the car." Bob leaned forward and smiled. "He wouldn't know what to do with it if he caught up with one, but he loves the chase. I remember going to bars several years ago. I'd walk in there profiling, but only be interested in the girls who ignored me." He laughed as he continued.

"There could be a whole room full of gorgeous women just staring at me. I'd go for the one girl who ignored me. Even if she may was really, really ugly!" He gestured emphatically with his hands as he spoke.

"Then, if she finally started paying attention to me, I'd ignore her too." He paused for a few seconds. Leaning back in his chair, he looked at the ceiling and continued. "I'll tell you what. I guess I've thought about it now for a long, long time. I just didn't want anything to do with a woman who'd have anything to do with me! I figured I was just trash. If a woman liked me, she had to be pretty trashy too. I hate to admit it, but that's exactly how I felt."

Everyone desires intimacy. If you were lucky as an infant, you found it in your mother's welcoming arms. Perhaps you found it at a funeral when you lowered your defenses to embrace a family member. Or it could have occurred the first time you realized you were in love with that significant other and began opening up to him or her. But over time, you were hurt, rejected, or worse—ignored. You began to respond to intimacy like you would respond to a lion caged in a zoo. You admire the lion's beauty, but are not sure you want to get too close. It happens daily.

> "Yes" I answered you last night; "No" this morning, sir, I say:
> Colors seen by candlelight will not look the same by day.
> —Elizabeth Barrett Browning, "The Lady's 'Yes'"

Many years ago, I counseled a family whose daughter epitomized the way many of us react to intimacy. The parents were worried about her behavior. Her father had confronted her about the notes she'd brought home from school. One of her teachers had written her parents that she was still playing chase with little boys on the playground. She had missed some recess time for this infraction.

"It's not fair!" She exclaimed, emphasizing her words by placing her hands firmly on her hips. She was an attractive, red-haired nine-year-old. I noticed that when she got angry her freckles seemed to blend together. "Why should I get in trouble? The boys are chasing me. All I do is run from them. It's not my fault. It's just not fair."

"It doesn't matter if it's not fair," her father spoke up. "You're the one who gets in trouble, and you're the one who's got to make them stop."

"I've told them to stop a thousand times," she pleaded. "They still chase me. And they chase me more now than they used to. What do you expect me to do?"

I cleared my throat before I finally spoke. "What happens if you don't run?"

She looked up. "Huh?" She squinted her eyes. "What do you mean?"

I walked over and sat beside her. "So, some little boy wants you to play chase. It takes two people to play chase. A little boy comes up and says 'Boo!' or whatever little boys say now. You have to run to make it start. I mean if you don't run, there's no game."

She turned her head sideways and stared up at me. "What are you talkin' about?" she asked with a certain amount of curiosity.

"Look," I continued, "if you refuse to run, nobody can chase you. The little boy comes up and he runs toward you. Turn around and tell him you don't want to play. Tell him it's a stupid game. Eventually he'll quit. One person can't play chase alone. Just don't play. If you don't run, the game's over."

Two weeks later, she explained the results to me. "Well, he started to run after me and I just stopped, and turned around and said, 'I don't want to play chase. It's a stupid game. It's a kid's game. I'm too old to do that any more!' Then I turned and walked away."

"So what did he do?" I laughed aloud.

"Oh, I don't know." She shrugged. "He just stood there and stared at me with his arms hanging down at his sides, looking real sad."

I laughed at the story, but I honestly felt somewhat sorry for the deflated young boy. Just like that, his power was gone. Zelda and Scott played a similar sequence of chase their entire lives. Unfortunately, neither stopped until their deaths put an end to the game. Either of them could have put a halt to it; it could have been as easy as it was for the redhead. With Zelda, the playground was the fire department. She continually climbed out onto the roof, pushed the ladder away, and persistently waited to be rescued—although it never happened after the age of nine. She opened herself to the possibility of intimacy. But when it didn't work, she retreated into depression and mental illness. It was a pattern she and Scott followed throughout their brief lives together. Both of them violated one of the basic requirements for intimacy.

For any measure of intimacy to occur, you must develop trust. You need to believe that there's nothing to run from on the playground of relationships; there's no reason to play chase. To find intimacy, you need to feel accepted enough to disclose your private self. And you have to believe these disclosures won't overwhelm your partner. This usually requires time. Partners who succeed most often share small parts of their intimate selves gradually. If a superficial message is accepted, then, gradually, a deeper one is risked.

Scott was fearful of deepening his relationship with Zelda. He presumed, probably correctly, she would reject his more sensitive and less masculine side. By all indications, he was correct—at least in the early phases of their relationship. Zelda was sickened by Scott's increasing insecurity. When he did attempt to discuss the more vulnerable parts of himself, she threatened to have affairs, and she occasionally did. Scott seldom understood himself and was incapable of verbally expressing his true feelings. They had tremendous difficulty communicating, even about mechanical things such as money and child rearing. Unable to open up to each other, they became caught in a vicious cycle: attack, defend, and counterattack. Their meager attempts at intimacy were blocked at the most superficial level. This became their biggest obstacle to intimacy.

Pretense such as playing chase can thwart any hope of intimacy. Bob, mentioned earlier in this chapter, was too busy running and hiding to grow close. Between his wife and his girlfriend, he had just enough of his needs met; he needn't risk anything more. David and Walt created so much conflict in the workplace that it prevented an entire company from achieving its goal. In their case, it wasn't a quest for traditional intimacy; they were unable to achieve harmony. Jack and Sandra were secure at a distance from each other, but experienced tremendous conflict when attempting to get closer. Gary and Katie wasted energy and time battling for control. Their anger prevented either from achieving their potential.

"When I hold back," Katie later explained, "I feel like I'm in charge, you know? I'm in control. I can prevent him from hurting me deeply. I might not be able to avoid pain altogether, but it's easier to maintain damage control. I can't be overwhelmed by Gary if I'm in control."

Bob once defined intimacy in the following way. "When I compared what I had to what it could be, there was always a gap," he explained. "So I figured I'd have two women. Between the two of them, I could have everything. One woman would be wild and crazy. The other would be better grounded and provide roots. I figured I'd just shift back and forth, depending on what I needed. Of course, that worked well till I got caught. Then I'd have to back off for a while till things settled down. Later, I'd start the whole thing over again."

Like many people, Bob purposely selected the wrong partner. He was afraid of having only one relationship. He was so frightened of being abandoned, Bob purposely picked women who would require him to fragment his efforts. That way, if he lost one relationship, he still would not be alone. This pattern probably did serve the purpose of helping to avoid the pain of abandonment, but it also prevented Bob from attaining what he really wanted. He never experienced intimacy.

We arrive at truth, not by reason only, but also by the heart.
—Blaise Pascal, *Pensers*

One of the biggest complaints I hear from wives in marriage counseling is: "My husband won't talk about his feelings." There are times when the roles are reversed, but they are, overwhelmingly, the minority. Viewed collectively, our society is one where feelings have been discounted. People either avoid them or become totally intoxicated by them. At times, it appears to be a cyclic ritual. This is especially true for men.

Intimacy begins the moment you understand your inner experience—the wide range of emotions, thoughts, and what's generally identified as consciousness. Identifying these experiences is the first step toward intimacy. The second is being willing to communicate them to another. The third step is translating that awareness into meaningful, descriptive language. And the fourth is being fully and uncritically accepted and understood by another person.

Alexithymia is a term used to describe the inability to discuss or even be aware of one's emotions or moods. It's rarely used in psychotherapy today, yet, in my opinion, it's the most common dysfunction among men today. Alexithymics have difficulty with each step toward intimacy. The term itself is fascinating. The prefix *a* means "not." *Lex* originated in Latin and refers to language or vocabulary, as in "lexicon." *Thymia* comes from the Greek word *thymos*, which means having to do with soul, spirit, or feelings. Alexithymics, then, are not capable of using language (lex), to describe things of the spirit or mind (thymia). Statistically, this problem is seen more frequently in the male population than in the female population.

From infancy, men are socialized not to cry. "Don't be a sissy!" boys are admonished when they're hurt. If they do occasionally tear up, they are called names and bullied by others—sometimes by family members. It has been an unwritten rule, probably for centuries, that men are supposed to be emotionally strong. Unfortunately, the word *strong* has been interpreted as being out of touch with emotion. In some ways, it has become socially desirable for men to be alexithymic. But the problem arises in the power of emotional energy. Lost contact with all emotions can develop into either schizoid or antisocial tendencies. Neither is desirable.

In general, women deal with emotions far better than men. Women are more expressive and better communicators, and they generally have wider social networks. This is probably one of the biggest reasons they live longer. There is one emotion, however, that is not acceptable for women to express in our society. That emotion is anger. As a result, many women are unable to identify their angry feelings. Instead, they express sadness, or depression. Anger kept inside can indeed lead to depression, and possibly suicide. Zelda's mental deterioration probably had more to do with suppressed anger than anything else.

Men, on the other hand, generally communicate anger successfully. It is socially acceptable for men to show anger. As a result, many other emotions—frustration sadness, fear, grieving, and hurt—are expressed as anger, which can escalate to inappropriate and sometimes dangerous rage. The high incidence of violent crime, including spousal abuse, is evidence of this. Men repress most emotions. They deny or ignore them to the point that the pressure finally explodes.

Some suggest these gender differences result from vastly different brain structures. Scientists now postulate that the female brain has a greater capacity to interact between the two hemispheres. Recent research has demonstrated that the female brain has a more developed corpus callosum, the band of commissural fibers that unites the two sides of the brain. As a result, women are more likely to integrate the mind-body and mind-emotion connection. Researchers suggest this is responsible for women having fewer problems expressing their emotions.

The consequences of alexithymia can be dangerous, for both alexithymics and those with whom they interact. Feelings do not disappear by repressing them. They inevitably surface, as either rage or medical problems such as ulcers, high blood pressure, or depression. The solution, however, is what alexithymics fear most: intimacy. Through intimacy, a powerful bond is created between two people. The comfort created by someone accepting you completely, in spite of your weaknesses, is a special phenomenon. When two people experience such intimacy, their relationship is permanently changed. A feeling of attachment and belonging occurs and brings a sense of empathy into the relationship. Empathy comes from the German word *ein fuhling* and literally means "in feeling." When intimacy occurs, you begin to feel as though you are inside the other person. The person is woven into yourself to the point you either understand, or will take time to understand, him or her.

Sidney Gourard, author of *The Transparent Self*, described open and intimate relationships as the substance of a healthy life. He also indicated the time and energy required to build intimacy was tremendous. After researching the subject and experimenting honestly with his own relationships, Gourard came to several, fascinating conclusions. One was that some people can't handle others' self-disclosure. Care must be exercised in determining who the recipients will be. He also suggested limiting intimate friendships to no more than three, because of the time and energy involved.

> *This communicating of a man's self to his friend works two contrary effects,*
> *for it redoubleth joys, and cutteth griefs in half.*
> —Francis Bacon, *Essays*

The Fitzgeralds were doomed from the beginning. In a personal letter to Scott, Ernest Hemingway wrote, "We are both bitched from the start." Perhaps the marriage was doomed before it began. When Scott was ready to be honest with Zelda, she made fun of him. Later, as she matured, Zelda sought intimacy from Scott. But it was too late. He had retreated into his own anger and alcoholism. Both Scott and Zelda detached further from their feelings; they became alexithymic, and both paid for it with their lives.

In his classic book *Twilight of the Idols*, Friedrich Nietzsche wrote "That which does not destroy me makes me stronger." As I look at my life, it becomes clear that I learned more and hurt more from my own Zelda relationship than anything I had ever experienced—other than actual combat, that is. I paid a tremendous tuition, but the learning was probably worth it. One of the many important lessons: nobody is immune to the Zelda Complex; even if you have some understanding of it, you may still be vulnerable. I also learned that no matter how cerebral your relationships or life have been in the past, you can still find yourself intoxicated by the Zelda Complex.

Most important, I learned the significance that patterns play in relationships. My father died when I was ten years old. It created multiple problems for my family, but especially my mother. She probably needed therapy at the time, but it was nowhere near as available as it is today. When she went off the deep end, I decided it was my responsibility to cure her. Although I was incapable of such an enormous feat at that age, it didn't prevent me from trying. I failed to rescue my mother, but apparently never gave up on the need.

In retrospect, I now recognize that one of the things I was most attracted to in my own Zelda was her sickness. She was the same age my mother was when my father died. She had a young son who was in desperate need of parenting. Most of all, she was already a step or two "off the deep end." Apparently, she provided me an opportunity to finally rectify my mistake. I was too young to fix my mom, but I was primed for "fixing" my Zelda. Since she was extremely attractive, it made the process that much more inviting. I was confused and frustrated during this time. I desperately wanted her approval, which she withheld. At the time, I really thought it was her. But it wasn't her at all. By fixing her, I was finally completing the work I had begun some thirty years earlier.

After my father's death, my mother was preoccupied with her own pain. She had neither the time nor the capacity to help me or my sister, Sonia, heal. Sonia and I both began looking for intimacy elsewhere, a search that wouldn't end, for either of us, until adulthood. It was a powerful pattern that actually began with my mother's biological parents.

They had given my mother up for adoption to the people I called my grandparents. Apparently, her biological parents were unable to provide intimacy, so they found someone who could. Perhaps, in my own way, I was trying to fix three generations of problems by rescuing my Zelda. If so, I failed miserably. I feel lucky, however, to have escaped with any degree of psychological health. Some people never escape. Unfortunately, Scott and Zelda's only escape was through death.

One of my clients had married three, alcoholic wife beaters in a row. She divorced them after each had been admitted to a treatment program. Once they were sober, she sent them packing and found some other soul to rescue. A teenager came to see me when his girlfriend told him she was pregnant. In the course of therapy, we eventually discovered that the same thing had occurred with his father, grandfather, and great-grandfather. These and other patterns accomplish one thing. They prevent people from being themselves, and experiencing intimacy.

At times, it appears these patterns are passed on in DNA, like eye color or height. More likely, it's the lure of the familiar. Zelda illustrated the lure of the familiar in many ways. The men she dated were familiar. The one she ended up marrying was different at first, but became a caricature of himself while trying to prove his masculinity. Zelda was an accomplished dancer; she danced around intimacy until it destroyed her mental health and her life. Scott's heroines were all familiar representations of Zelda. The women to whom he was attracted were familiar. The last friendship he had before his death was with a younger version of Zelda. In many ways, he repeated his father's path. Like his father, Scott experienced nagging financial problems his entire life. He felt inadequate as a provider. He became the psychologically unavailable father he disdained as a teen. He never became the gallant male he dreamed of. It was familiar. It was predictable. It was painful. It was painfully familiar.

The way to love anything is to realize that it might be lost.
— G. K. Chesterton

The opposite of intimacy is emotional loneliness. It can haunt you even in the presence of friends. Society has generated a frenetic pace of technological change, encouraging superficial attachments. One marriage is nothing more than a boot camp for the next. Friendship has been replaced by the Internet; e-mail is considered interpersonal communication. Regardless of technology's pace, however, our emotional needs have not changed significantly over time. Loneliness has become a sickening way of life. Those values left by the "me generation" have led to a fragmented society where the words *dysfunctional* and *family* seldom appear by themselves.

As a result, we seek relationships that provide it all. Our expectations soar drastically out of proportion to reality. We seek white-hot sex, total communication, a spiritual guru, and a hard-bodied lover, all in one. Instantly. We want to pop our psychological messes in the microwave and, two minutes later, bring out a perfect, intimate relationship. It never happens. So we discard that relationship, beginning our quest once again. These fantasies are the biggest enemies of intimacy.

True intimacy is grown over time, like a garden. If you cultivate it, you will eventually reap tremendous results. If not, there is little chance of success. There are two elements that will help you harvest healthy intimacy. Both require effort and the willingness to make intimacy an extremely high priority.

The first element, interestingly enough, is simple longevity. Intimacy takes time. The longer you know a person, the more likely you are to become intimate. This factor cannot be replaced, but it can be sped up by increasing the frequency of informal contact. Today, most society revolves around the workplace. With its formal structure and emphasis on job-based roles, little opportunity is provided for the ingredients of intimacy. Intimacy is nourished through low-pressure interaction, relaxation, and the gradual lessening of defense mechanisms. Society used to provide a vehicle for intimacy through town squares, where folks gathered to gossip. Families promoted intimacy by gathering on front porches, rocking or swinging while greeting neighbors. Extended families, living within walking distance of each other, created a safe, social network and a sense of security. For most of us, however, few of these commodities exist any longer. Today, if you truly want intimacy, you have to make it a goal and go out of your way to make it happen.

It's not formal structure that leads to intimacy. A dinner party is less likely to create intimacy than an informal gathering that leads to a relaxed give-and-take. Nor is it likely that a five-hour meeting held three times a year will create closeness. Actually, one hour every week would be much better. Brief, low-pressure gatherings are usually far more conducive to deepening relationships. And small, infrequent pauses from formal interaction are much better than major productions, with accompanying degrees of major expectations.

The second element that helps to create intimacy is gradual, but persistent, revelation. Slowly revealing your inner self gives the other person a glimpse of your vulnerable side. Some people consider revelation almost synonymous with intimacy, because of its power. It usually precedes the crucial shift from a perfunctory relationship to an intimate one. Revelation, or unmasking, is a gradual process that deepens as trust increases. Occasionally it can occur rapidly, but this is usually after months of more superficial communication.

Revealing oneself relieves emotional loneliness. The listener usually experiences honesty of this sort as a gift of trust and affection. For the speaker, it relieves shame, fear, and guilt. If acceptance is the response, the bond created can defy explanation. In all the couples I've mentioned thus far, revelation was unwelcome, or, in some cases, not even allowed. Zelda rejected Scott's sensitivity. Scott later reciprocated and rejected Zelda's attempts at honesty. My own Zelda mocked my attempts to unmask myself, walking out of the relationship on four, separate occasions. Bob refused to unmask with either Debbie or Sam. Each saw only portions of who he was. Katie was unable to handle Gary's success. Uncomfortable with his own emotions, Gary could not accept Katie's unmasking. David and Walt were too defensive and angry to get even superficially close. The jealousy and rivalry they perpetuated ultimately infected hundreds of people. Jack and Sandra simply played with each other. When one pursued, the other would distance. Then, within days, they would switch roles.

All failed to meet the necessary requirements for a healthy relationship, and they ran from the same thing. It was not fear of intimacy. It was the fear of total, emotional annihilation that could occur with rejection. As Dr. Pennebacker demonstrated, intimacy and friendship should be valued. They are important for your mental as well as physical health. An intimate relationship is probably the most important emotional asset a person can have. Even the most introverted person needs to reveal him- or herself. The consequences of not finding a relationship in which it is safe to do so can be devastating, as it was with the Fitzgeralds. Actually, it is tragic. It is a tragedy Zelda tightly embraced. And it was the beginning of the end for both of them.

CHECKLIST

Instructions: Check each statement that applies.

_____1. Even when I am around people, I sometimes feel terribly lonely.

_____2. I enjoy debating different points of view on various issues, but stray from conversations about feelings.

_____3. I have never experienced a close, personal relationship I consider satisfying.

_____4. I have lots of acquaintances, but not really any close friends.

_____5. I have been married more than twice, or in long-term, committed relationships more than twice.

_____6. I have used sex as a means to get closer to my partner.

_____7. I have no desire to share my feelings with anyone. It's really none of their business anyway.

_____8. Discussing everyday issues, such as child care or finances, with my partner often results in disagreement.

_____9. When I am criticized, I feel I should have the opportunity to defend my actions. If they would just understand my motives, they would see I am right.

_____10. I'd like to have closer friendships, but I really don't have the time.

_____11. When I am with my partner, I feel as if I cannot be myself.

_____12. I excelled in math and science in school.

_____13. Quite frankly, I don't have a good opinion of people who can't control their emotions.

_____14. I have been accused of being a workaholic.

_____15. I am more comfortable in large gatherings than in small groups.

Scoring: Total the number of statements checked. Scores less than five suggest you are fairly comfortable with intimacy. Scores between five and ten indicate that achieving intimacy may be a problem for you. If you checked more than ten statements, you probably actively avoid intimacy. It may be helpful to share this checklist with a friend, to determine why intimacy is uncomfortable for you.

Journal Session

1. It may be interesting for you to try to define what intimacy means to you. Sandra and Jack had very different ideas about what it meant. It is likely that intimacy means something totally different to your partner as well.

2. After writing your own definition, ask your partner for his or hers. Obviously, you cannot help each other achieve intimacy if neither of you understands the other's need for, or definition of, it.

Chapter 4

THE BARRACUDA WALTZ
THE DANCE OF ZELDA COUPLES

*So close
Yet so far away
We believe in tomorrow but we're stuck in today
We're so close yet so far away.*
—Daryl Hall and George Green, "So Close"

Y ou can use any substance to create distance. Zelda had affairs; Scott had alcohol. Both played mind games. Jack and Sandra did all of the above. Their fourth counseling session was tedious and tiring; their wavering was beginning to wear on me. Like the Fitzgeralds, Jack and Sandra danced around closeness. Unlike the Fitzgeralds, they had not yet become terminal. In many ways, I felt more like a fortune teller than a therapist.

Finally, trying to hide my exasperation, yet still sound analytical, I suggested: "You know, you two came here telling me you wanted a better marriage. I believe you. You are both obviously intelligent. But what you are doing is not so bright. It's not going to create a lot of problems, but it's not going to help things either. What your behavior really does, or what your patterns really do, is to prevent you from getting close. Now, to me, that's bad enough.

"The problem is, if you keep this up, you're about a year away from causing some serious damage. This is just the beginning. If you really want a good marriage, you've got to stop what you're doing. If you don't want to stop, that's your business. But you're never going to have a happy marriage."

The couple glared at me, silently. Jack started to speak, but restrained himself. I realized I'd perhaps overreacted and began to apologize. "Look, folks, I'm sorry if I'm coming on too strong. But I know where this is headed, you don't. You act as if this is harmless. It's not. What you're doing is, at a minimum, wasteful. At best, it will keep you apart. At worst, you'll end up driving each other to divorce. You tell me you want to stay married. If that's the goal, maybe you'd better start moving toward each other, instead of dancing around one another.

"You know what you remind me of?" I leaned over to emphasize my point. "A barracuda I played with while I was scuba diving." In actuality, theirs was a fairly common pattern among married couples: The wife pursues her husband until he begins to pursue her. Then she retreats. When the husband gets tired of pursuing and stops, she pursues again. This pattern actually does resemble the movements of a barracuda with which I came eye to eye in the Florida Keys.

A group of friends and I had chartered a boat and were several miles out in the Atlantic. I was the first of my group to enter the water that day. After the bubbles and silt cleared, I looked up. There he was: a five-foot barracuda staring at me, grinding his teeth back and forth in a sinister way. Initially, I froze. To move, I reasoned, might provoke him. To sit still might invite an angry snap of his razor-sharp teeth. I wasn't aware of any barracuda attacks on scuba divers, but I didn't want to be the first! We both hovered motionlessly and stared at each other. Neither of us moved for what seemed like minutes but was probably only seconds. He continued to stare, grinding his teeth rhythmically. I remained frozen, breathing very slowly.

Finally, I inched my hand forward slowly, reaching out to touch him. Matching the pace of my arm, he and backed off. But he swam only far enough away to escape my reach, still maintaining eye contact and grinding his teeth. Breathing a sigh of relief, I smiled, backing ever so slowly away. As I retreated, the barracuda mirrored my movement, advancing methodically toward me, yet remaining the same distance away.

When I stopped, he stopped. When I swam toward him, he swam away. When I swam away from him, he followed me. He mirrored my movement, but remained an arm's length away. We continued this hypnotic rhythm until I looked at my air gauge and realized I was about to exhaust my oxygen supply. As the barracuda and I surfaced, I noticed the other divers had gathered to watch. Later, one of them commented that it looked like the barracuda and I had been waltzing back and forth on the ocean floor.

For years, I had forgotten the experience. Then, one day I realized that in relationships we repeat this experience. Like the barracuda, most people never get much closer than just beyond arm's reach. The barracuda waltz is repeated millions of times a day, although not on the ocean floor.

To this day, I have no idea what it would have been like to actually touch the barracuda. He could have bitten me. We could have had fun together. I could have scratched him. Or perhaps, some suggest, I could have taken him home and had 'cuda fillet. With increasing closeness, there was increasing risk. There was opportunity for fun, but at the same time there was opportunity for injury or pain to either one or both of us. So, instead of caressing, we waltzed. In relationships, people do the same.

> *Fear always springs from ignorance.*
> —Ralph Waldo Emerson, *The American Scholar*

At one point in their relationship, Jack and Sandra had been close and vulnerable to each other. But it had all changed. The dance had become so complex that nobody could figure out how it started, or who was leading or following. They had an intellectual understanding and an acute awareness of the dance, but it had apparently taken on a life and power all its own. Now, the barracuda waltz—not Jack or Sandra—was in charge. Although both could discuss the intellectual aspects of the relationship, neither was willing to talk about its emotional health.

In the song "So Close Yet So Far Away," the lyrics poetically lament a couple's consistently unsuccessful attempts at getting close: "And the dream that pulls us together, Girl / Is a dream that keeps us / So close yet so far away." Scott and Zelda struggled with this process. So did Jack and Sandra. Probably so have you, at some time in your life. A 1987 study of divorce attorneys found lack of communication coupled with divergent personal growth patterns to be the leading cause of divorce. When I initially visited with Jack and Sandra in psychotherapy, they claimed to have a communication problem. Yet the problem's origins were deeply rooted in their vastly different directions of growth. As with most couples, the two areas were interrelated. Sandra had grown more toward needing emotional connectedness. Jack had become more detached from his emotions as he became more involved in work and intellectual pursuits. His alexithymia was Sandra's biggest complaint. Yet, like many women, she was also developing her own alexithymic tendencies in response.

Women's disgust with men's general emotional unavailability is likely universal. I hear it daily in psychotherapy and on radio talk shows. Volumes of books have been written on the subject. In the film *Fatal Attraction,* the character Glenn Close played had a field day with this idea: "I woke up. You weren't here. I hate that." And women across the globe applauded. Perhaps the theme was exaggerated. But thousands of women identified with the character's frustration. The psychological unavailability of men is a major component of the barracuda waltz. The result is a failure to communicate, which leads to vastly different directions of growth. This results in a lack of attention, which often leads to extramarital affairs or divorce. The vindictiveness of Close's character dramatically illustrated the frustration most women experience. Thankfully, few go to her extremes to make the point.

As frustrating as divergent growth patterns are, the barracuda waltz is even worse. If you have a distant relationship, at least you know what you have. The waltz is deceptive and seductive in that you occasionally get glimpses of intimacy. You literally become "so close yet so far away." This glimpse of intimacy makes it difficult to sink into the complacency of simply maintaining distance as some people do.

It takes two people to dance this waltz. As with any dance, it is cooperative. In the midst of it, you cannot ascertain who's leading, who's following, or who started. The goal of the dance is not to please either partner. Its rhythm is avoidance; its tune is one of mutual fear. It's often danced perpetually, and can take one of several directions: It can end by consent of the dancers. It can advance to a higher level of the Zelda complex. Or it can end in psychological or physical devastation.

The pattern Jack and Sandra illustrated represents Stage One of the Zelda Complex. It is marked by a mutual awareness that problems exist in the relationship. This awareness is accompanied by an inability to simply stop the pattern. The couple feels powerless to control the dance. Occasionally, both partners may be fully conscious of what they're doing but impotent to change. At other times they're unaware of what's going on at all. They are, however, completely aware of their dissatisfaction.

Sometimes it was worth all the disadvantages of marriage
just to have that: one friend in an indifferent world.

—Erica Jong, *Fear of Flying*

There are four stages of the Zelda Complex. A couple may advance through all four stages, remain at Stage One or Stage Two independently, or get out of the Complex completely. All couples we've observed at advanced stages, however, began at Stage One. It has also been observed that some couples can exhibit Stage One symptoms temporarily and never develop the full-blown Complex. This usually results from the relationship terminating at this stage, or some form of severe trauma jolting the couple out of the dance. Just like the little girl who quit playing chase with the boys on the playground, the dance can easily stop. One partner can simply quit cooperating. Unfortunately, neither Jack nor Sandra ever did.

This pattern is found most often among highly verbal people who are intelligent and articulate. Though their verbal skills may not be demonstrated in the marriage, they are usually quite successful communicators otherwise. Their verbal skill could be part of the solution; instead, it becomes part of the problem. They use communication skills to keep them apart; they spar verbally rather than risk an emotional embrace.

I liked Jack and Sandra from the first minute I met them. I wanted their marriage to succeed. They were in their late forties, but had an attitude about them that seemed much younger. She was a high-energy, special-education teacher at a local high school. Jack was a chiropractor with his own busy practice. They led low-profile lives, and didn't socialize a great deal. They had raised two adopted children successfully. The children, now grown, were living on their own.

"When I first realized we had these problems," Sandra began, "I thought maybe I was just having empty-nest syndrome or something. You know, with the kids gone, perhaps my attention was deflected from them onto the marriage. As long as I was busy raising the kids and working, I really didn't focus on our relationship that much. I guess I woke up one morning and realized we were so far apart, we were just like strangers. Friends, yes. But as far as deep relationships go, I didn't even know Jack."

I glanced over at Jack. "What do you think about all this?" I asked. "She says you guys are strangers. How do you describe your marriage right now?"

Jack looked at Sandra briefly and then back at me. As he began to speak, he focused his eyes in my general direction, but on some imaginary spot over my right shoulder. I noticed he specifically avoided eye contact. "I don't know how she comes up with this about us being strangers. My God! We spend a lot of time together. People see us as the ideal couple. Financially we're okay. I give her a lot of attention." He looked over at Sandra. "Don't I give you a lot more attention than any of your friends' husbands give their wives?"

She nodded. "You give me attention all right. In fact, you give me a great deal of it. We can discuss politics, books, and movies. We discuss a lot of things. But we never talk about our lives—our souls. Yes, we have a great intellectual friendship. You are a fine companion. But I can have all that with my colleagues at school, or with students. I need a soul mate. We have never been that with each other. That's where the problem really is."

We had several other insightful conversations. But they had difficulty going beyond insight. When they made plans to seek more closeness, something always sabotaged them. On one occasion, they had planned an intimate getaway at a vacation area two hours away from the stress of home and work. They talked about it and planned it for weeks. The day they were supposed to leave, Jack began complaining about money. His business was down, yet he had recently given one of his employees a substantial raise. In spite of Sandra's request not to spoil their weekend together, he continued to obsess about the problems. Then he began a harangue about the cost of psychotherapy and eventually the money they had spent on the upcoming weekend. Finally, in an angry outburst, Sandra refused to go; they stayed home, silently allowing the weekend to simmer away.

Scenes like this happened regularly. Their verbal skills, although incredibly strong, didn't help them communicate, but kept them away from each other instead. Strong verbal skills are necessary to have a good relationship; this couple used them as barriers. Fascinatingly enough, when asked what attracted them to each other, each independently cited their mutual ability to talk about things. They could discuss things completely and comprehensively, and still do. It was their inability to talk about each other that created the problems. It was as Hall and Oates described: "the dreams that keep us together are the dreams that keep us apart."

Jack and Sandra's communication pattern was ultimately reduced to a series of messages and responses, motivated by one-upmanship and the need for control. Their struggles at defining the base of power in the relationship became more important than exchanging information. What was said became far less important than how it was said. The time and energy once devoted to children was now directed toward debate. There were sporadic lapses: Their daughter's miscarriage resulted in an undeclared truce. And when Jack's mother died after a serious stroke, hostility ceased once again. But in the end, the barracuda waltz triumphed.

It's important to understand that boundaries can be communicated both with and without words. Gestures, postures, and physical stance all send powerful messages, as do facial expression, tone of voice, and inflection. Albert Mehrabian discovered in his research that when it comes to an emotional response, 55 percent of its impact is caused by the speaker's facial expression. Tone of voice is responsible for 38 percent. Only 7 percent had anything to do with the words used.

The March 27, 1995, issue of Newsweek, which explored gender differences in brain functioning, reported that men do a very poor job of interpreting facial expressions other than those having to do with anger. Combining these two studies, we can infer that men can be expected to misunderstand emotional communication 55 percent of the time. Sandra suggested that perhaps 93 percent would be more accurate. "The biggest problem in the world today for women is men," she once described emphatically. "They can talk about the weather. They can talk about business. They can talk about sports. But they can't talk about life." To her, and to many other women, life is about emotional honesty.

Unfortunately, women are increasingly experiencing problems in this area. Several years after my barracuda experience, I took another scuba-diving trip. We were off the Florida panhandle, in the Gulf, having tremendous fun scuba diving. During one dive, however, something happened that illustrates these principles in a powerful way. We were at a depth of about forty feet when I looked up and saw the outline of a huge, eerie-looking hammerhead shark passing above me. In the grayness, he appeared to be about ten feet long. While there may be no documented cases of barracudas attacking scuba divers, sharks have done it repeatedly. I hurriedly swam to my dive buddy's side and tapped her shoulder. She turned toward me, and I pointed upward with my forefinger, indicating we needed to surface. She shook her head, no, and continued to swim.

Once again, I tapped her and pointed toward the surface. This time she literally placed her hands on her hips, and emphatically shook her head and entire body, No!

I realized this was becoming a power struggle. But try as I might, this was not the time for emotional empathy. I had just seen a prehistoric-looking hammerhead, who was probably ready for lunch. I usually respect protocol, but at that moment I realized the danger present. Finally, in exasperation, I reached over and turned off her air. I offered her my spare regulator as we surfaced together. As soon as we found the boat, she unloaded on me.

"Why did you do that!" she shouted.

"Hammerhead," I breathed. "A huge hammerhead was hovering around us."

"Well, I didn't see it!" she rationalized.

"Yeah, I could tell. But you don't have to see a shark for him to eat you."

That's truly the way it is. You don't have to see trouble in your relationship to be affected by it. You don't have to understand the waltz you're dancing to end up too far away. It's not a requirement that your partner warn you before leaving the relationship. Similarly, you don't have to be aware of what's going on to be devoured by the dynamics of a relationship. Just as the hammerhead's attack can be deadly, so can the barracuda waltz.

Zelda's histrionics and Scott's drunkenness were notice enough; problems existed. Although signals are rarely as dramatic at this stage. The Fitzgeralds' Stage One symptoms began while they were dating. Their correspondence reveals that they were aware some problems existed. Jack and Sandra had been married for twenty-six years, stuck in Stage One. As long as they focused on their children, they did quite well. There were few dramatics and no drunkenness. But you don't have to see trouble to be affected by it.

Trouble soon struck.

I have always made a distinction between my friends and my confidants. I enjoy the conversation of the former; from the latter I hide nothing.

—Edith Piaf

As we looked back at the evolution of Jack and Sandra's marriage, neither could pinpoint when the distancing really began. They couldn't explain or understand; nevertheless, it affected them. Their intellectual style of communication kept them in Stage One. They got neither too close nor too far away and became addicts in mutual misery. Jack could not understand or express his real feelings. Sandra understood her feelings, but was unwilling to express them in a way Jack could understand.

But Charles understood her. They had been friends for ten years and had even attended graduate school together. He was paraplegic as a result of an injury incurred during the Vietnam War. He was an English teacher and a poet, who had been divorced from his only love since his injury some twenty years earlier. Because of his injury, Charles was unable to have sexual intercourse. Earlier, he had befriended Jack, but understood Jack's shortcomings as a communicator. He did not exploit their differences. Like most affairs, it just happened. By the time Sandra entered into therapy, she and Charles had been intensely involved for more than three years. The affair was brought to my attention by Jack's suspicions.

Eventually, Sandra came to see me and confessed, looking for direction. "So that's the truth," she concluded. "It's an affair of the heart. Technically, we haven't committed adultery. Yet the only reason we haven't is because Charles can't. Jack is hot on our trail right now. He's spoken to both of us and to some of our friends. We've all denied it, and, probably, I could convince him we're not doing anything. I mean, seriously, Jack knows Charles can't have sex. I guess my question is, what do you think I should do? Should I tell him what's really going on?"

I hesitated, attempting to think my answer through before I responded. "It all depends on what your goal is," I began. "I mean, what do you want from this? Do you want to be married to Jack? Or do you want to divorce him and marry Charles? Or do you want to do neither? Perhaps you want things to continue the way they are. I don't know. This is a critical time for you and Jack. I do know that. You have to determine where you want to go from here. And you really don't have a lot of time. You need to think this out very clearly before you go much further."

The waltz begins as a communication problem. It can evolve into a far more serious conflict, including affairs, among other things. It can also develop into an advanced stage of the Zelda Complex. Sandra began a relationship with Charles as a direct result of not being able to talk on a deep level with Jack. That does not make it Jack's fault. But if they could have achieved a deeper, more rewarding level of communication, it probably would not have occurred. Certainly, in this case, the relationship with Charles was not about sex.

"I really don't want to end my marriage," Sandra continued. "I'm not sure why not. Other than materialism and tradition, it doesn't add much to the quality of my life. There is also the religious factor, as far as getting a divorce is concerned. I've got tremendously deep-seated injunctions about divorce. But I don't want to give up my relationship with Charles either.

"He really is my best friend. He doesn't expect me to get divorced. We've talked about it. We can talk about anything. That's the point. I can talk to Charles, and he will listen to me. He listens to me and it makes me feel special."

Listening accurately is extremely difficult. Some researchers indicate that the message sent is received only about 15 percent of the time. People hear the words, but 85 percent of the time, they miss the meaning. Jack listened while staring out the window, flipping through the newspaper, or watching TV. When he decided to talk, it was most frequently while Sandra was cooking supper or, for whatever reason, using the bathroom. Either way, it was very difficult for her to listen intensely and empathetically to Jack. The way Sandra described it, they often conducted duologues—two separate conversations taking place simultaneously. For example, Sandra would talk about the children, while Jack would answer, telling something that happened at the office. They listened to themselves rather than to each other. But it wasn't that way with Charles.

"Charles listens to what I'm saying. He listens with his heart," Sandra explained. "He listens with his mind. He listens with his soul. He looks at me. He leans over toward me. He'll hold my hand. He's cried with me. He's opened up with me. He's told me about his life. I feel like I really know him. I don't really even know Jack, though I've been married to him for some twenty-five years now. I know my girlfriend of two or three years far better than I know Jack. But I don't want to end the marriage. And I don't want to give up my relationship with Charles."

I held my first position as a psychotherapist in 1974. Since that time, I have worked in various settings including universities, alcohol rehabilitation centers, psychiatric hospitals, and outpatient clinics. I don't know exactly how many women I've spoken to in psychotherapy over those years. It probably numbers in the thousands. I feel very lucky to listen to women as I do. They have told me of their fear, their joy, their pain. They have also told me on multiple occasions about their affairs. I have not once heard a women suggest she had an affair because her lover had a cute bottom, large penis, or nice face. I have, however, heard men express such sentiment on multiple occasions. What I have heard women say is they had an affair because their lover listened to them and made them feel special. And I have heard that explanation on dozens of occasions.

Sandra's story was not a new one. I'd heard it dozens of times before. However, this situation was vastly different. It truly was not a sexual relationship in the technical sense of the term. Her love for Charles was more altruistic than utilitarian. They were good friends. I contemplated for quite some time what to say before answering. "I can't make the decision for you," I finally told Sandra. "You have to live with yourself when all is said and done. I mean, you guys will either get a divorce, or Jack will die first anyway. Statistics illustrate one of those will happen first. Ultimately, you'll be alone, regardless of what happens in this situation. You have to do what you can live with. You've got to be your own best friend.

"If you ever want to have a real, intimate relationship with Jack, you will have to be honest with him. But if you're honest, it could result in him leaving you or abusing you emotionally for the rest of your life. That's probably what would happen. I mean, I doubt he would leave you, knowing him like I do. But let's face it. If you guys have been playing games for twenty-five years, why would you stop now? From what I can tell, your parents did the same thing. It's like a family tradition with you guys."

Dance is the hidden language of the soul.
—Martha Graham

How something is said can dramatically contradict *what* is said. Jack and Sandra had a history of mixed messages. On one occasion, I illustrated the way they communicate by having them stand and grasp each other with both hands. I had them push with one hand and pull with the other. The result: they went in circles, which was precisely what they were doing in their relationship. They went neither forward nor backward; they wasted time going in circles without making any progress toward closeness.

On another occasion, I had them stand facing each other. Once again, I had Sandra beckon Jack toward her with her right hand, gesturing him to come forward. At the same time, I had her hold up her left hand in the traditional blocking, or "halt," position. In essence, they were saying "Come here. Now go away," over and over again. And that's exactly what occurred. They would step forward, then back—forward then back—and do so repeatedly.

These physical demonstrations were intended to dramatically illustrate the impact their communication patterns were having on their marriage. The frustration they experienced in doing such drills merely represented what they felt in their life together. The difference is that real-life frustrations have real-life consequences. That consequence: Jack and Sandra's relationship continued to function at a distance. They continued to be "so close yet so far away." They were waltzing through life rather than living it.

I later brought this observation to their attention. By this time, we had diagrammed many of the destructive ways they communicated. Jack had worked through much of his anger. Sandra had convinced him that she had nothing more than an emotional attachment to Charles. She had characterized Charles as no different than many of her girlfriends, and Jack had finally accepted her explanation. They continued to play verbal games with each other, but were now able to laugh when they realized what they were doing. At this point, they still did not have intimacy. They continued their waltz while trying to analyze their mistakes. It was not much better, but it seemed to work for them.

Yet they remained on a verbal merry-go-round. Attacks and counterattacks continued, and they took turns initiating them. When Jack was attempting to improve their relationship, Sandra would distance through verbal sparring. Jack would eventually tire, giving up in disgust, and then Sandra would attempt to patch things up, only to be met by Jack distancing through verbal disagreements. This pattern was so familiar they could graph it. They switched roles in nine- to ten-day cycles, despite fully understanding the process. But they remained incapable of interrupting it. As I later discussed this with them, Jack and Sandra both claimed to be powerless.

Intellectualization is one of the problems with which most people who get stuck in Stage One struggle. It's as if they intellectualize for its own sake. Analysis and debate become the goal, rather than problem solving or getting close. Verbal sparring becomes such an integral part of their communication pattern, it becomes part of the waltz. Its purpose, much like other patterns in relationships, is to maintain distance. Couples become obsessed with playing the game, rather than focusing on what's important. For Jack and Sandra, it became a very significant part of their life. On one occasion, they actually brought in a chart detailing the different categories of arguments and a breakdown of who started them. This chart also included the direction the arguments took, and their type.

Jack and Sandra had charted five major categories of arguments. These are common styles of conflict, and most people participate in them at one time or another. The first category was called *mind reading*. This was Sandra's favorite strategy, and the one she used most frequently. In this exchange, Sandra acted as if she knew Jack better than he knew himself. She could read his mind.

"Oh no," she would yell. "I know what you're thinking. I know you better than you know yourself!" Another approach she took: "Oh, sure. That's what you say now. But I know what you really mean." On other occasions, she would communicate her knowing nonverbally as well. She would roll her eyes and shake her head, suggesting, "I know what that means. I'm not stupid, you know. And I don't have to put up with this."

Jack resorted to mind reading occasionally, but according to the couple's data, Sandra specialized in it. "How can I argue with her?" he asked. "If she can read my mind, there's nothing to do other than let her." This pattern was particularly frustrating for Jack because whatever he said, or didn't say, could be immediately dismissed. "When she gets into this," Jack said, smiling, "I just shake my head and call her 'The Great Karnack.' She's a supreme clairvoyant, and there is nothing I can do."

"Yeah," Sandra agreed, "I do that. But it's only because he won't talk. He clams up and says nothing. I don't know what I'm supposed to do. He won't respond to me at all. He doesn't answer me. He doesn't look at me. Sometimes he won't even grunt! So, yes, I mind read." She crossed her arms. "And I do a great job at it!"

Sandra called the second category of arguments *psychiatrist*. "Oh yes, indeedy!" she laughed. "Didn't you know that Jack's a psychiatrist as well as a chiropractor? He's 'bilateral!' He's got all my problems figured out. Let me tell you, he can diagnose me just like that!" She snapped her fingers.

Finally, Jack smiled and faced me. "She's right." He nodded his head. "I do that far more than she does. It's my favorite strategy. But actually, she plays psychiatrist more than I mind-read. What was it last night?" He looked at Sandra. "You said I was schizo or something?"

"I said you were schizoid." She emphasized the last syllable. "You're cut off from your feelings."

I interrupted and laughed. "He's actually alexithymic then."

"A what?" Jack asked. "What is that? Some kind of eating disorder or something?"

We all laughed as they continued to describe their patterns.

Sandra labeled the third category *TWD*, pronounced "tweed." "This is one of the biggies." She said, nodding her head emphatically. "Tweed stands for toxic waste dump. That's when you just dump everything. Name calling, talking about 'your mama,' last week's problems, last year's problems, problems from a past life—I mean, everything's allowed. And talk about distancing! I feel like a demon possessed when I do a tweed. It's mostly during PMS. Jack tweeds during his PMS time too!"

A lot of people dump. Most of the arguments Scott and Zelda had appear to fall into this category. These disagreements often began over something of substance and then deteriorated. Soon the original purpose of the discussion was lost. There appears to be no specific issue, but rather an undifferentiated mass of confusion, frustration, and anger during such outbursts. TWDs can be overwhelming, and often occur when both partners feel overwhelmed to begin with. I've worked with many couples who "tweed" during particularly stressful periods, such as after the birth of a child, during a move, or the process of rebuilding a house together. TWDs are very destructive and lead to violence in many instances.

Jack called the fourth category of arguments *Double O.* "It's overgeneralized omniscience," he mocked condescendingly. "It's when you turn your nose up and look down at the other person through your glasses. Then you kind of tilt your head and say something like . . ." He hyperextended his shoulders, tilted his head, and exaggerated his already-snobbish tone.

"Oh, Sandra! Everyone knows you're difficult to get along with. Your boss knows. Several of your friends have discussed it with me. I even got a call from a board member about you last week." Jack resumed his normal posture. "It drives her crazy." Jack and Sandra both laughed.

"My favorite Double O is this," Sandra joined in. She stood up, placed her hands on her hips, and began shaking her head back and forth. "You just hate women!" Sandra screamed toward Jack at the top of her lungs. She shook her head violently, her hair flinging wildly as she moved.

"Your mother told me you hate women. Your sister told me you hate women. Even your girlfriend, the one you had an affair with—told me you hate women! I'm not the problem here, Jack. You are! You hate women! That's the problem!" As quickly as she began, she suddenly stopped screaming, looked up, smiled, and sat down meekly.

"Bravo!" Jack applauded. "Encore!" Sandra continued to smile quietly.

"Whoa! Wait a minute." I held up my hand. "Hang on just a second. Now, what do you mean, Jack had an affair? Did I overlook something? I don't remember hearing anything about Jack having an affair."

"Oh, he probably didn't have one." Sandra explained. "That's just the point. When you Double O, you just sort of cover all the possibilities. If he ever did have one, then this way he thinks I know about it. And, of course, his mom is dead, so he can't check in with her over whether or not she said he hated women. That's what it's all about—overgeneralized omniscience. You sort of throw all this stuff out and see what sticks. It really makes him crazy and fills him with doubt. He begins to think maybe I know something that he didn't think I knew. And I feel like a genius! It's a great way to put your partner on the defensive."

"And a great way to waltz too, huh?" I asked.

"Sure." Jack nodded. "But there's one that's even better. We call it the *do/do argument.*"

"Yeah." Sandra nodded. "It's a killer. You're damned if you do, and damned if you don't. Do/do. And that's exactly how you feel when you get into one of those. You feel just like doo-doo. They're awful."

The do/do argument occurs when a listener is trapped in a no-win situation. Regardless of his response, he is wrong. As a result, the listener will often internalize his response and, eventually, act self-destructively. This is usually done in response to contradictory cues sent by the speaker. A powerful dilemma ensues. A prominent family therapist and researcher, Jay Haley, suggested years ago that such messages were responsible for a large portion of mental illness found in the world. He specifically found such communication patterns consistent with those of many schizophrenics he had interviewed.

Jack described a do/do pattern he and Sandra played out fairly often. Sandra would tell Jack something like, "I need you to tell me you love me more often." Later that day Jack would tell Sandra he loved her.

"Yeah, sure," she usually responded with her arms crossed. "You're just saying that because I asked you to." You're damned if you do.

If Jack had said nothing, Sandra would have complained with equal intensity. You're damned if you don't. And it would have been difficult for anyone to deny it was a legitimate complaint. Jack was well aware of his shortcoming in that respect. It was that awareness that contributed to his feeling helpless, which, in turn, was the root of Jack's frustration and anxiety in these do/do patterns. Severe do/do arguments can result in self-destructive responses. Sandra described one occasion when Jack cornered her in a no-win argument. It was so painful, she was unable to recall exactly what had been said.

"I don't really remember the exact situation," she admitted, tilting her head upward to look at the ceiling. "It is the entrapment that stands out. It was almost like I faced a psychological death sentence. My only alternatives were to recognize his deliberate meanness and incredible coldness, or turn totally within myself and sort of decide I must be crazy. It was like gradually detaching from reality by pretending to be someone or somewhere else. It's just an awful, awful feeling. Even now, I shudder just thinking about it."

I turned and looked at Jack, and then back at Sandra. I shook my head back and forth, while resting my elbows on my knees. "You all understand this stuff more than I do. You have more understanding than any three or four people I know, put together. You've got more experience and insight into this than the people who originally researched these ideas.

"So with all this insight, why don't you just stop doing this to each other? Can't you stop intellectualizing and start learning to avoid it? Can't you put some of this incredible brain power you both have into ending these destructive games you're playing?" I leaned back in my chair, rocking back and forth several times without speaking. Finally, I made eye contact with Jack and Sandra again.

"Folks," I leaned toward them. "How about just stopping the dance? Don't you ever get tired of waltzing?"

Jack and Sandra glanced at each other, then back at me. They showed no expression, nor said a word. They stared at one another without speaking for a few minutes. And then I realized their answer. They would probably never quit waltzing. It was the only way they knew how to relate to each other.

The deepest need of man, then, is the need to overcome his separateness, to leave the prison of his aloneness. The absolute failure to achieve this aim means insanity, because the pain of complete isolation can be overcome only by such a radical withdrawal from the world outside that the feeling of separation disappears —because the world outside, from which one is separated, has disappeared.

—Erich Fromm

Jack and Sandra were both brilliant people. There was no questioning their intellect. They are also extremely likable people. Although I no longer see them in therapy, I do consider them my personal friends and see them socially on occasion. Interestingly enough, I think they would be flattered if they knew I included them in this book. That, too, is part of their problem. They would be better off if they felt sad at being depicted as accurately as I have described them, because their plight is a sad one.

Erich Fromm once said, "Infantile love follows the principle: I love because I am loved. Mature love follows the principle: I am loved because I love." Sandra loves Charles. She will probably always love Charles. Neither of them is ready for the commitment of marriage to the other. Neither of them is prepared for the commitment of marriage to anybody. That is Sandra's problem. She chooses a relationship with Charles simply because it eliminates the question of legalistic sexual contact. Her religious values will not allow her to commit adultery. Charles can never penetrate her vagina with his penis. To her, that means she is safe by definition from adultery. Therefore, she will never have to commit completely to Charles. Nor will she have to commit to Jack, simply because they constantly waltz. They will never gain closeness. At the same time, I doubt they will ever divorce.

So they waltz. They will never get too close, yet they will never get too far away. Sandra reaches out to Jack. He grinds his teeth and hovers a little more than arm's length away. When she turns to leave, he follows her, but maintains his distance. When she turns toward him, he distances again. They can do this till the day they die. They've taught it to their children. And beyond their death, their children will perpetuate the dance. Jack and Sandra will likely remain at this stage of the Zelda Complex, rather than advance to the more dangerous stages.

Stage Three is where Scott and Zelda spent most of their lives. The classic case of a Stage Three Zelda relationship is one in which one partner does not have an identity of his or her own. Both Jack and Sandra had strong identities. They had meaningful careers and enjoyed their lives outside of the marriage. They were not economically or psychologically dependent on one another. They were not in competitive career patterns. Jack's career was his; Sandra's, hers. Had Sandra been working as Jack's office manager, for example, the possibilities for difficulty would have been vastly greater.

Sandra did not have difficulty with the amount of attention Jack received, although Jack did occasionally have trouble with the success he perceived Sandra enjoying. In some ways he would have felt more masculine had she remained more dependent on him. It certainly would have given him more control. But he had married her as she was, and was willing to accept her success. Their waltzing was the problem. Yet in some ways it was functional. The waltz kept them fixated at this level, preventing them from becoming more destructively involved with each other. Jack and Sandra were together for more than twenty-five years before they came to see me. That doesn't mean they had a good relationship, however. Actually, it did have some excellent qualities: They had never been separated for any length of time. Their arguments were more intellectual than emotional. And, while they didn't get exceptionally close, they certainly didn't get too far away.

> *Every calamity is a spur and valuable hint.*
> —Ralph Waldo Emerson

My own Zelda was in my life only for a period of months. After leaving the last time, she would have returned, had it not been for the intervention of my office staff. Their main concern, however, was not what she was doing to me. "Let her make a nut case out of you if you want to," Bud had confronted me. "It's your kids and the business we're concerned about."

My Zelda's waltz was far more intense than that of Jack and Sandra. Where theirs was a slow-paced waltz of some twenty-four years, ours was more like a slam dance in a punk-rock bar. There was nothing subtle about my Zelda's approach. When she was finally convinced I was not going to let her return, she actually broke into my house. She took most of my financial records, several Christmas presents, and hundreds of dollars in cash as well as some checks. Although she spent the money and forged the checks, I realized it wasn't about money. The entire episode was about her attempting to continue the connection—the connection was vital if the waltz was to go on. During one telephone discussion with her I laughingly explained, "I don't mind dancing with a barracuda, but dancing with you is like dancing with that hammerhead shark." She found no humor in my explanation, and showed no appreciation for the metaphor.

I wanted to remain friends with my Zelda. I had asked if we could be pals, and it was a sincere request. I now realize she was incapable of agreeing to such a truce. For her, it was much easier to hate. As with most Zeldas, she was extremely dichotomous. Life was either black or white, hot or cold, right or wrong. In her mind, she was right and I was wrong. That made it far easier for her to distance once the dance stopped.

Similarly, her dichotomization eliminated risk. If she had agreed to be friends, she may have felt affection for me. That would have meant risk. Zeldas don't handle uncomplicated friendship well. They can deal with emotional intensity. They can use relationships. They can manipulate extremely well. But Zeldas don't "do" simple affection. Friendship is more difficult to dance with. It's really too bad. We could've been friends.

CHECKLIST

Instructions: Check each statement that applies.

_____ 1. I often have discussions with my partner during which I find it difficult to remember what the original issue was.

_____ 2. I pride myself on my ability to debate either side of an issue.

_____ 3. When my partner and I disagree, I find it necessary to strengthen my case by bringing up past injustices or resentments.

_____ 4. I share my deepest feelings with someone other than my partner.

_____ 5. My partner has told me more than once that I don't listen to what he or she says.

_____ 6. If I have to tell my partner to do something for me (such as bring me flowers), it doesn't count. If he or she only does it when I ask, then I know it's not sincere.

_____ 7. I have had, or am currently involved in, an affair.

_____ 8. I often say hurtful things that would have been better left unsaid.

_____9. During arguments, my partner has accused me of things that weren't even true. Or I have accused my partner of things I'm not sure were factual, just to catch him or her off guard.

_____10. In order to prove a point, I have made up comments that were purportedly made by other people, so my partner would think I wasn't the only one with my point of view.

Scoring: Total the number of check marks. Scores of three or less indicate you have not been caught in the trap of the barracuda waltz. Totals between three and seven suggest you use arguments as a means of maintaining distance in your relationship. If you have a score of more than seven it would probably be helpful for you and your partner to see a professional.

Journal Session

Analyze your relationship for the five major categories of arguments. How many of them do you employ? Which ones are used on you? What would happen if you discontinued using them?

Mind Reading: Acting as if you know what your partner is thinking.

Psychiatrist: Diagnosing your partner's emotional requests in terms of being mentally ill, which shifts responsibility for the problems in your relationship onto your partner.

TWD (toxic waste dump, or "tweed"): Clouding the issue by bringing up past injustices that have already been discussed or resentments never before mentioned.

Double O (overgeneralized omniscience): Making up facts or opinions to support your point of view that cannot be verified, or which seem plausible but are not necessarily true.

The Do/Do Argument (damned if you do, damned if you don't): Asking your partner to improve in a certain area, and then dismissing his or her efforts as insincere because you had to suggest the change.

Chapter 5

A Seductive Dance
ENTRAPPED IN THE ZELDA COMPLEX

Yeah, a man loves a woman but he can't understand
Why she's sad when she stares at the ring on her hand.
　　　　　　—Daryl Hall and George Green, "So Close"

There was a beauty and gaiety in the 1920s. Zelda and Scott had great style and flair. They reflected as well as defined their decade. On the *outside*, they lived excessively and without regret. They were passionate people living in a passionate time. Their lives were marked by incredible highs and lows, by intense periods of productivity and stagnation, and equal periods of frivolity and despair. It's so easy to look at the sickness and overlook the joy they undoubtedly experienced. But the world around them changed; they did not.

What brought the Fitzgeralds down was their inability to deal with changes *inside* their relationship. Scott and Zelda were dreadfully and painfully enmeshed. They were dependent on alcohol. They were dependent on sensationalism. But it was probably their dependency on each other that led to their greatest difficulty. It didn't change—even when they were apart. Their lives, correspondence, and books reflected this. The Fitzgerald marriage was the epitome of a dysfunctional relationship. But most of all, it was a commentary on hostile dependency.

Like the Fitzgeralds, couples can speed through the various stages of the Zelda Complex. Some people remain in Stage One virtually their entire lives, never going beyond it. Scott and Zelda leapt through Stage One during their courtship. Even before marriage, they had already entered Stage Two. The hostile dependency continued until their deaths, although their marriage certainly moved into more destructive stages.

Stage Three, the most visibly dysfunctional stage of the Zelda Complex, is similar to the other stages. Couples can remain in Stage Three, move in and out of it, or progress to Stage Four. By the time the relationship enters Stage Four, the danger has already occurred. Couples in Stage Four are at risk of injuring each other. It can lead to psychological or physical death, as it did with the Fitzgeralds.

A couple can move through Stages One, Two, and Three, toward Stage Four, within a matter of weeks. Other couples may take thirty or forty years to reach Stage Four. The pace depends primarily on the mental health of the individuals involved. Alcohol or drug use can also expedite the process, as can external stressors such as finance, extended family, and children.

Scott and Zelda rotated within the last three stages throughout their marriage. Though their high degree of hostile dependency was indicative of their illness, they actually experienced all the phases. They competed with each other unmercifully. Scott's plagiarism of Zelda's work is evidence of this. His inability to allow her an identity, other than that of the heroine in his novels, likely contributed to her series of psychiatric hospitalizations. He was jealous of her talent. She was jealous of the attention he received. When she attempted to make a place for herself with her art or dancing, he belittled her efforts. This led to her further withdrawal and retreat into depression.

Their dependency was not only emotional, but functional as well. The Fitzgeralds epitomized the couple who can't live with or without each other. Their neediness, as demonstrated through their early writings and correspondence, illustrated their dependency. They were a couple that never seemed to be complete as individuals or satisfied when together. They ultimately entered Stage Four and became obsessed with each other. Their relationship became more a disease than a marriage. At this point, they became very dangerous, together or apart. Scott's alcoholism worsened as Zelda's insanity increased. Each seemed to retreat into their private hells. Neither of them ever returned. Zelda's psychological death occurred rather quickly. Scott's creative death was almost immediately followed by his massive heart attack. Zelda not only burned her paintings and Scott's writings, but ultimately burned herself to death. The Fitzgeralds' lives are exaggerated versions of others'. Thousands of couples have found similar paths. Because of the intensity with which they lived and the intensity of the era, Zelda and Scott took the process further than most could ever imagine.

Anger is momentary madness, so control your passion or it will control you.
—Horace, *Epistles*

Hostile dependency is a very dangerous process. Many adolescents who enter their first intense relationship experience dependency as romantic. They think it's cute when a boyfriend or girlfriend is jealous. In fact, when someone is not jealous, it's considered a lack of affection, or a lack of love. "If you're not jealous, obviously you can't love me"—it's a common sentiment for this age group. At this age, love and dependency are experienced as the same phenomenon. But in reality, the two are quite different.

Love can strengthen you. Dependency will only weaken you. You cannot experience any type of dependency without an accompanying degree of hostility. Dependency, by definition, makes you require something. It's the literal opposite of independent. A person can be dependent on a mere substance, such as caffeine, or on something more powerful, such as alcohol, cocaine, or a prescription medication. At the same time, someone can be dependent on another person. Relationships are at least as addictive as a drug, and maybe more so.

I've never met a drug addict who was a happy individual. Addiction comes from the Latin root, *addictus* which means to be a slave or to be enslaved to. Author Dr. Wayne Dyer once said, "There's no such thing as a well-adjusted slave." Similarly, I've never met a well-adjusted addict. You really can't be dependent on anything, and be truly happy about it. Dependency is like having a crutch. Addicts need the substance they're addicted to in order to feel normal. As a result, they end up being angry at whatever they're dependent upon.

Psychologists and psychiatrists describe hostile dependency as the state many adolescents go through with their parents. In reality, the definition is far more expansive. We have perpetuated a society where dependency is a way of life. People are dependent upon each other; people are dependent upon the government. People are dependent on stimulation—from whatever source. To the degree they don't feel sufficient as individuals, hostile dependents are correspondingly angry. The hostile-dependent cycle can go in vastly different directions. It can be internalized and create incredible problems. Zelda experienced problems with depression. Scott experienced problems with alcoholism. Both were caused by internalized anger and hostility. Scott and Zelda also externalized their hostility. They had many public quarrels. They each had fits of rage. Neither extreme seemed to work.

It's possible to reconcile hostile dependency through a more rational approach. Apparently the Fitzgeralds made some superficial attempt at this. Scott met with Zelda's psychiatrist on multiple occasions. But just as Zelda used the hospitals as a way of controlling Scott, he used the visits to criticize psychiatrists and Zelda. As long as they remained in this hostile-dependent cycle, nothing could be accomplished. They were unable to heal the resentment of the past. They were unsuccessful at halting their recurring bouts with anger. As a result, they perpetuated the cycle.

The hostile-dependent cycle can happen to virtually any relationship. Although we see it most often in families, it can and does occur in all relationships. People who reach Stage Two are openly competitive and appear angry with each other. Waltzing no longer works. The individuals are competitive, usually bound together through family or business relationships, and the level of hostility released periodically escalates to the point that it becomes detrimental to the people or organization involved.

We don't receive wisdom; we must discover it for ourselves after a journey that no one can take for us or spare us.
—Marcel Proust

Several years ago, I worked as a consultant with a large, family-owned manufacturing company. The company had gone through tremendous stress when the reins of power were handed from the father to his two sons. Each son had grown up in, and with, the business. Their father had started one of the first modern manufacturing plants in the area. He had built it through sheer strength of will and old-fashioned work. Though he passed control of the company on to his two sons, he was unable to pass on his work ethic. I had worked with the father and mother in marriage counseling. After one particularly difficult session, they asked if I would be willing to work with their two boys. After explaining the circumstances to me, I agreed to do so.

The meeting took place in a plush conference room at their large corporate headquarters. The room dwarfed our small meeting gathered in the corner. I felt somewhat intimidated by the size and splendor of the extremely well-decorated interior. It was more suitable for a board meeting of twenty than a small consultation of three. Their youngest son, David, leaned toward me, elbows on his knees, staring blankly at the floor. He sighed deeply, tilting his head as he inspected me with a cynical eye. Walt, his older brother, sat in the opposite corner. He crossed his legs and leaned back in a leather chair, fidgeting nervously with his glasses. He smoked in a peculiar, erratic fashion, driving his cigarette back and forth like a rapid-fire piston. Smoke poured from his mouth as he coughed, his eyes fixed hypnotically at a point on the wall, just beyond David and me. Finally, David began to speak.

"The bottom line is, Dr. Baucom, neither one of us wants to be in this meeting. This was Dad's idea, not ours. He ran this damn company for forty years. Now he's trying to continue to run it in fact, if not in name. Yeah, Walt and I are having some problems. The truth is Walt never gives us anything positive. You know, we're in there busting our butts in the plant all day long, and we don't get any feedback from Walt and his group of sissies over in marketing. And I'll tell you the truth. It gets old after awhile. The only time we ever hear anything is when we screw up, and he is the worst one of all. He never tells you when you do anything right. Ever since he took over marketing, it's been like this, and—"

"I just can't believe this crap," Walt interrupted. "We have gone over this time and time again. I'm spread out too thinly as it is. I honestly do not have the time or the inclination to go around pumping up the guys in the plant every day. That's not my job. That's your job, David." Walt stopped speaking as abruptly as he had started. He leaned back contemptuously and forced the cigarette into his mouth. Smoke circled around his head as he gazed at the ceiling, appearing detached.

"Besides," Walt continued, "I'm the president this year. You're the president next year. As long as I'm the president, I'm going to do it my way. When you're the president, you can do it your way."

Their father had made somewhat of a devil's agreement. Rather than name one son president over the other, he had them alternate each year. Regardless of the title, David was in charge of manufacturing and Walt would always be in charge of marketing. Truthfully, that's where their skills lay. But in this particular case, Walt was asserting his position as president simply to get his way.

"That's just absolute garbage!" David shouted. He stared defiantly in Walt's direction. Walt continued to ignore him. "You know what, Walt? We've had this discussion since we were boys. We've talked about running this company all of our lives. We discussed and planned how we would do it. We always talked about how it would be, running the company and getting Dad out of the way. Implementing some of the things we'd learned at Georgia Tech—the quality control program—really making this a leading company in the industry. And now, all of a sudden, since you're the God-almighty president, you just let it go to your head. It's stupid! I'm tired of it. I don't have to cooperate with you. With my stock and Mom and Dad's put together, we can overrule you anyway."

"David," I spoke up. "What's going on inside of you? What are you feeling emotionally?" I asked. "I mean really, what's going on?"

He glanced in my direction as I broke his concentration. He seemed startled. "Mostly pissed off is what I feel right now," he immediately responded.

"And how about underneath that?" I questioned.

"I don't know." He shook his head, disappointed. "This whole mess is the story of my life. It's the story of my relationship with my parents for sure. It's the story of my relationship with my brother. Frankly, this company has made everything else meaningless. I mean, why does it have to be this way? I'm tired of competing with my brother. We have competed all of our lives. In wrestling, he was state champion first. And then, finally, I won the state championship. I swear if I hadn't, I might have committed suicide. In football, I felt like I always had to be as good as he was. The same thing in track, and with grades at school. I was always following in his footsteps, and competing against this bastard over here who kind of walked on water.

"Then, when we went to work at the company, he got the marketing position because he can 'B.S.' better than me. I got stuck in manufacturing. Now, admittedly, I've got more technical background than he does, since I've got the degree in engineering. But, you see, marketing is a glamour position and I got the grease-monkey job. And it's been that way our entire lives."

The last of the human freedoms —to choose one's attitude in any given set of circumstances, to choose one's own way.

—Victor Frankl

Walt and David demonstrated a very significant factor in the Zelda Complex: It doesn't occur only in romantic relationships. Walt and David represent two different components. They not only are business partners, but brothers and colleagues as well. Siblings can enter the Zelda Complex. So can people who work together. Occasionally, when family members are thrust into business situations not necessarily of their own choosing, the possibilities of a Zelda Complex increase exponentially.

At this level, the hostile dependency includes almost obsessive competition. At some point, it is openly destructive. Other times, the intensity simmers underneath a glossy layer of superficiality. In most Stage Two relationships, the people seem somehow obligated to remain enmeshed. They are caught up in the relationship and, for whatever reason, feel powerless to get out. Many people at this level report feeling immobilized. Sometimes this is the result of religious beliefs, business obligations, or financial restraints.

As an example, Walt and David both had to remain in the family business or risk having their father sell it from beneath them. The bylaws were written such that if either son chose not to cooperate with his plans, their father could unload the business and write off the two of them financially. In many ways, they felt financially imprisoned by his actions, yet, theoretically, were free to leave any time they chose. To Walt and David, theory and reality never coincided.

Other people have remained in unhealthy marriages out of similar feelings of entrapment. There are cases where people have remained married their entire lives because of religious beliefs. They felt that to leave their marriage would be damning their souls to eternal punishment. Some couples have remained married for financial reasons. They haven't wanted to face the economic devastation they feared divorce would create. As a result, they have chosen the emotional devastation that unrequited love often brings. Still others remain married "because of the children." Although this has a noble ring, theory and reality seldom coincide here either.

One of the primary differences between Stage One and Stage Two is the lack of disguise. People in Stage Two realize there are problems. They know about their anger. The waltzing of Stage One no longer works. As a result, they exchange hostilities both covertly and overtly. In families, Stage Two Zeldas will belittle each other in front of other family members—including children. Yet they claim to be staying together for the kids' sake. Such paradoxes permeate Stage Two. Often the relationship and all involved are psychologically destroyed.

Sometimes Stage Two Zeldas sabotage the workplace beyond repair. They often create unnecessary conflict by belittling other workers, complaining about management, and generally being very critical of the company's policies. Though they usually remain dependent on the employer for both economic and emotional reasons, they are very angry about it. Most frequently, the anger will be expressed in very destructive ways. Tremendous stress is created as a result, and very few people benefit.

It's almost comical to observe Stage Two Zeldas in their recreation. They can't even go on a leisurely walk together. One of them always feels he or she must win. Gary and Katie decided against my advice to begin jogging together as a way of improving their relationship. The jog turned into a frenetic foot race and led to further arguments. Someone always had to win, which meant someone also had to lose. Jack and Sandra experienced this when they gardened together. While landscaping a new piece of property, they competed over who could transplant pecan trees more quickly. When working on the same transplant together, they had heated discussions about how deep the holes should be.

Bob and Sam experienced the same hostile dependency while sailing together. Although they actually did compete on the racing circuit, their competition expanded onto their own sailing vessel. When captaining the ship, one would always find it necessary to criticize the other who was a member of the crew. The same thing happened when the other captained the vessel. Competition and conflict becomes pervasive during the hostile-dependent, Stage Two cycle. Unfortunately, it also becomes immobilizing.

During Stage Two, the Zelda Complex becomes a chronic, progressive, debilitating disorder. People who enter Stage Two literally get out of control. Fighting continues to a point that the relationship can be permanently fractured. The theme for Stage One of the Zelda Complex is the waltz. The theme for Stage Two is hostile dependency. At both extremes of that paradigm, hostility is the most powerful. Some maintain that anger is a *normal* human reaction. While that may be debatable, what is indisputable is that anger is a *common* human reaction. People get angry.

If you do not wish to be prone to anger, do not feed the habit;
give it nothing which may tend to its increase.

—Epictetus

Webster defines anger as "a strong feeling of displeasure." Although every human has such feelings, the way in which these feelings are expressed varies considerably between individuals and cultures. One writer defined anger as "a feeling of being hurt, annoyed, furious, and enraged." Another described it as "a positive reaction that does us harm here and now." The Icelandic word for anger has a meaning of grief or sorrow. Whatever the cultural definitions, however, there are common physiological changes human beings experience in response to anger. Blood rushing throughout the body increases blood pressure. The pulse quickens, and the heart occasionally pounds within the chest. The stomach expands, and the throat and head occasionally tighten. Muscles also tense, particularly those near the face, teeth, stomach, and fist.

Karl Meninger believed anger was something a child was born with. He suggested anger was caused by impulse or self-expression being thwarted. Over the years, various researchers have supported his explanation. Initially most people attempt to suppress their anger. This is probably out of fear that others will stop loving them if they express it. This is a learned response that begins with disapproval in early childhood. A few people are quite successful in keeping a lid on their rage. They ignore their anger and assume it's gone away. Actually, it becomes displaced, surfacing in other ways. Anger that isn't expressed directly will often lead to various health problems including ulcers, headaches, and more serious maladies. Some express anger in a passive-aggressive manner. They operate under the disguise of benevolence in order to appear "nice." Yet in reality, they do small things to get even while maintaining the mask of being well-mannered, helpful, or friendly.

My sister was once stuck in a hostile-dependent relationship. Because of her spouse's domineering nature, she was unable to express her anger directly. As a result, she maintained her smile and outwardly demure appearance. On one occasion, she literally caught him with his pants down, embracing another woman. Rather than interrupt them, she poured sugar into the gas tanks of their vehicles. When the engines were destroyed, she comforted her husband and expressed great regret that anyone would stoop to such behavior. That was true passive aggressiveness.

In its purest form, passive aggressiveness indirectly resists the demands of others in a nonconfrontational stance. Passive-aggressive individuals can become very stubborn. They are habitually late for appointments, do not return phone calls, procrastinate, and often "forget." In many instances, they have so successfully suppressed their anger that it is completely beyond their awareness. They think it doesn't exist, but it always comes out indirectly. In the hostile-dependent cycle, it's simply a way of getting even without assuming responsibility.

Zelda was a master at the art of passive aggressiveness. During their engagement period, Scott was in New York trying to make it as a writer. Zelda, who was awaiting him in Montgomery, began sending him letters about her escapades with other men. Her sole purpose was to make Scott jealous and angry. In her own writing she described, "I keep thinking how these men think I am purely decorative . . . they are just fools for not knowing better."

Scott and Zelda both were ultimately consumed and controlled by their rage. When they did express it, both were out of control. Zelda's rage eventually led to her demise. Rage can eventually become the focus of one's life. It grows so prominent in some people's lives that it becomes their purpose for existence. In many ways, the emotion itself becomes addictive.

Anger arousal involves both our minds and our bodies. Our hearts beat faster. Our breathing accelerates. Our faces may flush, and our hands may shake or become clammy with perspiration. These symptoms are involuntary. They are part of the physiological reaction that gets the body ready for action. Interestingly enough, such responses are also common with drug use, sexual desire, or anything that alerts the body to be prepared for special efforts. Two researchers found that anger, fear, sex, joy, and drug arousal all arise from the same general biochemical and physiological state.

The explanation for this is fairly scientific. The brain control centers that appear to mediate sex and rage are clustered quite closely together. Stimulation of one part of the brain may well result in an erection. Stimulation in another area of the brain less than a millimeter away produces rage. Stimulation to another part of the brain—again, only another millimeter away—can produce a hallucinogenic response. This has led to several conclusions. It's postulated that anger may be so closely related to these other responses that a misunderstanding between lovers could easily explode into violence, caused by brain stimulation in the wrong area.

Another conclusion is that such reactions can be as addicting as any drug. Even the hormonal reactions of adrenaline, norphrenaphin, and seratonin can be addicting when interacting simultaneously during periods of anger. Many people report feeling "high" in response to the rush of anger. In most ways, it is a drugged effect. Others describe an odor or taste that accompanies rage. People can subconsciously seek the sensation simply as a way to regain the rush. This can contribute to what's described as a conflict-habituated relationship. And it can speed the couple through to Stage Four of the Zelda Complex.

Fascinatingly enough, hostility often creates a connection between people. The apathetic void is filled by a powerful rage. Some individuals fantasize about their partner dying. Others pray that something terrible will befall their spouse to free them from the relationship. Zeldas perceive rage as being better than no feeling at all.

William Faulkner once said, "If I had to choose between pain and nothing, I'd always choose pain." The pain or, in this case, the anger, often becomes the only phenomenon two people have in common. As levels of hostility increase, the sickening dependency on anger increases as well. Yet at this stage, the anger is rarely dealt with successfully. These people are dependent on anger both for its rush and its ability to perpetuate their relationship. To remove their anger would leave them without their drug of choice.

*Everything that irritates us about others can lead us
to an understanding of ourselves.*

—Carl Jung

Walt and David were fully aware of their hostility toward each other. It went beyond sibling rivalry, and was complicated substantially by the employment agreement with their father. From infancy they had been bound together both as brothers and rivals. Their parents had frequently compared their personalities, school performance, and athletic prowess. They each had a natural need for approval from their parents, especially their father. Yet they never received it. This led to obsessive strife and competition about who would become the favorite son.

Unfortunately, neither of them was favored. As teenagers, they remained in trouble at school and had difficulty during their early college careers. However, their anger and intense need for approval drove them forward until they ultimately began succeeding in their own, individual ways. David was more charismatic and likable. He seemed to be a born salesman. Walt possessed mechanical aptitude and excelled in engineering classes at Georgia Tech. He eventually earned his degree in industrial engineering.

Meanwhile, David flunked out of Georgia Tech, spent eighteen months as a ski instructor in Steamboat Springs, Colorado, and then went to work as a sales representative in his father's company. Both sons climbed quickly through the ranks to their current positions. Yet they still competed for their father's ever elusive approval. Even the games their dad played—annually alternating the presidency, for example—kept them out of balance and under his control. It was a classic maneuver: divide and conquer. Their father had them exactly where he wanted them. They were hostile toward, yet dependent upon, each other. And both were dependent on him. As an added bonus, their hostility toward each other prevented them from more appropriately focusing their anger at their father.

My Zelda spent a great deal of time in the hostile-dependent phase. I enjoyed the stimulation, entertainment, and general fun she created. She brought out the child in me. No one had done that, up to that point in my life. She was dependent on me for financial support, stability in general, identity, and psychological health. She despised her dependency and expressed it in many ways. She felt weakened and vulnerable by it. She was angry because she couldn't control me. She was angry because my personal happiness and notoriety did not rub off on her. She was angry because I put my children first. She was jealous of the love, devotion, and commitment I felt toward my mother. Shortly after the confrontation with my staff, her anger finally exploded.

That particular staff meeting had gotten my attention. Although it was the fourth wake-up call, I still wasn't convinced. Within days of that meeting, however, my fifth wake-up call occurred. My Zelda physically attacked one of my children and cursed at both of them. At this point, I finally ejected her from my home. Everyone around me had seen it coming. I had been warned by my staff, my mother, and even my children. Yet I didn't want it to be true. I still thought I could fix her. That is the nature of hostile dependency and the power of its addictiveness. People become so blinded, they miss the obvious, or simply lose perspective. They miss what's really important. This happened with Scott and Zelda. It happened with Walt and David. And embarrassingly enough, it happened to me as well.

A man who has not passed through the inferno of his passions has never overcome them.

—Carl Jung

My first consulting session with Walt and David focused on information gathering. Before beginning to deal with their conflicts, my goal was to understand the relationship they had. Such work is like putting together a huge jigsaw puzzle. You first turn the pieces over, and then piece together the relationship. If successful in connecting the pieces, the meaning of their separate identities surfaces. Ultimately, the pieces come together to form a complete picture. The bigger the picture, the more comprehensive the understanding. This is the way it unfolded with them.

As I worked with Walt and David, several things became obvious. They were very dependent on each other. Their entire livelihood was hinged on their ability to work together. Their father had succeeded in binding the two boys together in a way that created an almost "damned if you do, damned if you don't" lifestyle. The only difference was that the *entire* relationship revolved around a do/do response. By this time, their hostility was obvious. They alternated between the extremes of hostility and dependence. The intensity of the cycle had become an issue within the company. The entire corporation was being adversely influenced by the conflict between Walt and David. Employees were choosing sides. It was becoming an atmosphere more like a wrestling tournament than a corporation. Anytime there are winners, there must be losers. In this particular case, if anyone lost, it would probably be the entire company.

Yet both Walt and David seemed competent in their jobs. They were uniquely qualified in their respective areas. I believed if they overcame the hostile-dependency cycle they could successfully run the company. My primary concern was the longer the conflict persisted, the more twisted and sick it would become. During our second session, we uncovered more pieces of the jigsaw puzzle. Walt leaned forward as we sat around the conference table. They had decided it would be easier if we sat in a more formal setting. Somehow the barrier of the huge oak table gave them a sense of security and safety. The conversation progressed more quickly in that setting.

"I don't know," Walt began. "David's my brother and we've always been close. But hell, we've never gotten along. We've fought all our lives. We've got old eight-millimeter home movies of birthday parties. They show us fighting then, when we were five and three years old. It's just incredible. And I don't know if we're trapped in this thing or what. One thing's real clear. We are destroying the damn company. What you brought up last time is the truth. Every day is like a tick on the clock of a time bomb. I'm scared we'll never get this thing together. We could lose our family, the business, our inheritance—we could lose everything!"

I turned toward David, gesturing for him to speak. "Sounds fairly reasonable to me, David. What do you think?"

David sighed and shook his head. "Well, this whole thing has gotten outta hand. It's kinda like what Walt was saying. It's really crazy. We've got so much to lose, but I feel hopeless to change things. This is our entire lives. You know how it is, John. We really don't have any choice. We have to work together, or die together. But we know it up here in our heads." He tapped his forehead with his fingers.

"We know the problem, but we just lose control. I get caught up trying to win and beat my brother, or be the top dog—I don't know what it is. It's definitely beyond logic. Our wives know about it. Our employees know about it. Our parents know about it. The whole damn industry knows about it. In fact, I think we're kind of the laughing stock of the industry. People make jokes about our family. People make jokes about our company. The truth is, if we didn't go shooting ourselves in the foot all the damn time we'd be the industry leader right now. But we're too busy fighting with each other, you know? We're so focused on each other that we can't concentrate on profit or productivity. We can't focus on sales. And I guess the truth is, if we don't change we are going to die, economically at least. The real question I have is, what do we do about it?"

Walt and David simultaneously looked toward me expectantly. I cleared my throat as I began to speak. "Most of us can change. But usually you have to hurt enough first. The pain is what gets your attention. It's what motivates you to change. But it's only when you finally have hurt long enough and deep enough that you are ready to create change. The real question is, Have you hurt enough? For some people, only a little bit of inconvenience is necessary to motivate them. For others, they practically have to die first. Y'all have been caught up in this so long, I don't know if you are ready.

"I can tell you how to get through this, but I can't make you do it. It's the same as if some guy were to ask me, How do I get to Atlanta? I can tell him five or six different ways he can get there. But he's the one who has to make the trip. You guys have some good understanding about what you're doing. Now let's see if we can put it into practical application and help you get out of this mess."

Over the years, I have discovered that businesses are usually more willing to follow a plan for change than are families or people in individual psychotherapy. As a consultant, I can usually go into an organization and give them a strategic plan for change and know it will be followed. Families function on a more emotional level. They are more hesitant. They get caught up in the emotional traps far more easily. Working with family-owned businesses presented a strange combination of the two.

Walt and David, although in business together, were inextricably family. The sibling rivalry they experienced needed to be removed, not only for the good of the company, but for their own health as well. I wasn't sure if they could follow a plan or not. But I was ready to recommend one to them, and to their father.

Do not be afraid of the past.
If people tell you that it is irrevocable, do not believe them.

—Oscar Wilde

Walt and David both described the intense awareness of being out of control. Most people in Stage Two report a similar awareness. Later, that awareness is lost. Walt and David were willing to work toward resolution. Unfortunately, most people's perspective is so twisted over time that working through the problem is unlikely.

People in Stage Two of the Zelda Complex usually feel trapped. The hostile dependency is so oppressive they literally get lost in other areas. One woman I worked with insulated herself in the study of genealogy. To me, this was poetically appropriate. She could not be angry or hostile toward dead people. It gave her a sense of control and power she didn't have in her own marriage. She became so obsessed with genealogy it became more than a full-time activity. She avoided her parents, ignored her kids and grandchildren, and only had "genealogy friends." Her own mother, who was bedridden, joked that her daughter didn't have time for her since she was still living. From her perspective, you only got attention if you were dead.

Other people insulate themselves through a wide variety of superficial relationships. (These people usually avoid intimate relationships altogether.) They scatter their energy over a wide range of people. They are never alone, and are rarely with only one other person. In this way, they hide from hostility and avoid any problems with dependency. These people fear spending too much time in one relationship, thinking if someone gets to know them well enough they'll confront them. They simply don't want to deal with it.

Other people become compulsive about involvement in civic clubs or civic projects. Many bury themselves in their work and become workaholics. In the South, one of the most common ways for people to deal with their hostile dependency is to bury themselves in church work. Church helps them defuse their hostility, which enables them to cope with it. Through their belief in God, they begin to pray or meditate and are provided hope. Some churches provide emotional outlets as well. High-energy, emotionally expressive churches can provide catharsis. This can funnel hostility in a socially acceptable and often healthy direction. Sometimes it can backfire, however, as when an individual becomes fanatical, or single-minded. Examples of this would be individuals who blow up abortion clinics. Churches also try to help squelch rage that has been expressed as violence. All too often, however, this merely masks the problems and encourages passive-aggressive behavior.

Nevertheless, strong religious beliefs can sometimes be the only factor that prevents some people from becoming actively involved in Stage Four–level violence. In this way it acts as a buffer to prevent dangerous acting out. Yet in other ways it's still a part of the endless cycle that perpetuates Stage Two and prevents people from exiting the cycle. Stage Two behavior is usually socially acceptable. Although anger and dependency are out of control, the people are not. Beyond Stage Two, however, the relationship can become quite dangerous and does result in physical and emotional harm.

Men often make up in wrath what they want in reason.
—W. R. Alger

The capacity for avoiding hostile dependency is the key to all successful relationships. It defines the limits or heights of someone's ability to love and achieve as well. It requires a renewal of trust. One must be confident enough in his or her own inner strength to be honest. One must be able to expose the most private and vulnerable parts of him- or herself, and accept the other's vulnerability.

It takes tremendous courage to openly discuss hostile dependency. Such discussions can be easily misunderstood, and often are. To do so successfully requires two people who have the same goal. In the past, women have been more skilled at this, and were the de facto monitors of relationships. But more and more, women are backing out of the responsibility. They are refusing to accept the caretaker role. This is probably healthy for women, but unhealthy for men. With neither partner responsible for caretaking, hostile dependency can quickly evolve into a Stage Three Zelda Complex. Walt and David avoided Stage Three, primarily because each of them had their own identities. They felt competent and confident outside of their sibling relationship. Had Walt simply had no life other than that as David's brother, Stage Three would have likely occurred.

In her relationship with Scott, Zelda felt inadequate. In some ways, Walt felt less skilled than his brother. After all, David was the first to win a wrestling state championship. David was the first to start on the football team. David was also two years older than Walt, so it was expected. Yet Walt had his share of fame. In comparison, Zelda did not. Another factor contributing to the Fitzgeralds' Stage Three Complex was that Scott literally robbed Zelda of her glory. Any time one is prevented by another from pursuing his or her dream, adverse consequences are inevitable. Walt and David never did this to each other.

Walt and David competed with each other. But they each felt adequate to compete. Zelda felt superior to Scott originally. Later she felt too inadequate to compete at all. And Scott contributed to this inequity of power. Inequity never existed for Walt and David. It also didn't exist for Jack and Sandra. Each of them had their own lives. Historically, it has been wives who sacrificed their identities for the sake of their husbands. Their satisfaction then became hooked on the star of his success. Husband gets success. Wife gets a relationship.

No one knows how women got appointed caretakers of relationships. Perhaps it was a task they assumed, primarily because of their advanced social skills. (As described earlier, men historically spent more time on tasks and women spent more time with people.) Several days before writing this material, I met in psychotherapy with a couple who illustrated this. The husband had worked for more than thirty years in the insurance industry and was very successful. His wife had been a homemaker and mother and by all standards did a great job. Now, in their late fifties, she was experiencing tremendous fear of abandonment. She was afraid he would leave her. It had already happened to several of their friends and, in my opinion, there was a very real possibility it could happen to them.

I recognized that they were locked in a hostile-dependent cycle. She was dependent on him for her income, identity, and position. He was dependent on her because her father had tremendous amounts of money invested for them jointly. It was akin to a modern-day dowry. She could not afford to leave him; most of their assets were in his name. He could not afford to leave her, because most of their investments were in both of their names. There was also a clause that if they divorced all would be left to her. The woman described it poetically, between sobs. For her husband, it was an economic and practical issue. For her, it was obviously emotional.

"I spent all my life building his career. I raised his children and kept his home spotless. Now I have nothing to show for it. He could do the same thing our friend did. If he wanted to, he could leave me for a thirty-year-old or a twenty-five-year-old blond. And I would have nothing. He doesn't even need me anymore. And I need him. And I hate myself for it!"

Her husband denied any intention of leaving the relationship, yet his denial was hollow. Later, he expressed his anger privately.

"There's nothing I can do about it. I'm locked in this relationship for the rest of my life, like it or not. The truth is, I don't love her like I should. There's nothing wrong with her. She's a good person. I've spent all my life on the road. The fact is, I've had lots of women. I never intended to stay married after the children left home.

"Yet now, if I leave, I lose everything. The children wouldn't have anything to do with me. She would get all the investments. At best, our assets would be split down the middle, or probably worse. I'm sure I'd have to pay alimony, till she remarried, which she would never do. I could get me a new wife and start me a new family. But what would be the use? For the first time in my life, I realize I'm trapped. I'm out of control. And I simply don't like it."

As he discovered, there is a way out. But it came later.

CHECKLIST

Instructions: Check those statements that apply.

_____ 1. I do not feel I can break off this relationship because of family, financial, or religious restraints. In many ways, I feel trapped.

_____ 2. I do not have a means of earning any money for myself. I have to rely on my partner for spending money. Or, I feel empowered knowing my partner is dependent upon me.

_____ 3. When my partner ignores me, I find myself picking arguments to gain attention.

_____ 4. I frequently forget to accomplish small tasks my partner asks of me.

_____ 5. I am late for dates or appointments with my partner.

_____ 6. I do not feel adequate in comparison to my partner.

_____ 7. I fantasize about my partner becoming ill or dying.

_____ 8. I have considered suicide.

_____ 9. I feel competitive toward my partner in many aspects of our relationship.

_____ 10. My partner has belittled my efforts to improve myself or scorned my accomplishments.

Scoring: Total the number of check marks. Totals less than three suggest little difficulty with hostile dependency. Scores between three and seven indicate that hostile dependency may be a problem for you. Scores above seven suggest full-blown crisis. It would probably be a good idea to discuss with a professional healthy ways of dealing with your anger and realistic approaches to lowering your dependence.

JOURNAL SESSION

1. It may be helpful to list the areas where dependence is an issue in this relationship. Consider such areas as education, finance, child care, business, etc.

2. List those areas where change is possible. What changes would be necessary to make you more comfortable? Consider discussing a minor one with your partner to determine if he or she is receptive to making changes.

Chapter 6

ENMESHED AND JEALOUS
AN ADDICTION TO AFFLICTION

Then she sits in some club where the long shadows fall
Drops a coin in the juke box not the phone on the wall.
— Daryl Hall and George Green, "So Close"

Control seemed to be a major theme with both Scott and Zelda. In the early years, before *This Side of Paradise* was published, Zelda was definitely in charge in the relationship. From the summer of 1918 until the spring of 1920, Zelda was more powerful in all ways. She was as perpetually flirtatious as Scott was jealous. Even during their engagement, she played the field in a visible and celebrated way. Photographs taken of Zelda during this time show her to be stunning. Her skin was almost milky white. She had a deceiving appearance of naiveté and innocence. There was an allure about Zelda that was attractive to men and a daring equally seductive.

Zelda enjoyed being the center of attention. During her adolescence she was continuously quoted in southern newspapers. Zelda would go anywhere to be written up in the society pages. Her escapades in Montgomery, Atlanta, Birmingham, and even her trip to Lookout Mountain, were widely reported. She dated a different man each night, and appeared to get her way with most of them.

To say Scott was smitten with Zelda would be unfair. At the beginning of the relationship, he was mesmerized by her. Zelda had been used to dating physically aggressive, large, athletic men. Football players, aviators, and the like constituted the stable from which she chose her partners. Scott was different. Though he fancied himself as one of the men normally attractive to Zelda, he was very much the opposite. He was small, creative, and sensitive. He was a poet. These qualities were an enigma for Zelda. She was simultaneously attracted and repulsed by what she saw in Scott. In many ways they were mirror images of each other, although neither realized it at the time. Zelda was definitely more socially adept and she took advantage of Scott.

Until *This Side of Paradise* was published, Scott had really not succeeded at anything. Although he was a military officer, he never saw combat. Nor did he become an aviator, which was, up to that point, a central focus of much of his and Zelda's existence. To Scott, aviators were more gallant than infantry soldiers. They were knights; their planes, steeds. The armistice prevented him from proving himself as a soldier and aviator. He had not succeeded at sports. He virtually flunked out of Princeton. In essence, Scott had not succeeded at anything.

This made him more vulnerable to Zelda's garyarious manipulations. Especially during the early years, Scott seemed insecure about his masculinity. They began a relationship based on his inadequacies. She, in turn, ruled the relationship and controlled Scott. Yet everything changed with *This Side of Paradise*. By September 1920, the book was a hit. It had sold thirty-three thousand copies and the Fitzgeralds were the talk of New York City. Zelda chopped off her hair and began the series of histrionics which later resulted in her being identified as the quintessential flapper. Friends described the Fitzgeralds as drinking and fighting constantly. In October 1921, their daughter Scottie was born, and within six months *The Beautiful and the Damned* was published.

The tables had turned so dramatically the relationship was in continuous uproar. They entered the relationship with one set of understandings. Though unspoken, the understanding was that Zelda would ultimately be in control. Now, things were upside down. Scott was getting all the attention, and Zelda was envious and jealous of that attention. Scott had gained control of the relationship. But it's far more complicated than that. In many ways, Zelda created F. Scott Fitzgerald.

Perhaps she only inspired *This Side of Paradise*, but it appears she wrote major portions of *The Beautiful and the Damned*, both in spirit and in truth. Yet she received no recognition or appreciation for her efforts. In the winter of 1928–29 Zelda wrote six short stories. Five were published under both Scott's and Zelda's names; on the sixth, Zelda's name was omitted altogether. Scott later admitted that those and other stories bearing both names were entirely Zelda's work. In effect, Scott received notoriety for writings that were Zelda's. Considering Zelda's desperate need for attention, this profoundly affected her, and was extremely destructive to their relationship.

Despite his own successes, Scott still appeared to be jealous and envious of Zelda's talent. He was well aware that the success of his last two books partially resulted from his plagiarizing her material. That awareness only added to his sense of failure and dependency. All of this became the basis of their illness. It marked the beginning of their premature end. Scott and Zelda's relationship define Stage Three of the Zelda Complex.

Heaven has no rage like love to hatred turned.

—Congreve

The Zelda Complex is a chronic, progressive, debilitating disorder that occurs between two or more people. The beginning of Stage Three represents the core of the Zelda Complex. It begins when one partner perceives the other as succeeding beyond a level initially expected in the relationship. It is success outside of one or both partners' comfort zone. It's important to understand, success is a relative term. *Perception* of success is the key.

People enter relationships with unspoken agreements. These agreements can include intentions of behavior, love, and intimacy. Another such unspoken agreement is how the couple will handle perceived success. Zelda and Scott formed an unspoken contract based on Zelda's being the center of attention. Scott went along with this agreement. Scott wasn't concerned about being the center of attention; he wanted to be an excellent writer. Yet along with his success as a writer came attention. Zelda, on the other hand, thrived at being the center of attention. It was one of her goals in life. Although she was infinitely talented, the thing she most wanted was to be the center of attention and to be taken care of.

There appears to be an implied agreement in all relationships as to what the tolerable level of focused attention will be and who will receive it. As long as this unspoken contract was kept, the Fitzgeralds' marriage survived, although not necessarily in a healthy way. So it is with most couples. Stage Three is a pre-critical stage for relationships. It is dangerous psychologically, but usually not physically. People in Stage Three are jealous of each other. One usually envies the other's success. But it goes beyond that.

I've never met anyone who wanted to experience a Zelda Complex. Most people are completely unaware of its existence. When I ask most couples how they arrived at Stage Three, they have no idea. That's no surprise. I said the same thing when my own Zelda and I attempted to understand what we were doing to each other.

Oh jealousy! Thou magnifier of trifles.

—Schiller

I am predominantly a shy, introverted, quiet individual who has only a few friends. Those friendships are long-standing, however, and their depth can be staggering. My wake-up calls were a direct result of the choices I had made. I can understand the divorce I went through quite easily. I acknowledge my contributions to the demise of that relationship and truly don't blame my ex-wife for the decision she made. Most of the relationships in my life have been logical. My Zelda relationship was not.

As I look back on it, several things become quite clear. Regardless of her physical beauty, my Zelda was a deeply troubled woman. She was attracted to me, frankly, because she wanted to be like me. I certainly was no match for her in physical beauty. Many people, including my closest friends, suggested my Zelda was initially interested in me because she thought I had money. I tried to deter that by allowing her to talk with my bookkeeper and accountant. The divorce I went through had cost me far more than emotional pain. It was not simply that I didn't have a great deal of money, I was indebted and extended as far as I could possibly be without going under. Recovering from the divorce and going from a two-income to a one-income family had devastated me. Since I had been told money was the logical attraction for my Zelda, I tried to make sure the facts became known.

But that was part of the big problem. I looked for a logical explanation to the relationship. The truth was not to be found in rational thinking. The truth was found in the pathology of the Zelda Complex. I had no money. My Zelda saw happiness and mental health in me. Regardless of the suffering I had experienced, I was still a happy person. She had never found mental health, much less happiness.

Like Zelda Fitzgerald, my own Zelda was a good actress. She pretended to be all the things I wanted in a partner. She pretended to be domestic. She pretended to be attracted to my children. She pretended to be calm and supportive. Deep down, however, she was Zelda Fitzgerald made over. She craved the attention I received from radio, TV, and speaking engagements. She hoped that attention would rub off by association. The opposite occurred.

Like Zelda's response to Scott, my Zelda could not handle my success. In fact, she could not handle anything over which she had no control. Yet I was blind to this. Others around me saw it almost for what it was. I was oblivious to reality. The relationship is now over. It's not over simply because I exited the relationship. It's over because I refused to perpetuate Stage Three, or to enter Stage Four. I stepped outside the cycle.

My Zelda fantasized I would make her well. There was a part of me that thought I could. She dreamt that the happiness she saw in me could be hers through osmosis. This never happened. When it didn't, the pretense crumbled around her. The bitterness and anger she had repressed finally surfaced. Although it was painful, I finally saw the relationship for what it was. And then I had a decision to make. Some people look in the mirror and don't like what they see. At this point, they can begin to change what they're looking at, buy a new mirror, or quit looking at it altogether. My choice was to change myself. Scott's and Zelda's choice was ultimately to quit looking. That was the difference.

> *Whoever envies another confesses his superiority.*
> —Samuel Johnson, *The Rambler*

Scott and Zelda Fitzgerald were certainly not the first two people to enter Stage Three. People have struggled through similar relationships throughout time. The Bible is filled with accounts of such patterns. The first occurred, according to biblical tradition, before the Earth was even formed. According to creation lore, Lucifer and Michael were both angels who lived in heaven. Lucifer was uncomfortable with the degree of attention Michael was receiving from God. He began a rebellion in heaven that resulted in a conflict between Michael and his angels, and Lucifer with his rebellious horde. Ultimately, Lucifer was banned from heaven, sent to wander the earth. The story of Joseph and his conflicts with his brothers describe a similar pattern. So does that of Cain and Abel.

The theme of the Zelda Complex is found throughout literature as well. Shakespeare described it in his epoch *Macbeth*. In it, Macbeth is encouraged by his wife to kill Duncan and take over the throne. A series of other murders and, ultimately, Macbeth's own death resulted. Lady Macbeth, like Zelda, resorted to insanity and ultimately to suicide. King Arthur also experienced his own Zelda Complex. Through the triangle of Lancelot, Guinevere, and his own obliviousness, his kingdom was destroyed. Similarly, Julius Caesar, through the envy and jealousy of Brutus and his band of thugs, experienced a Zelda Complex with fatal results. If one subscribes to Oliver Stone's presentation of *J.F.K.*, the Kennedy White House was one disastrous Zelda Complex. It changed the course of the Vietnam War, the presidency, and global politics. The validity of Stone's account may never be known for certain, although most historians agree there was enough envy, jealousy, and destructive behavior to create a Zelda Complex among those involved.

In the examples described above, there are several things these groups have in common. First, they were forced together in circumstances that led to a degree of hostile dependency. Second, those circumstances frequently precluded the characters from truly getting close to one another. Some waltzed around closeness, catching occasional glimpses of it. Others were enmeshed in their closeness to some degree. Cain and Abel were brothers. Joseph and his persecutors were all from the same family. Some brothers were angry at their father's favoring Joseph. Lucifer and Michael were considered the two angels closest to God. Lancelot was King Arthur's favorite knight. Brutus was Caesar's closest ally. Each of these individuals developed a sense of dependency that led not only to hostility, but to enmeshment. They had no separate identity.

With other people, it may not be enmeshment as much as it is immaturity. Watching someone whom you've helped achieve success or stardom higher than yours takes an unusual degree of maturity. Actually, very few people are capable of it. The key to avoiding these problems is simple to explain, but difficult to accomplish. Each person in a relationship needs to succeed on his or her own without creating a sense of unnecessary distance. At the same time, it's vital that each person not only have a separate identity but the chance to develop and succeed independently. Unfortunately, it is most often women who are not allowed this opportunity.

Love must have wings to fly away from love, and to fly back again.
—Edwin Arlington Robinson

Gary and Katie met in college, and had been married since their early twenties. When Gary went to law school, Katie worked to pay for their livelihood. She continued to work through the early stages of his career, putting off her own development. Interestingly enough, they had originally been attracted to each other because both wanted to be attorneys. They decided early on that Gary would go to law school first and Katie would work. Initially, the agreement had been that she would work until he graduated. Then he would work and she would attend law school. It seemed plausible at the time.

Gary flourished in law school. He had truly found his calling. He was extremely successful and worked on the staff of the school's legal review. Upon graduation he was granted an internship with a federal judge and Katie followed him to a different city. He was later offered a position in a major law firm and gratefully accepted. Unfortunately, the closest law school was more than four hours away. This prevented Katie from pursuing her dream. Initially, she was so excited about Gary's success that it didn't bother her. But it did create conflict between Katie and her parents. Katie is a brilliant, articulate woman. If the truth be known, she is probably more intelligent than Gary, though less outspoken. When he was in law school, she had completed many of his assignments and wrote his papers for him. She had put off her personal goals and gratification to help Gary. She had lived through him. Her parents thought it was a mistake. Over the years, Katie came to agree with them.

When I first met Gary and Katie, they were in the midst of a Stage Three pattern. Katie was well aware of it and willing to discuss the difficulty. Gary was hesitant. He was in denial and refused to acknowledge the obvious. After meeting with them initially, I asked Gary if I could see him privately during the next appointment. That particular session highlighted the dilemma. Gary wanted to stay married, but seemed to be unwilling to do the necessary work.

I glanced at him across the room. A white shirt and maroon tie accented his navy pin-striped suit. A lined face and gray temples gave him a distinguished but stiff appearance. When he smiled—which was rare—it appeared almost strained. He dressed, spoke, and acted his part: a successful attorney preparing to run for district attorney general.

"I'm certain you're probably right, John," he began, enunciating each word slowly and thoughtfully. "I've analyzed it since our last session, and the paperwork you had me fill out really made me think. But I just don't see what Katie's trying to prove. Can you go over that part again? I just can't figure how it adds up."

I reflected a moment as his words trailed off. Gary's academic and professional qualifications were impeccable. Throughout the community, his reputation was that of a hard-driving achiever. Yet he was so stoic I wondered how his relationship with Katie had survived up to this point.

"I just don't understand the bottom line," he continued. "You see, I understand most things. They're logical. But this doesn't figure at all. Probably the smartest thing we could do would be to go ahead and separate. Yet, I don't think it would be good for my political career. I have aspirations beyond the attorney general's office."

I considered his carefully chosen words. His language was in quantitative patterns, fitting someone with his background. I made a mental note to respond similarly. There was an obvious tension in his voice. His resistance to emotion suggested that perhaps Katie's complaints were fair; Gary had distanced himself emotionally from her. At this point, there was profound conflict. She was having a problem with his career advancements. He was having difficulty with her emotional demands. The truth was, she had put him through school. He had obtained no loans or help from his parents. But Gary had never kept up his end of the bargain. He was the one who had failed in that respect.

Currently, they had three children in private schools and massive obligations. It was unlikely Katie would ever go to law school. She now needed Gary financially far more than he needed her. Though he claimed no outside sexual involvement, I would have been surprised if there were not. They had not had sex together in more than nine months. Yet both described themselves as sexual people. Katie resented his political aspirations; they prevented her from pursuing her own life. Gary said she was nonsupportive, and he was probably right. She had spent her entire adult life supporting his goals. Now she wanted to pursue her own.

What began as a simple disagreement had evolved to the point that their conflicts were public. In many ways, I feared it was too late for them to change. Katie was painfully depressed. In the past weeks, Gary had choked her. Although they said it was the first time, I wondered if they had entered therapy woefully too late. The truth was, a divorce could affect his political future. They were in trouble.

Trifles light as air are to the jealous confirmations strong as proofs of Holy writ.
—Shakespeare, *Othello*

Of the twenty-five different factors that influence the Zelda Complex, several contribute predominately to Stage Three. They begin with the need for approval. At least one person in the relationship will have an intense need for approval. This need goes beyond the normal level, however. His or her desire approaches dependency. This person is usually the same one who possesses the sense of entitlement. Both factors blend to create critical vulnerability. Stage Three Zeldas feel entitled to love, bordering on an expectation of being worshiped. When the expectation is not met, they don't see it as something wrong with them. They blame their partner. This perpetuates their unrealistic expectations. They not only want, but often demand, to be treated far more regally than what's typically expected.

Another series of factors critical to Stage Three are those found under Factors of Achievement. Most people who experience the Zelda Complex are gifted intellectually. This does not mean they achieve at a level commensurate with their skill. In fact, the opposite is usually true. When harnessed, this intelligence can lead to competitiveness with their partner. It is not always the most intelligent partner who is the high achiever, as in Scott and Zelda's case. I will always believe that Zelda was, by far, more talented. It appears, however, that Scott had just enough task-oriented skills to complete his works. Zelda saw her task as finding a man strong enough to take care of her and give her attention. Scott wanted to be a writer. Scott achieved his goal. Zelda never did.

The final factor from this grouping critical to Stage Three is obviously the inability of one partner to handle the perceived success of the other. It usually revolves around the one who is more visible or receives more public attention. In one case I worked with, the husband was a highly paid accountant. His wife was working at a television station in a small community, barely making minimum wage. Yet she hosted an early morning talk show and was quite popular in the community. When they went out to eat, everyone noticed and was interested in talking to her. Though the husband made about five times what his wife did, he perceived her as being more successful because of her notoriety. His perception of success had more to do with appearances than quantitative measurements.

Regardless of their level of education, most people who experience the Zelda Complex are emotionally quite unadvanced. They have extremely immature expectations of what love may or may not provide. As a result, one person is usually attracted to the relationship because of what he or she sees in the other. They both feel incomplete and hope to find wholeness through the relationship. Katie was attracted to Gary because she wanted to be an attorney. Another woman I saw in psychotherapy wanted to be a jet fighter pilot. She didn't pursue her goal because of religious convictions. She was a member of a denomination that would not look kindly on a woman getting an advanced education or serving in the military. As a result, she married a fighter pilot, and experienced the Zelda Complex.

The only thing that prevented Walt and David from progressing into Stage Three was their individual competence. (Business partners frequently experience the Zelda Complex, especially when one feels inadequate in some way.) Though Walt and David struggled with sibling rivalry, each had achieved on his own. This contrasted with the fighter pilot illustration. Walt did not want to *be* David, or vice versa. Their strengths actually complemented, rather than competed, with each other. The intensity they experienced was caused more by their being siblings than their being business partners.

Intensity is one of the serious risk factors in Stage Three of the Zelda Complex. Its seeds are found both in emotional and sexual relationships. Intensity contributes to fluctuating mood swings and feeds off of itself. If one partner begins to withdraw, the level of insecurity peaks and the other may feel humiliated. Withdrawal is a way of controlling the situation indirectly. But violence is often the result. I have never been exposed to a case of physical abuse which was not preceded by perceived humiliation. Rarely was it intended that way, however. It was most often meant as a way of getting the other person's attention. Usually it's a passive-aggressive effort to lure the other back into the Complex and make the more insecure partner feel safer.

If the relationship evolves into one where perceived humiliation is prolonged, it is likely that the couple will enter Stage Four. This occurs quickly in many relationships; in some Stage Three relationships it takes longer. Once the element of perceived humiliation arises, however, the stakes have increased and it is only a matter of time before Stage Four occurs.

I was angry with my friend:
I told my wrath, my wrath did end.
I was angry with my foe:
I told it not, my wrath did grow.

—William Blake, *A Poison Tree*

Scott and Zelda Fitzgerald demonstrated virtually all Stage Three characteristics in their own relationship. They did escalate to Stage Four on multiple occasions, but primarily oscillated in and out of Stage Three during the productive years. The same was true of my own Zelda relationship. Because of her needs, we spent most of our time in Stage Three. By the time we would have naturally evolved into Stage Four, I had stepped outside of the relationship. I had tried to convince her on several occasions that the approach she was taking would lead only to emotional devastation. She seemed unwilling to accept my explanation. Finally, and only briefly before it was too late, she agreed. To her credit, she exited the relationship before allowing it to evolve to Stage Four. The other alternative would have been to experience her own bout with insanity.

A Stage Three or Stage Four Zelda Complex requires the cooperation of two people. Once I had stopped contributing to the problem, my Zelda had a choice: She could attempt to ignore my withdrawal and remain attached to the relationship, or she could get out and start over somewhere else. The paradox is, by continuing to contribute to a dysfunctional relationship, you remain in it. Scott and Zelda certainly did. Sometimes, Zelda relationships end only when one person refuses to play chase any longer.

When one person quits contributing to the Complex, it is common for the other to attempt to entrap him or her back into the pattern. In many ways, this is a last-ditch effort by the partner who remains. It's a distorted cry for help and attention. It's akin to a drowning person who climbs all over you in an effort to save themselves. I have seen several instances where Zeldas attempted suicide as a way of jerking their partner back into the Complex. Some people would rather have a bad relationship than no relationship at all. Nevertheless, exiting at this level is usually the kindest thing you can do. It gives both the opportunity to get help, and prevents escalation to the more dangerous Stage Four. Unfortunately, it's rare for people to independently exit relationships at this stage. Outside help is usually required. It is more common to remain fixated at this level or advance to Stage Four.

It's crucial to understand that it's not necessary for a couple to experience each of the twenty-five factors for a Zelda Complex to occur. Some symptoms are so problematic that only a few can create a toxic relationship. The factors present in the Zelda Complex between the paramedic and his wife were those involving family background and level of achievement. His wife was outrageously spoiled. She was so indulged as a child, she felt entitled to happiness and success without working for it. She had been the center of attention in her family of origin and fully expected to continue in that role after her marriage.

As the paramedic once explained, this made their relationship very difficult. "Hell, she was a full-time job. I mean, she wanted what she wanted—when she wanted it. I don't think she was really jealous of my job. She was jealous that I wasn't there to kiss up to her all the time. When another guy came along and had more time to give, she just quit our marriage and moved in with him. But it was easy for him; he didn't work. All he had to do was sit there and stare at her, and she liked it. But when there wasn't any money to support her spending habits, it wasn't so great after all."

In this particular case, attention appeared to be what his wife wanted. She had difficulty making the transition from spoiled and indulged child to responsible wife. She also demonstrated a problem with accepting the perceived success of her husband. When he started getting more attention than she did, the sparks began to fly. Literally within six months of his becoming a paramedic, her first affair began. Yet he was actually home more in this job than in his previous one. Working twenty-four hours on and twenty-four off left a lot of time for him to attend to her. But it wasn't enough. Not only did she want his attention, she wanted all of it. When she didn't get it, she initially became disturbed and ultimately got out of the relationship.

Another example is that of the morning talk show host and her husband. Because of her visibility through TV, she was perceived as being more successful. Her husband made five times her annual income and had a graduate degree, whereas she had only a bachelor's. Yet he had difficulty handling the recognition and public affection she received. They entered therapy committed and intelligent enough to get out of their Stage Three Complex. But he had tremendous difficulty admitting what was really wrong.

"Are you saying I'm jealous?" he laughed out loud. "I mean, is that it? We're paying this much money and all you can say is that I'm jealous of her success? By all standards, I'm more successful than she is! How can you say I'm jealous?"

"Really now, I didn't use that word," I responded calmly. "This isn't about jealousy. It's far more than that. It's not jealousy. It's not envy. It's not greed.

"You have been extremely successful in your own business. What's going on has more to do with visibility. It has to do with perception. It has to do with emotions. No, this isn't jealousy. It's a lot different than that."

In a similar situation, a quite successful and well-paid bricklayer entered a Stage Three Zelda Complex when his wife got a job in an attorney's office. Although he made far more money, he perceived her as more successful because she held a white collar job. This man reacted to his emotional perception rather than the economic reality. To him, the fact that she dressed up to go to work and associated with attorneys represented success. His unhealthy response rapidly led to a Stage Three Zelda Complex.

Katie and Gary represent the factor of perceived success as well. Her problems began early, but escalated when he began to run for public office. Regardless of whether or not he was elected, the perception of success influenced her. If elected, he would end up taking a substantial pay cut from his private practice. But that was irrelevant. When it comes to the Zelda Complex, perceived success is far more important than reality.

It's amazing how much can be accomplished if no one cares who gets the credit.
— Blanton Collier

Some people wonder if the Zelda Complex applies only to women. Obviously, it doesn't. It's true that women are more often in a passive, or observer, role. That occurs for a variety of reasons. In spite of an ever more progressive society, women still suffer discrimination. Additionally, women continue to support their husbands' careers at the expense of their own opportunities. Katie didn't go to law school, but married an attorney. Then, she supported his career to the detriment of her own. But, there's another reason women are often times more symptomatically identified in the Zelda Complex.

Historically, women have not been socialized to work as members of a team the way men have. This has changed somewhat in the last twenty years, but there is still a vast difference. Historically, young girls were placed on their daddies' laps and told how wonderful they were. They were pampered, coddled, dressed up, and admired. Boys, on the other hand, wrestled with their fathers and played Little League football. There they learned the rudiments of getting along as a member of a group.

In Little League football, boys learn that the entire team is important.

They also learn that each member is valuable and necessary. Certainly, one person may get more attention. The quarterback scores the winning touchdown and gets the glory. But he and everyone else knows it would have been impossible without the offensive lineman. Typically, the first thing the quarterback does is congratulate his lineman. This is teamwork, and it is learned in sports. I've never read of a three-hundred-pound offensive tackle having a Zelda Complex. As indicated, things have changed somewhat in the past twenty years. Opportunities such as those found in women's sports are reversing that trend. Girls growing up today have more opportunity to participate in organized sports, and are learning teamwork and cooperation more than in the past. Nevertheless, women still have a long way to go in learning these areas. During one of our sessions, I was attempting to explain this concept to Sandra.

"Don't say another word," she interrupted. "I know exactly what you're talking about! It's like the difference between Boy Scouts and Girl Scouts. I know they both have similar goals and values. But, I swear, they're as different as night and day."

"Maybe they're just as different as men and women," I joked. "But tell me what you mean. I thought they were pretty much the same."

"I was a Girl Scout leader for ten years," Sandra continued. "When I moved up here, I had to repeat my Girl Scout leader training. I couldn't believe it. Even though I only moved one county away they wouldn't accept my training from another council. Leader training takes several Saturdays and it has to be completed within a certain period of time. I had to take time off work to get it done. But it's the same in every council I've worked. Lots of paperwork, detailed leader guidelines and manuals, and mandatory meetings. Everything has to be done just so.

"If I wanted simply to have a camp out in my backyard I had to go on an overnight training session, have extra trained leaders with me, and fill out tons of paperwork. Who's got time for all that stuff when you're volunteering your time in the first place? I felt like someone was always looking over my shoulder to see if I had every *i* dotted. It created a lot of hard feelings between volunteers and the paid council staff. A lot of time was wasted just establishing a pecking order—especially by the volunteers. I didn't feel part of a team, that's for sure.

"I worked for the Boy Scouts even before my son was old enough to be a Scout. I sort of got roped into it—you know how it goes—I just couldn't say no. I stayed until he was an Eagle, then I got out. But there was no problem transferring training from council to council. Even Red Cross training counted. They had monthly roundtables, for leaders to go and get ideas for meetings and ask questions. Of course, they wanted you to attend, but there wasn't any 'you have to be there or else' stuff. There was just a whole different feeling to it. There are lots of women who work in Boy Scouts, but men run the show on the council level. They do a good job of doing what you're talking about—of making you feel part of a team."

The word "love" has by no means the same sense for both sexes,
and this is one of the serious misunderstandings that divide them.
—Simone de Beauvoir

Another factor marking a Stage Three Zelda Complex is the couple's lack of ability to properly define love. People who experience the Zelda Complex tend to see love as something to cure their ills. It's perceived as salve or medicine to make them healthy. As a result, they develop unrealistic expectations for any relationship, whether personal or business. Zeldas may be extremely successful businesspeople. They may be quite wealthy or have extremely high IQs. I've met several Zelda Complex members whom I would define as academically brilliant. Yet when it comes to love, they are woefully immature. When love does not conquer all, they blame the person they're involved with. It would be healthier to look at their own expectations, which often are vastly out of line with reality.

After a series of these relationships, Zeldas begin to blame love itself. They blame all men or all women. This overgeneralization makes it easy for them to avoid responsibility. The healthier approach would be to take a look at their immature expectations. But Zeldas rarely do. More often, they remain in one unhealthy relationship until it ends. After a brief period of detox, they begin another.

Zeldas are usually looking for combustibility, though it may be on a subconscious level. Intensity, melodrama, and high energy fuels them. Even if this comes in the form of physical abuse—which it commonly does in Stage Four—it doesn't matter. The main ingredient is the energy itself. I have often heard Zeldas say they get out of relationships where people treat them well. They find such relationships boring. "It doesn't give me the kind of feeling I need," they explain. "He doesn't excite me.

I'm not attracted to him." What these comments really say is that their partners aren't sick enough for them.

It's this attraction to the mixture of diesel fuel and fertilizer that creates difficulty for the relationship. Zeldas simply don't want to live without such combustible energy, despite its dangerous potential. At the very least, it will lead to psychological problems. But those can be relatively benign. The more serious threat is the possibility of physical harm, illness, or even death.

Katie seemed to have a similar affinity for the combustible. After a few visits, I began to realize the seriousness of her Zelda Complex. She had grown woefully depressed, sometimes remaining in bed for prolonged periods of time. She had abandoned her family psychologically and had retreated into her own world. The children had started to assume more responsibility and align themselves with their father. From their perspective, mom had freaked out. Though they recognized their father's instability, they knew their mother couldn't protect them. "My mom's a psycho," one of her sons explained to me.

But Katie wasn't a psycho. She was depressed. She was in serious psychological trouble. In fact, by the time I saw her in counseling, she was experiencing marked hopelessness. At this point in my career, I had seen this same response occur in dozens of Zelda Complexes. She was being consumed by the relationship. As Zelda had done after Scott plagiarized her diary, Katie had lost her identity and soul. She was a gifted woman in her own right, and Gary even admitted that she probably would have been a better attorney than he was. Yet after putting Gary through school and getting pregnant, she had given up on any life of her own. As her children aged, Katie saw her entire reason for living vanish in front of her. As he increased his political aspirations, Gary gave her less time. By nature, he was a workaholic. By choice, he avoided Katie rather than deal with the legitimacy of her concerns.

Like many others who end up in psychotherapy, the nature of their relationship had changed. Gary no longer needed Katie's support to make it through law school. He no longer needed her to write his papers. He didn't even need her to run the household. He could afford a housekeeper, groundskeeper, and nanny. Gary had surrounded himself with staff to do all the things Katie once did. The only reason he had not sought divorce already was his concern about politics. So they hung on to each other, in spite of their deteriorating health.

Katie was clearly the more symptomatic of the two. Her depression and withdrawal were visible to anyone. Gary's symptoms were less obvious. Few knew of his ulcers, his anxiety attacks, or his addiction to Xanax. Gary abused Xanax the same way some people chew gum; he mixed it with Librax for his stomach problems. The anxiety attacks had begun within days of Katie's first disappearance. She had left home for the weekend to stay with friends, but had not informed Gary where she would be. By doing so, if divorce occurred, she could be accused of abandonment and would have far more difficulty getting custody of the youngest child. This functionally stalemated any movement from the relationship. Gary wanted to hang onto the marriage for political reasons. Katie now could not get out, even if she chose, without the likelihood of losing everything. It became a catch-22 and prevented the relationship from going anywhere.

Katie spiraled downward, becoming ever sicker. Gary smiled, and took more Xanax. Not satisfied with my responses, he took Katie to see a physician who put her on Prozac and another anti-depressant. She was told her problems were caused by a chemical imbalance and psychiatric hospitalization was needed. Against my advice, Gary insisted Katie agree to be hospitalized. He threatened to file for divorce and take the children if she didn't. If she did, he promised to remain married to her. Katie gave in, but chose a treatment program of her own liking.

"I know you told me it was a mistake," she explained later. "But at that point, I just wanted some rest. I was tired of fighting. I was tired of the contest. I was tired of the games. I was just tired. I don't know when I've ever been so totally exhausted and wiped out.

"I'd like to think that even though he is an attorney this whole thing wasn't a manipulation. Yet I know, deep down inside, it was. In fact, it was nothing but a con. He was a shrewd, manipulative attorney at work. That's all it was. But, like I said, I was so wiped out it didn't matter. I was ready to get away, but I had no idea of the consequences.

"Treatment was really a nice rest. It was good to be pampered. I did get my act together a little bit more than before. But I paid one heck of a price for that luxury. I've got a nineteen-year-old, a seventeen-year-old, and a fifteen-year-old. And all three of them think I'm a fruitcake. If they had talked to a judge, there's no doubt in my mind that they would have said they wanted to go with their daddy. And he'd come out of this smelling like a rose.

"Poor old Gary," she lamented mockingly. "Poor old martyr. Married to a crazy woman. Yet look how he's stood by her. He's just the salt of the earth, isn't he, John?" She looked up, smiled, and shook her head sarcastically. "It's really pretty disgusting isn't it?

"You've nailed what's going on. You understand, it for sure. It's just like you said—that material you gave me to read—it's that Zelda thing. And I really feel sorry for her, mainly because I know her. I am her. And I hate it."

By the time a person has achieved years adequate for choosing a direction, the die is cast and the moment has long-since passed which determined the future.
—Zelda Fitzgerald, *Save Me the Waltz*

Stage Three is a pre-violent and critical phase of the Zelda Complex. It's an emotional morass that occasionally involves a balance of physical risk. People who remain in Stage Three for any length of time will inevitably suffer emotional damage. One of the most damaging aspects of Stage Three is that one member of the relationship is typically labeled as the "wrong" one. "Wrong," "sick," or "crazy"—whatever they are called is irrelevant. The problem is, any Zelda Complex is a two-person process. One person cannot be "the problem."

One has to dish it out and the other has to accept it. It takes two people to experience the Zelda Complex. In Stage Three, one partner ultimately uses his perceived success as a weapon against the other. Gary could have encouraged Katie and arranged for her to go to law school on her own. If she had other aspirations, he could have encouraged her to pursue them as well. Rather than squelch Zelda's creativity, Scott could have used it. He could have acknowledged Zelda's contributions to his writing, but, publicly at least, he never did. Had I recognized what was occurring in my own Zelda relationship, I'm sure it could have been avoided as well. I could have done more to help my Zelda find her individual happiness. But at the time I really didn't recognize what was going on.

In the Fitzgeralds' marriage, first Zelda and then both had problems. In Katie and Gary's case, she looked like the troubled one initially; Gary's problems surfaced later. In my own Zelda relationship, my children showed symptoms first. The fact is, anyone who remains in the Zelda Complex long enough will experience problems. Both members will become symptomatic. Yet, unfortunately, the way our mental health system works, one person is usually isolated and labeled as the problem. This is not only unfair, but grossly inaccurate.

Zelda was diagnosed as schizophrenic. Katie, upon her hospitalization, was diagnosed psychotic. Diagnosticians take great liberties with the labels they assign people. Once someone is diagnosed severely, much of their credibility and opportunity in today's world is neutralized. Perhaps, by stretching the definition, someone could call Zelda schizophrenic. From what I've read about her, and by her, however, I think she was anything but schizophrenic. As I read the current psychiatric diagnostic and statistical manual, I find nothing defining Katie as psychotic either. This type of reductionistic thinking takes the dynamics of a troubled relationship and places all the negatives on one participant. Most often, such diagnoses are placed on wives.

Zelda had problems. She was spoiled rotten as a child. She was too attractive for her own good. She was seldom required to pay any consequences for her choices. She was undisciplined, gave in to her impulses too easily, and had trouble keeping commitments. However, nothing was wrong with her that could not have been reconciled. If she had been willing to let go of her manipulation, she could have gotten help.

Katie was troubled as well. She was a woman who lived nowhere near her potential. The gap between her potential and what she actually achieved was the depth of her depression. And like Zelda, Katie was not troubled by the things she had done. She was traumatized by things left undone. Both of these women suffered extremes of the Zelda Complex. They felt trapped inside their relationships. They each were troubled in their own ways. The Zelda Complex destroyed their lives. It took Zelda's life. Katie had to make some very difficult decisions, or it would take hers as well.

CHECKLIST

Instructions: Check those statements that apply.

_____1. Since this relationship began, my partner has received a promotion, finished school, or distinguished himself or herself in some other way.

_____2. Lately I am restless and dissatisfied with my job or circumstances.

_____3. I have argued with my partner in public.

_____4. I have been told by others I am wasting my talents.

_____5. I really need approval from my partner.

_____6. My partner has a high-profile occupation.

_____7. People who treat me well seem rather boring.

_____8. I don't feel needed anymore. I feel I need this relationship more than my partner does.

_____9. I am afraid of being abandoned.

_____10. I've been in more than one relationship where I was abused verbally or physically.

_____11. I think the main reason I was attracted to my partner was because I wanted to be like be like him or her.

_____12. Rather than pursue my own talents and education, I have worked to support my spouse or children so they could pursue theirs.

_____13. I have an awareness that something is lacking in my life, but I'm not sure how to fix it.

_____14. My partner is already considered successful in areas I would like to develop.

_____15. I fantasize about changing places with my partner.

Scoring: Total the number of check marks. Five or less suggest you are not currently a candidate for Stage Three of the Zelda Complex. Scores between five and ten indicate tendencies toward Stage Three symptoms. Totals of more than ten indicate you are likely in Stage Three of a Zelda relationship and are experiencing serious difficulties. It would be wise for you to consult a professional.

Chapter 7

The Reality Blur
ESCALATION
TO VIOLENCE

So close
Yet so far away
Who would have thought that we'd end up this way
We're so close yet so far away.
—Daryl Hall and George Green, "So Close"

Ginevra King first met Scott Fitzgerald at Christmas of 1914. She was visiting one of Scott's childhood friends, Marie Hearsey, in St. Paul, and was introduced to him there. He was immediately smitten with her and apparently never overcame it. Ginevra was Scott's first obsessive relationship. For a three-year period, he couldn't get her off his mind. Scott demonstrated this obsessiveness through some of the correspondence he wrote during his sophomore and junior years at Princeton. The same kind of single-mindedness was illustrated in his fictional letters to Isabel in *This Side of Paradise*. Twenty years later, he was still obsessed with Ginevra.

Scott was obsessive-compulsive. Whatever he did, he did to excess. "Nothing in moderation" was his motto. For him, falling in love was more disease than emotion. He literally and figuratively worshiped Zelda. When pursuing her, he was totally consumed by thoughts of her. He flooded her with letters, telegrams, and gifts. He gave her all of his emotional energy. He gave Zelda what she wanted, and most of the time it was his attention. More than anything else, that was probably the attraction he held for her.

Zelda was the perfect outlet for Scott's intense energy. She desired to be the center of attention and, in his eyes, was just that. But she was in many men's eyes. The fraternity to which Auburn football player Pete Bonner belonged formed a Zelda fan club. Their entire purpose: to keep her entertained. She constantly was pursued by aviators from the nearby military base. Pilots did tailspins around her house and an infantry officer once stood in her front yard and conducted the entire manual of arms with a rifle. Zelda would actually write Scott telling of her exploits and conquests. He was overwhelmed with jealousy. It enraged him. It fueled his intensity.

The same series of interactions occurred in May 1924, when Zelda had a very public affair with the French naval aviator Edouard Josan. Scott confronted Zelda and Edouard. There is speculation he actually attacked them. Edouard left the French Riviera despite being assigned there by his military commander. He was so fearful of Scott's reaction that somehow he arranged a transfer. In response, Zelda attempted suicide.

Between 1918 and 1924, when Zelda had her affair, there are countless reports of she and Scott arguing. Many people tell of them drinking excessively, screaming, and raging toward each other. The day after such scenes, people report noticing Zelda with black eyes or bruises. This incredibly vicious cycle continued the entire length of their relationship. Each of them was careful not to attack the other when friends were present. Yet there are reliable reports they were violent to each other on multiple occasions. Regardless, there can be no debate over the immense psychological warfare. There are countless examples of psychological subterfuge by each of them throughout the history of their relationship. But Zelda was the master.

This contributed to Scott's fears and he became even less confident. In spite of his accomplishments, he was always insecure. This probably began with his lack of opportunity as a youth to prove his masculinity. On at least one occasion, he dressed up as a showgirl and appeared in a chorus line. This resulted in a great deal of gossip and speculation about his sexual orientation. One of the problems was that he looked quite attractive in the garb. He wore the same costume to a University of Minnesota dance and created quite a sensation. Using Zelda's writings in his own work probably increased his sense of insecurity as well. Even his greatest accomplishments, his books, were not entirely his own. Scott was deeply insecure even to the point of his death. And his obsessive-compulsive nature left him obsessing constantly about his self-doubt.

Zelda was just the opposite. She did have some obsessive-compulsive qualities, but they were small by comparison. For the most part, she was confident and as sure of herself as Scott was insecure. Scott considered himself inferior to Zelda. He continually described her as stronger and more confident, and complained that she thought of him as a woman. If Zelda ever questioned her self-confidence, it didn't last long, and there is no obvious record of it. She saw her entire life as an exercise in impulse; others were there for entertainment value. This was true with her father and with every man she dated, including Scott and her psychiatrists.

Scott adored Zelda but needed her. She envied his productivity, but held him in contempt. As a result, they argued constantly. Their drinking lowered their defense mechanisms, which led to even more violence. To their credit, they did not kill each other directly. That is sometimes the result of obsessive, violent relationships. Instead, they killed each other in more subtle ways. Their rage ultimately took its toll. It happened in the Menendez family. It happened in the Betty and Dan Broderick triangle. It could happen to you as well.

> *I love her and she loves me, and we hate each other with*
> *a wild hatred born of life.*
>
> —August Strindberg

Stage four of the Zelda Complex is the obsessive-violent stage. Typically, at this point, usually both partners—but at least one—are slowly losing contact with reality and their boundaries. It could almost be the definition of psychosis, but most Zeldas are logical and rational in every other way. People who enter Stage Four are not troubled in all of their relationships. They are usually pictures of stability in most ways. In fact, they can be extremely successful in business, but totally "wacko" when it comes to this particular relationship.

A Stage Four male may be described as rational and calm by virtually all who know him. A Stage Four female might be called gracious and dignified, and the description may seem accurate. It's usually just one relationship that is problematic—and, in most cases I've worked with, it's usually a romantic one. Stage Four Zeldas have already advanced though the first three stages. This can occur in a matter of weeks, or take years. No one we have studied begins the relationship at Stage Four. Whatever the pace, it is a methodical process of advancement.

Stage Four Zeldas are completely afflicted with each other. In the cases where there are two obsessive-compulsives, they are even more afflicted and intense. At this level, they are addicted both to each other and to the intensity. The relationships can become violent, and move in and out of a cycle similar to that of the Fitzgeralds'. The relationships can be not only dangerous but also in fact quite deadly.

Statistics indicate that every eight seconds, somewhere in our country, someone is a victim of spousal abuse. In most cases, the victims are women. More and more frequently, however, women physically abuse men. Some studies indicate that as much as 32 percent of all domestic violence comprises women abusing men. Such violence is less likely to be reported by men than women. But it definitely occurs.

In the recent hysteria surrounding the O. J. Simpson trial, new attention has been focused on domestic violence. Yet little study has been given to *how* these relationships become violent. As a therapist, I have worked with many violent couples over the years. Once the dynamics were understood and analyzed, I found there was more than enough responsibility to go around, in every occasion. Certainly in the cases of repeated violence, whether committed by the husband or the wife, a cyclical pattern begins to appear. In each case I've studied, one of the twenty-five factors of the Zelda Complex consistently shows up: the presence of perceived humiliation.

Perceived humiliation is an important concept. It seems to be the one isolated component present in all Stage Four relationships. This process occurs when one partner interprets the other partner's behavior as humiliating. This is especially true when it happens in the presence of others. In one of the 911 transcripts released during the trial O. J. addressed this. Screaming at Nicole, he told her, "You can't treat O. J. like that! You can't treat O. J. like that!" And though violence occurred frequently between these two people, they continually ended up together.

My Zelda had her own violent nature. Near the end of the relationship, I was attempting to convince her to move out of my home. Finally, in exasperation, I began to take the clothes out of her bedroom closet to start the process. In retaliation, she grabbed a wooden coat hanger and attacked me. I tried to block the onslaught with my hand. The coat hanger sliced through the first three fingers on my left hand. They bled profusely. Then she threw the coat hanger down and started beating me on the back, telling me to put her clothes back in the closet. Initially, I laughed and asked her if this was a new kind of foreplay. When she started screaming at me, I turned and stared at her, dropped the clothes on the floor, and walked away. She screamed that if I didn't return the clothes to the closet she was going to call the police and report a domestic dispute. I ignored her, so she called 911. Later, she attempted to cancel the call, but the police came anyway. I explained the situation to them, showed them my hand, and explained there was indeed violence going on, but I was not the perpetrator. I asked them to inspect her physically to make sure there were no bruises in case it ever arose in court. Obviously, at this point, she felt out of control and publicly humiliated, which is not a good feeling for any obsessive-compulsive person. Yet it was she who was attempting to humiliate me.

Most Stage Four relationships do have an extremely dangerous component to them. These individuals may be stable and nonthreatening when alone; when placed together, they are like sodium and water. An explosion can result, the results of which can be devastating. Sadly enough, they often are.

When anger arises, think of the consequences.

—Confucius

Each of the stories presented in this book is true. Details have been changed to protect the confidentiality of those involved, but the essence of each couple presented and each illustration given is 100 percent accurate. The following case is probably the most memorable I have ever dealt with in psychotherapy. The triangle was indeed a rare group of people. They are unique in the variety of factors they illustrated. Like an exclamation point at the end of the sentence, they add emphasis. This is exactly what they did for my understanding of the Zelda Complex.

I first met them shortly after my own Zelda experience had concluded. They were further inspiration for me to write this book and, in many ways, deserve acknowledgments for their contribution. Bob and his wife, Debbie, first came to see me for marriage counseling. They both appeared to be in their late forties and, during their first session, reported a fairly typical pattern of distancing. As we got further into the counseling process, however, the story grew more complex.

Bob had been a very successful salesman over the years. He was different than many typical sales personalities. He looked more the part of an accountant or computer programmer than he did a stereotypical salesman. Yet that was part of his success. Through his demeanor and dress, he communicated a sense of reliability and professionalism. People with large amounts of money to invest seemed to trust him. He and Debbie both appeared reserved and controlled, yet articulate. They lived in an exclusive neighborhood, drove the finest cars, and always appeared very concerned about image. This made Debbie's revelation all the more startling.

The third counseling session began the same as all the others had. They were congenial and the picture of upper-class happiness. Debbie appeared far younger than her forty-six years. Her jet black hair was thick, long, and perfectly styled. Her dark eyes and aquiline features provided her an appearance of wealth and class. She had an athletic build, yet carried herself like the model she once was. Bob always wore a gray suit with a tailored shirt. He was one of the few people who would come to therapy on a Saturday afternoon with a starched white shirt and cufflinks. He always wore a charcoal gray suit, but explained there were six different shades of charcoal gray. His coiffure would have been fashionable with people of a military background; it was short and trimmed, yet stylish. They both sat and smiled. I was beginning to think these people were so filled with denial we would never get anywhere when Debbie finally opened up.

"I don't know if anything could ever surprise you." She leaned toward me, still smiling. "You've probably heard everything by now. I don't know what you think about us or what kind of people you think we are. We've discussed whether or not to tell you what's really been happening. But, of course, having gone through what you have in your own life, we feel confident you won't judge us too critically." I laughed at her explanation and shook my head in agreement. She laughed back, seeming a bit embarrassed.

"Oh my goodness!" she exclaimed. "I didn't mean that the way it sounded. It's just that you are so open about your life. I guess what I meant was—oh well, never mind!" She waved her hand back and forth. "It's just that we figure you're easy to talk to, because you certainly talk to us openly."

"Yeah" I nodded my head. "Someone told me the other day I probably don't have any skeletons left in the closet by now. Some people don't like that, and wish I'd left them there! I figure I'll just be honest and that way, people will know what they are dealing with."

She leaned toward me and reached out her hand as if she was going to touch me. "No" She said, gesturing. "Believe me, its easier this way. I am saying this as a compliment. But anyway, let me get to the point before I stick my other foot in my mouth.

"Bob's had this little thing going with his office manager for about six years. He has been fairly honest about it, as far as I can tell. I guess, to put it bluntly, he's been having an affair with Sam and it's just getting crazier and crazier. We call her Sam. Her real name's Samantha. She knows that I know. And I know that she knows. He has gone back and forth between us during all these years. They live together, and he'll come home and we'll live together. I've asked him to fire her but he isn't ever going to. So it's just a mess.

"Oh, this is so embarrassing," she said, covering her face. "I've never told anyone about all this. The police have been called on her. They've been called on me. They've been called on Bob! It's really worse than any soap opera I've ever watched, and it probably isn't going to get any better real soon. It all came to a head about three weeks ago. It was just like a scene from some disgusting movie." She looked at Bob and shook her head back and forth in disbelief.

"Go ahead, Deb!" he encouraged. "Don't look at me! You're doing a great job. Just go ahead and tell him the truth and get it over with."

Debbie sighed and then looked back at me. "I guess the easiest thing is to go ahead and tell you what happened." She continued, "The best way to put it is, there was a huge argument. And before it was over, Bob was chasing Sam down the interstate at about 130 miles an hour. He was shooting at her out of his window with a pistol. And I was chasing him. There were four police cars chasing all of us. And we went right down the interstate, around the city. It was the absolute worst thing I have ever been involved in. At least we all ended up in jail, instead of in the hospital! If it hadn't been for the sheriff being a friend of ours and the judge being one of Bob's clients, I don't know what would've happened. As it was, all of us ended up getting speeding tickets, but they were reduced to a seventy in a fifty-five to keep it from being too terrible.

"And I don't know how it all started. I know that he came home and we'd had an argument. He'd gone over to her house. I'd called her and bitched her out, before he got there. Bob doesn't have any tact at all. He has no tact whatsoever when it comes to marriage.

"Now he may be good at his job—obviously he is—but he is just pure hell as a husband. He and Sam drink too much. One time, they got caught having sex on the interstate. They pulled over their car, and were in the median of the interstate stark naked, having sex—and got arrested by a patrolman who just happened to drive by!" Debbie shook her head back and forth, and then paused, turning back to Bob.

"Am I exaggerating at all?" she asked.

Bob shook his head and then said, "No." He nodded. "No, you're telling the truth; unfortunately there is probably more you're not telling."

People in Stage Four of the Zelda Complex are usually extremely sexual. They will have a history of high sexual energy, usually accented by infidelity and multiple periods of sexual experimentation. They can be extremely violent, both during sex and otherwise. At a minimum, they are verbally combative and extremely critical. They usually have extended abusive episodes, marked by episodes of violence. These can include actual fist fights, stabbings, and occasionally murders. At times, they seem to actually enjoy fighting.

The problem is, violence can be addictive. The body responds to the "rush" and physiological changes that occur with violence as it does to a drug. I've heard a number of people describe domestic violence as habit forming. The rush can become foreplay. Violence creates a cycle that often results in sex. The conflict begins as a verbal disagreement. This is usually followed by threats and excessive profanity. At some point, one partner will attack the other. This often results in retaliation, which is when the physical violence escalates. The confrontation will usually proceed until one partner becomes excessive and hurts the other. When he or she realizes the other is actually injured, he or she will comfort the other person while expressing remorse. Ultimately, this apology leads to an episode of intense sexual intercourse, which can itself appear violent. This cycle is a very dangerous one, as John and Lorena Bobbitt demonstrated. Yet it is one that occurs rather frequently.

> *Keep violence in the mind where it belongs.*
> —Brian Aldiss, *Charteris*

By 1938, Zelda was having difficulty relating to Scott, or to their daughter, Scottie. She was becoming more reclusive. She would isolate herself and remain sequestered in the bedroom for several days on end. She began to be tense around everyone. This changed somewhat when

Dr. Thomas Rennie was assigned to Zelda's case. He was a young bachelor who was infatuated with both of the Fitzgeralds. Dr. Rennie was an aspiring writer himself and appeared to be mesmerized by Scott, and attracted to Zelda. He apparently became obsessed with the case, and appears to have worked fervently to help them. Scott was distressed by Zelda's novel *Save Me the Waltz*. Dr. Rennie attempted to resolve the conflict over her writing, but was unsuccessful. Zelda ultimately saw him as one more man who failed her. And, ultimately, she had a love-hate relationship with him, just as she had with other men.

Years after the passion is removed, it's easier to see things more clearly. In a letter to his daughter Scottie, written in 1940, Scott recognized he should never have married Zelda. Scott described Zelda as not having the "strength for the big stage that she sometimes pretended, and pretended beautifully." Zelda pretended to be in control. She pretended to be somebody she wasn't. She spent all her psychological energy pretending. And finally all the pretense was gone.

The same thing was true of my Zelda. In retrospect, we both realized it. While writing this book, I had the opportunity to speak with her. I apologized for my contributions to the deterioration of our relationship.

"I made more mistakes than you did," she responded. "I learned a lot from you. You were a great teacher, but I didn't want to be a student at the time. I wanted to be your lover. When I didn't get what I wanted, I started spending money compulsively, and became angry. And then we would get in a fight.

"I knew I had to leave. And when you made me go, it just made it easier for me to stay mad at you. But I knew it had to happen. You were a good teacher. And most of the stuff you told me was true—"

"I don't know," I interrupted. "Everything I said wasn't true. A lot of what I said was out of pain. I was being hurt, just like you were."

"Oh, I know," she nodded her head. "But most of the stuff you told me has turned out to be right. I learned a lot from you. I just wish I'd learned it earlier."

That's the difficulty. In the middle of Stage Four, reality is a blur. It's difficult to sift through the emotion to find reality. This is one of the things that makes Stage Four so dangerous. National headlines have been filled with reports over the last several years of people in the midst of Stage Four. Lorena Bobbitt made national news by cutting off her husband's penis after a quarrel. She reported to the first officer on the scene that she had done this because he had not given her a chance to have an orgasm. Later, she changed her story and said it was because he abused her. Regardless of her reasons, she severed his penis, rode around with it in the front seat of her car, and then threw it onto a suburban lawn. By now, everyone knows the story. His penis was later reattached and he proudly displayed it on pay-per-view television. Mrs. Bobbitt was retired to a psychiatric hospital. Mr. Bobbitt went on to be arrested several other times for committing violent acts against other women. Perhaps she learned from her experience, but obviously he did not.

Tanya Harding, Nancy Kerrigan, and Jeff Gilule entered their own Zelda triangle. Gilule and his thugs busted Kerrigan's kneecap with a tire iron. It was later discovered that Tanya Harding had conspired to plan the attack. In their own Zelda complex, the Menendez brothers killed their parents. The reality of what they did has not been debated, yet their case is still being tried to determine the nature of their responsibility. The O. J. Simpson case has been, and will continue to be, widely debated over the next few years. But it is obviously an advanced Stage Four Zelda Complex that includes all of the dynamics mentioned throughout this book. The Zelda Complex is real. The violence is real. The possibility of death, unfortunately, is real as well.

Never lose sight of the fact that the most important yardstick of your success will be how you treat other people—your family, friends, and co-workers, and even strangers you meet along the way.

—Barbara Bush

Most Americans can recite many details of the O. J. Simpson case. It has been so comprehensively reported and analyzed, it's as if it happened in our own families. The trial will continue to provide fodder for talk shows, probably for the next dozen years. Another Southern California story has been well reported. It didn't receive the national publicity of the O. J. Simpson trial, but it did make an impact.

Few people feel sorry for Betty Broderick. She was receiving $16,000 a month in alimony. She was living in a multimillion-dollar, palatial La Jolla estate. She was driving a jaguar, and had a boyfriend who cared deeply for her. Yet, in the face of all of this, she broke into her ex-husband's new home, and killed him and his current wife. The story of Dan and Betty Broderick has been reported, discussed, and was the substance of at least two movies. The purpose here is not to rehash the case, but to illustrate the dynamics and power of the Stage Four Zelda Complex.

Dan was an extremely powerful medical malpractice attorney and physician in Southern California. At the height of his success, he was making more than $100,000 per month. He and Betty had met while both were in college. After graduating, she taught elementary school to finance his education. Initially, he went to medical school and completed it, then went to law school and became a malpractice specialist. Theirs was no quick success story. Although both came from well-to-do backgrounds, they worked very hard and, over time, became quite successful.

Along with the trappings of success came the confusion provided by the Zelda Complex. After the birth of her children, Betty simply lost her identity. She committed herself to being a full-time mother and volunteered at her children's schools. She was now the wife of the most prominent malpractice attorney in Southern California. This is likely when Betty entered Stage Three of the Zelda Complex. Some of her friends reported she was having difficulty handling not only Dan's workaholic pattern, but also his success. He was extremely well recognized in the area. His practice was growing exponentially. And Betty was his wife and a mother. Originally, this had been her dream, but as she matured, she wanted her own success. But Dan encouraged her to stay home and raise the children.

Betty did not want the divorce. Dan had begun an affair with an attractive, young employee. Fascinatingly enough, the employee appeared to be a near clone of Betty, only twenty years younger. Betty suspected the affair, and grew more and more out of control as it continued. Not only was she angry, but she apparently lost contact with reality at some point. After committing the double homicide, Betty called and told several friends, "I think perhaps I killed Dan and his wife." Betty also reported to friends, "I'm not Mrs. Anything now."

The Broderick relationship is a classic Zelda story. Dan initially wooed the attractive Betty. They were both young, tempestuous, and somewhat wild. He was an attractive, Cornell medical student who fancied himself to be like Rhett Butler. She was a slender, blonde, effeminate coed who enjoyed his attention. They were obsessive-compulsive from the beginning. They went through all the stages of the Zelda Complex. Initially, the marriage was functional, but about the time Dan entered law school they entered Stage One. Upon graduating and moving to San Diego, it appears, they were caught in the hostile-dependent cycle. They needed each other for functional reasons, yet Dan was unhappy with the marriage. Stage Three began when he left the law firm to begin his own business. He quickly became successful, and Betty's difficulty with her own identity soared. This was soon followed by Dan's affair, and, later, marriage. During this time, Betty gained weight let and her personal appearance deteriorate. This added to her self-esteem problem, which she blamed on Dan.

Predictably, during the divorce trial, Dan tried to portray Betty as a lunatic. Apparently, he was somewhat successful. She got the house, the Jaguar, and huge alimony. Dan got the children and was the moral victor, if there can be such a thing in a divorce proceeding. The games continued. There were other lawsuits, after the divorce. Dan's new wife, a younger and prettier version of Betty, seemed insistent on rubbing it in. Dan, too, seemed to take pride in humiliating Betty publicly. The warfare escalated. At one point, Dan's new wife broke into Betty's home. Betty retaliated by breaking into their home on one occasion, even prior to the killings. Finally, the murder occurred, which put a tragic end to the theatrics, but not to the legal proceedings. Betty was convicted of murder and is currently serving her sentence in Chauchilla State Prison, near San Francisco.

The Zelda Complex contains many such tragic elements. Scott and Zelda did not shoot each other. Yet their deaths were a result of the same phenomenon. One can only speculate about the real facts in O. J. and Nicole Simpson's Zelda Complex. But no such speculation is necessary with the Broderick case. The verdict is not in question. The Broderick case is dramatic in its portrayal, but not uncommon. The deaths don't have to be as dramatic. Nor does the outcome. Psychological and emotional deaths occur daily. In *The Elvis Syndrome*, I stated that Elvis Presley died a psychological death the day his mother died. His biological death occurred some seventeen years later, but, in the end, it was simply a gradual slide to that point. It is my belief that literally millions of other similar but lesser-known deaths occur annually. And they are all unnecessary.

The Zelda Complex does not happen to one particular class of people. Like the Brodericks, one can be extremely well educated and suffer the phenomenon. One can be almost illiterate and suffer from it as well. Another misconception is that Stage Four happens only to a few. Stage Four relationships occur everywhere. And a person does not have to be chronically abusive to resort to violence. Anyone has the capacity for violent behavior. There is no evidence that Betty Broderick ever demonstrated any tendency toward violence prior to the murders. She was not a child abuser, or a husband abuser. There is no detectable history of abusive tendencies.

The same thing is true of men who occasionally abuse their spouse. Most people understand what a *binge drinker* is. Binge drinkers are people who may only drink once a year. Yet when they do, they go on a binge—they stay drunk for several days, in some cases, several weeks. In a similar way, people can go on binges of violence. In one case I worked with, the husband had been violent over a thirty-year period, on five separate occasions. That's an average of once every six years. But on those occasions he was violent, he caused tremendous physical harm to his wife: She suffered a broken elbow, a hairline fracture of the jaw, a broken nose, a broken forearm, and a fractured skull. This man was an educated engineer with a master's degree in business administration. His wife was a university professor with two master's degrees and a doctorate. They were very competitive and rotated between Stage Three and Stage Four most of their marriage. When I suggested they separate before someone got killed, the husband agreed. The wife, however, grew incensed and threatened legal action against him, and me! They remained together for several months longer, until he hospitalized her again in a fit of rage. Ultimately, they divorced. It was still against her wishes. Such is the twisted nature of a Stage Four Zelda Complex.

> *Who overcomes by force, hath overcome but half his foe.*
> —John Milton, *Paradise Lost*

When a person is *obsessive*, he or she has repetitive thought patterns. It is a perpetual process that requires tremendous energy. It results in a single-mindedness that can lead to tremendous success, or tremendous failure. Obsessive people rarely end up mired in mediocrity. They go to one extreme or the other. The word *compulsive* has to do with behavior. A *compulsion* is when you repeat a certain behavior incessantly. A compulsive drinker is a person who drinks to excess. A compulsive gambler is a person who gambles to excess. A compulsive worker is a person who becomes a workaholic. Similar to their obsessive thought patterns, compulsive people by nature are very dichotomous. They rarely end up in the middle of the road. A good compulsive motto would be "Nothing in moderation!"

You put the two qualities together and you have what is commonly referred to as an obsessive-compulsive personality. Every successful person in the world is obsessive-compulsive to some degree. Yet so is every alcoholic, drug addict, or person who dies from obesity. In reality, most people probably have some obsessive-compulsive tendencies. Then there are those who have extreme degrees of such energy.

Bob was obsessive-compulsive; Debbie was moderately so. To put it more clearly, Bob would have probably received an A in obsessive behavior on a report card. Debbie, on the other hand, would've received a B-. Bob's girlfriend, Samantha, would have received an A+! I agreed to see Sam at the insistence of both Bob and Debbie. I would have refused otherwise. Debbie was ready to get on with life. Bob had too much invested in keeping everything together. He had an extremely gorgeous, workaholic girlfriend who kept his business together. He had an equally attractive, yet older, wife who was society's darling. With Sam, he drank hard, worked hard, and played hard. With Debbie, he relaxed, balanced his life, and regained his sanity. It was a dichotomous exercise at its most extreme. And, frankly, it was one he wanted to continue.

Sam wasn't quite sure what she wanted. She said she didn't want to marry Bob. At the same time, she didn't want to give up the relationship. Sam had risen very rapidly in Bob's company, and occupied an office with enormous bay windows overlooking a nearby lake and mountains. It was more fitting for the CEO of a major corporation. On the wall was a life-size mural of Bob crossing the finish line in the Boston Marathon. It was record of a compulsive running binge that had occurred several years earlier. Much of Bob's success was directly attributable to Sam's commitment and work ethic. She had seen an opportunity to flourish with Bob and had seized it. At the same time, they had an intensely sexual relationship, enjoyed by both, along with other mutual excesses. Among them: gambling, drinking, and experimenting with illegal drugs, including cocaine. To their credit, cocaine was one compulsion they had decided to avoid.

Sam's personal appearance was impeccable. Everything matched. She looked the role of a perfect businesswoman, yet exuded sexuality. It was as if her conservative clothing attempted to restrain her sexual energy. She was a very attractive woman and I could understand Bob's affinity for her. She described herself as a perfectionist and said her modest home had a place for everything, and everything was in its place. Bob described it as "impeccable," and "clean to a fault." One of their recurring fights was about his messiness. She had not organized the house to accommodate a male's presence. Everything was categorized obsessively, to the point that she had different-colored hangers for different types of clothing. None of the hangers were designated for Bob's clothing, and she could not tolerate him draping things over chairs. The ensuing arguments were almost comical.

Sam and Debbie were not friends, but they weren't enemies either. They had openly discussed the affair and had frank discussions about Bob's faults. On several occasions, Debbie had told Sam she could have him if she wanted him. Sam usually laughed, saying "no thanks." She was satisfied with the way things were. That was probably true at the time. Debbie also recognized the importance Sam played in her life. The business could not have been as successful without Sam's help. Its success had a direct impact on Debbie's standard of living, and her future. The Zelda Complex is often complicated both by emotions and factual reality. Certainly, it was true in this triangle.

When two obsessive-compulsive personalities such as Bob and Sam get together, there is bound to be difficulty. A relationship can accommodate one obsessive personality without too many problems, as long as that person remains functional. There is almost no relationship that can stand the strain of two obsessive personalities. It is inevitable the two will combust. It may take months or years for the energy to break the two people down. But the reaction is inevitable.

The reason for that is understandable, but complex. Frankly, most relationships don't make sense. Most emotions don't make sense. Numbers do. Accounting ledgers make sense. Taxes, though complex, can be analyzed, categorized, and understood. Computers are logical and, if you study them long enough, will behave predictably. Obsessive-compulsive people are good at any logical activity. But emotions are irrational; they are not based on cause and effect, and certainly cannot be quantified. Most obsessive-compulsive people make tremendous accountants, computer programmers, or mathematicians. They are lousy at relationships.

Intimacy is the closest emotional bond. It requires the emotional energy of two people, both of whom are patient, understanding, and open minded. This is rarely the case with an obsessive-compulsive person. If one partner is obsessed with what he or she perceives as the other's failures, trouble will soon occur. When both people do the same thing, fireworks are inevitable. When obsessed with something that has a logical answer, obsessive-compulsives can ultimately find a conclusion. First of all, there is a logical answer.

Relationships are rarely logical. Emotions are seldom predictable. The obsessive-compulsive love affair, then, is to become engaged in a process that is terminally futile. There is no rational explanation, or winners and losers, in love. As a result, most obsessive people get caught up in being "right." That most often leads to finding fault with their partner. Since their intensity will not allow them to admit mistakes, they end up blaming their partner, justifying their insanity by finding fault. For obsessives, blame almost always lies outside of themselves.

The long-term, and usually short-term, effect of such thinking is disastrous. The couple is doomed to fireworks and ultimate failure. Dan Broderick had an affair, and, in my opinion, arranged to be caught. That was his way to exit what he saw as a less-than-satisfying marriage. Betty escalated the situation by gaining weight, becoming irrational, and ultimately killing her ex-husband and his new wife. Scott escalated by drinking and becoming threatening. Zelda escalated through setting fires, attempting suicide, and having herself hospitalized. Tanya Harding and Lorena Bobbitt escalated by becoming violent.

People in Stage Four will always find dramatic ways to escalate. It may be a subconscious cry for help, a bid for attention, or a way of expediting closure. My own Zelda escalated by attacking my children, attacking me with a clothes hanger, and then involving the police. At that stage of the relationship, there was nothing else that could be done. We had to either get out of the relationship or escalate further. At Stage Four, most relationships are beyond help. It is usually necessary to exit the relationship, at least temporarily, to get some perspective. If you attempt to reenter the relationship, it must be with completely new understandings, definitions, and expectations.

For whatever reason, Sam decided to escalate. She didn't wait for Debbie or Bob. She later explained to me in therapy that it was time for a conclusion to "the whole mess." At the time, I thought she was talking about suicide. She laughed and assured me that was not a possibility. I asked if it meant quitting her job and she assured me that would not do it either. She accurately explained that she and Bob and Debbie were locked in a cycle of hostile dependency. It benefited no one for Sam and Bob to discontinue their professional relationship. At the same time, she realized it was virtually impossible to separate their business and personal relationships.

Several weeks after that appointment, Bob called me, and explained what Sam had meant. When they had eaten supper together the evening before, she had informed him of her pregnancy, and that abortion was not an option. The dynamics were changed forever.

> *A man that studieth revenge keeps his own wound green,*
> *which otherwise would heal and do well.*
>
> —Francis Bacon

An obsessive-compulsive individual will ultimately make the absolute best, or absolute worst, of any given situation. This can also occur in vastly contrasting dichotomous styles. Equal degrees of intense compulsive energy will be directed toward success or failure. It can also occur within the same context. During one period of time, Scott pursued Zelda as no one had ever been pursued before. He later distanced himself from her just as intensely.

Betty Broderick supported her husband's career, put him through school, and tried to be the perfect lawyer's wife. Then, in exasperation, she did her best to destroy his business. When that didn't work, she destroyed his life. The Menendez brothers were described by friends of the family as almost perfect children when they were young, and later they killed their parents. John and Lorena Bobbitt had bragged to their friends about their intensely passionate and satisfying sex life. Then, their sadistic-masochistic rituals went too far and she cut off his penis.

Whatever obsessive-compulsives do, they will do with intensity. If they have a sexual relationship, it will be incredibly sexual. When they fight, the conflict will be equally passionate. And when they decide to distance themselves from each other, they will do so with a vigor that can be frightening. There is simply nothing that compares to an obsessive-compulsive turned cold. It is intimidating. This is what happened with Sam after she disclosed the pregnancy.

She oscillated between rage and complete withdrawal. She was no longer passionately sexual, or even friendly, with Bob. At this point, she had become enraged. It appeared her goal was to make the absolute worst out of their relationship. And she did virtually everything possible to achieve it. She began showing up late for work, losing phone messages, and failing to return calls to important clients. She went through marked personality changes, which many people attributed to her pregnancy. She began having open and public conflicts with Bob. Fascinatingly enough, her relationship with Debbie improved, despite Debbie not being aware of the pregnancy. Bob appeared beaten down and his drinking progressively increased. His effectiveness at work dropped, whether it was caused by Sam's withdrawal or his own dysfunction. Regardless everything changed.

I'm really not aware of how many people knew about the pregnancy. Shortly after Bob's phone call, they discontinued therapy. Debbie or Bob would occasionally call to keep me posted. Sam and I spoke on the phone several times as well. I continued to talk to them on the phone because I was intrigued by the case. I did see Sam on one occasion after the pregnancy, at her request. She was trying to make some decisions. She had decided to keep the child, but was contemplating ending the relationship with Bob. She assumed he would want to have nothing to do with the baby. She was also curious about which last name the child should be given. We had a prolonged discussion about this and I offered my opinions.

It is a biological fact that pregnancy does bring about mood changes. There are tremendous hormonal and biochemical consequences to pregnancy. One can never scientifically answer how much of Sam's change of behavior had to do with that. At the same time, it is my belief that she had grown weary of the pattern. The relationship between Sam, Bob and Debbie had taken an incredible toll on each of them. Sam had worked an average of sixty-five hours a week over the past seven years. I think she was tired of the grind. Developmentally, she was ready to have a child as well. It was simply a good time for her to become pregnant if she was going to do so. I believe she sincerely loved Bob. In other circumstances, I think she would have wanted to marry him. But in these circumstances, it was unlikely. Frankly, they never could have gotten along, and I think she realized this.

Sam was very angry at Bob for his insistence that she have an abortion. The conflict had escalated to the point that they were physically injuring each other, in spite of her condition. They seemed to be following a recipe for disaster. Every ingredient needed to assure tragedy was present. The high emotional energy was there. They had enjoyed intense pleasure, now it was time for the pain. The passion that had once been funneled into sexual energy, now became rage. There were equal volumes of anger, sadness, humiliation, and embarrassment. The sexual energy had disappeared. Their libido now was thwarted and was turning into stressful and destructive energy.

They had been combustible from the beginning. Now, their relationship had deteriorated into physically abusive bouts, accompanied by more chases down the interstates, Bob breaking into Sam's home, and Sam stealing documents from the office. The relationship had transcended combustible, and was now toxic. They were overdrinking, driving while intoxicated, and, in my opinion, behaving in an almost homicidal manner. The relationship had been the one place each of them could go to lower their defense mechanisms. Now it was gone.

Sam had always wanted to be like Bob. His success was something she could not have achieved on her own. She had overidentified with Bob and now she saw the entire process being threatened. She not only loved Bob, she wanted to become him. Yet Bob knew the truth. He could not have accomplished his goals without Sam's workaholism. They were enmeshed, and at this point, demise threatened not only their relationship, but also their sanity. In the advanced levels of Stage Four, mental health can deteriorate rapidly. Sam and Bob were losing it.

Neurosis is always a substitute for legitimate suffering.
—Carl Jung

F. Scott Fitzgerald began writing *Crack-Up Essays* at the Skyland Hotel in Hendersonville, North Carolina, in November 1935. This collection of writings and autobiographical pieces was published posthumously in 1945. Scott described it as "a desolately frank document for whom the salt of life has lost its savor." These essays document the deterioration of Scott's coping mechanisms. Zelda's deterioration was demonstrated more clearly in her artwork and photographs of her toward the latter years. She appeared cold, formal, and void of emotion before her death. It was more than the process of aging. Mileage had worn out Zelda. She was unable to attend Scott's funeral, eight years before her death. She was unable to attend her daughter's wedding in 1943, five years before she died. Gardening, painting, and religion were her outlets toward the end.

Her paintings had an eerie, if not bitter and tragic tone. After her hospitalization at Highland Hospital in 1936, Zelda became reclusive. She never really reentered society. It was her crack-up.

You can slow a crack-up if you're observant. Unfortunately, most people aren't sure what to look for. It's not a loss of control, though obsessive-compulsive people desire control. In reality, the only control a person has is self-control. Most obsessive-compulsives forget about that. They focus on things, activities, or other people. Zeldas need control more than most people. They react to their loss of control with sheer panic.

When I was attempting to move my Zelda's clothes out of her closet, I will never forget the words she screamed at me. "You put those damn clothes back! You've destroyed my closet. My closet was the only thing left in my life that was perfect! And now you've destroyed that too." She had been slowly losing control since moving in with me. Similar to Sam, the place in which she had lived before was extremely well organized. Although it was woefully small, everything had its place, and there was a place for everything. My house was just the opposite. People were continuously running in and out all the time. It was a massively disorganized, five-thousand-square-foot combination of a men's dormitory and martial arts dojo! Things around me were erratic, but my personal life was so ritualized it was boring. All of these things were the antithesis of what my Zelda wanted for her life.

Her closet, on the other hand, could be cataloged and organized. It was structured, divided, and alphabetized. I remember watching her walk into her closet and just stand there. Her arms would be crossed as she gazed at her clothes plaintively. She seemed mesmerized when retreating into that cave. She would stand there for a number of minutes, as if contemplating a million things around her. If I asked her what she was doing, she would always reply, "Looking." Her obsessive-compulsive need for structure could be found nowhere else but in her closet. Within its confines, she found solace. It was organized, structured, perfect. She felt at peace there.

Parting is all we know of heaven, and all we need of hell.
—Emily Dickinson, *My Life Closed Twice Before Its Close*

During the course of therapy, I received an unexpected telephone call from Sam and was asked to come to her house. She told me the back door would be unlocked and to just walk in. She said she wouldn't answer the doorbell if it rang. I was somewhat surprised and asked what was going on. She told me not to even ask, but to just come visit her. I did as she requested.

As I entered the back door, I noticed the house was dark, except for a muted glow coming from the living room. As I glanced around, I noticed the carnage which often results from Stage Four Zelda Complexes. At one end of the living room was a broken glass with ice and liquid soaking into the carpet. An end table had been overturned. The mantle had been swept clean, apparently by somebody's angry hands, and knickknacks were scattered on the floor. Magazines and books lay strewn around the carpet, like casualties on a battlefield. I walked gingerly to avoid stepping on the broken ashtray and cigarettes near the den.

"Sam?" I called out. "Anybody home? Samantha, are you here? Knock, knock. Where are you?"

"In here." I heard her voice coming from the den. "I'm in here. I'm on the couch." I walked toward the voice and saw her prostrate figure stretched out on the sofa. She was holding a towel of ice on her eye. She had scratches on her wrist.

"Damn. Where's Bob?" I asked. "Did he do this?"

She nodded her head silently, then responded, "I guess he's gone somewhere to cool off. Don't worry about it, he'll be back. He'll do it again."

"Sam, gee whiz!" I shook my head, letting the air expend from my lungs. "Let me take you to the emergency room or something. Geez, you look like you've been beaten all to hell. I'm going to call the police. This has really got to stop."

"No!" she insisted. "John, don't you dare. I'll hate you if you call the police. You know I can't do that. If you call the police, it will just make it worse. Just let me handle it. I only wanted to talk to you."

"Do you have any pictures of this?" I asked her.

She laughed out loud. "Are you kidding? I've got albums. This is not the worst one by far. I've got pictures. I've got dates. I've got statements from people. After this, I'm going to want one from you, too, by the way." She reached under the couch and brought up a Polaroid. "Take some shots of this, so I can put them in the album. Some day I'm going to nail this bastard and this stuff is going to be made public. Until then, I just need to stay calm."

"For God's sake, Sam. What are you waiting for?" I pleaded. "Don't you understand where this leads to? You've been lucky so far. I mean, do you want to end up dead? Besides, you're pregnant now. You can't do this stuff anymore."

"You're not telling me anything new," Sam responded. "He went out drinking again last night and you know what happens when he drinks. You know, maybe I'll learn my lesson this time. Who knows. Just don't preach to me, okay? Here, take the pictures and just tell me you love me or something."

I began taking pictures of her wrists, arms, and face. "Look," I began, "I don't want to preach. That's not what I'm trying to do. But I also don't want to see you dead. You guys have got to stop this. I mean, I've seen Bob almost as bad off as you are. You've done it to him, too. I love both you guys. It's not about love. It's not about preaching. It's about *life* and *death*. You guys are going to *kill* each other if you don't stop. That's about all there is to it. Why don't you guys get out of this thing? Get out of this craziness before it's too late!"

She nodded her head. "I know you're right. We really do have to stop this. But I can't do it by myself. I need help. I love him. Our lives are so tied together, I just feel like I don't have a future without him. I'm scared to death of being alone and not having any money. You know, I couldn't continue this lifestyle without him. And don't tell me some other guy would hire me. You and I both know that nobody's going to pay me what Bob does. It's just not going to happen. I feel trapped in this relationship, but I'm going to have a baby to think of. If we break up, what will I do then? Maybe next week it will be my turn, and I'll get even and beat the shit out of him."

I listened and was tempted to go ahead and call the police anyway, but I didn't. By not doing so, I became part of the problem. The Zelda Complex is a complicated equation that involves such interactions as those that occurred between Sam, Bob, and myself. For the process to continue, each person must cooperate with the deception. It usually takes one member to stop cooperating for it to stop. With Sam and Bob, the cycle stopped five weeks later.

The same thing happened a second time. Instead of going alone, I took Roy Glen with me, a detective at a local police department, and one of my best friends. Since he does a lot of undercover work, he doesn't look the part of a police officer. Sam opened up to him. Later that afternoon, he arrested Bob without her awareness. The violence between Bob and Sam ended. Unfortunately, it was only temporary.

CHECKLIST

Instructions: For both lists, check those statements that apply.

OBSESSIVE TENDENCIES

_____1. I often worry about problems for days.

_____2. I believe there is one "best" answer to every problem, and that answer is the one that should be followed. Or, my spouse believes there is one "best" answer.

_____3. Whenever I do something, I do it all the way.

_____4. I have one area in my house or at work (closet, drawer, desk, etc.) which has a place for everything.

_____5. If I can't win at something, I don't try it.

_____6. Being punctual is extremely important to me. If I know I am going to be late, I will sometimes cancel altogether.

_____7. I find it difficult to delegate tasks to others. I feel it's usually easier to do it myself and have it done right the first time.

_____8. I experience angry outbursts that surface for no apparent reason.

_____9. I feel I have no time for hobbies. It's necessary for me to spend as much time on my job as I can.

_____10. I have few friends other than those with whom I work.

STAGE FOUR FACTORS

_____1. I have exited and returned to this relationship more than once. Or my partner has.

_____2. My partner has repeatedly embarrassed me in public.

_____3. My partner and I often argue when we go out together, such that others around us have noticed.

_____4. The police have been called to our house to answer a domestic violence call.

_____5. I have had fist fights with my partner.

_____6. I don't feel as if we've really made up unless we have sex.

_____7. One or both of us has physically attacked the other during arguments.

_____8. I have experimented with drugs.

_____9. We have a passionate sex life.

_____10. I have attempted suicide. Or, my partner has attempted suicide.

_____11. I have threatened to kill my partner. Or, my partner has threatened me.

_____12. We have the best sex when we're making up.

_____13. I am successful and competent at work, but this relationship seems to have a mind of its own.

_____14. I have lied about bruises or scratches received during fights with my partner.

_____15. Our disagreements almost always degenerate into screaming sessions.

Scoring: Total the number of check marks in each list.

Obsessive Tendencies: Totals less than three indicate few problems with obsessiveness. A score between three and seven suggests you have obsessive tendencies that could cause problems. Scores higher than seven indicate extreme tendencies that should be monitored for possible problem-causing factors.

Stage Four Factors: A total of less than five suggests little problem with Stage Four factors. Scores between five and ten indicate problematic behavior that is causing problems in your relationship. You and your partner may need to see a professional to avoid hurting each other seriously. Scores higher than ten suggest a need for caution. Discussing this questionnaire with a professional is probably necessary to remain in this relationship.

Chapter 8

GREAT EXPECTATIONS
WHAT'S IN A GAME?

Some people think if you really believe
That's all you need to solve all the mysteries.

—Daryl Hall and George Green, "So Close"

There is no question that F. Scott Fitzgerald had difficulty with alcohol. Friends confronted him about it on several occasions. There is evidence he was even confronted by Zelda's psychiatrist. Scott became angry and defensive when they discussed his problems. He occasionally suggested that his drinking in no way compared with her schizophrenia, and if the doctors thought it did, he questioned their professionalism.

Zelda was definitely troubled. She was spoiled, manipulative, and depressed. She used her hospitalizations as a way to escape when nothing else was going her way. When too many demands were placed upon her, she would simply get sick. Zelda seemed to view hospitals more as retreats than places to focus on psychiatric treatment. She seldom cooperated with staff. Rather than learn from them, she flirted with her psychiatrists.

Scott and Zelda seem to have competed over who was most talented. He belittled her attempts at writing, art, and ballet. He called her a third-rate writer and dancer on many occasions. Yet, it was *her* writing that composed much of Scott's books. Both Scott and Zelda were insecure. They were too insecure to divorce, or to get along.

The Zelda Complex comprises many manipulative moves. They're called games, because they are indirect and dishonest ways of communicating. Scott's drinking and Zelda's multiple hospitalizations are examples of games. Zelda didn't go to the hospital because she felt ill; she went because nothing else worked. Of course, Zelda's most serious games involved fire. The message she was trying to send was, "Someone please notice and rescue me." The consequence, however, turned out to be death.

Because of their consequences, games can be disastrous. Scott would not even entertain the idea of giving up alcohol. He used alcohol as a way of escaping his emotions. When he had an eight-year dry spell as a writer, he blamed Zelda. He said it was her fault, because he was too busy caring for her. People afflicted with the Zelda Complex expend a lot of time and energy concealing the truth. It's often easier to be honest and accept the consequences, yet they seem unable to do this. Honesty is a rare commodity among Zeldas. It's almost nonexistent, except when all else has failed. Their motto seems to be "When nothing else works, as a last resort, divert to the truth." In the advanced stages of the Zelda Complex, it's difficult for anyone to sift through the lies.

Jack and Sandra played games in their relationship. The goal was multidimensional. On one level, they avoided intimacy; on another, they avoided the risk of rejection and pain that accompanies intimacy. Jack and Sandra weren't dishonest about everything. The were only dishonest about the important things. Having gotten to know them, I can say this with a degree of certainty. They were actually stuck in the relationship. They both wanted change, but feared it at the same time. They were frightened that change would cause the relationship to end, and they both wanted to avoid that outcome. Their investment was in maintaining the status quo at some manageable level. When we clarified that issue, the problem became a lot easier.

Walt and David played tremendous games. The stakes were personal as well as professional, but they were not intimidated by the risks. They played games by competing with each other. The atmosphere of the business was like a football game. Each was trying to win the game by getting his father's approval. Every transaction became another contest. Like the two astronauts from the movie *Enemy Mine*, Walt and David had to work together. But cooperation was difficult for them. It was more natural to compete and that's what they did, destroying the business in the process. They had developed an artificial hostile dependency. It was artificial in the sense that it was created by their father. They were not literally forced to cooperate. Yet if they did not, the consequences would have been severe.

Gary and Katie played games as well. She pretended to be a wife, mother, and career woman. Then she pretended to be an attorney's wife. She ignored her own talent and intelligence. She pretended to be satisfied in the role that had been cast for her. Yet nothing could have been further from the truth. Gary pretended to be politically correct. He pretended his wife was crazy. He played mind games with his children. He manipulated them into siding against their mother. It was a game that resulted in stalemate. No one could move. All players were compromised. And, in many ways, that was probably the implicit goal they had structured for themselves.

Debbie, Bob, and Sam played very harsh games. On one occasion, Bob returned home from a visit with Sam and said, "I've got good news."

"What's that?" Debbie asked.

Bob responded tritely, "Well, Sam's having her period. I can't have sex with her tonight. So I guess I'll stay here with you." Debbie and I later tried to figure out if he expected her to feel happy about the news, or if he was trying to insult her. Either way, the comment was stupid. He flaunted his relationship with Sam in a way that was rude, but not insidious. He never really lied to Debbie, as far as we know, until the final pregnancy. Bob and Debbie did occasionally have sexual relations, even though she knew about Sam. They went on vacations together, and carried on a publicly amiable marriage. Appearances can be deceiving, but to Bob, appearances were everything.

Sam played games with Bob as well. She pretended to be satisfied with the arrangement the three of them had. Deep down inside, she never was. She played games with the pregnancy. The pregnancy was a way to force the issue of marriage, or at least to get some closure on the triangle. It really wasn't about having a child. At her most honest level, Sam didn't want to be a mother. She wanted to work in the business. The pregnancy was a way of bringing everything to a head. She and Bob both played intense games with their rage. Their fights were frightening. On more than one occasion, people had told Bob that either he or Sam was going to get killed. Yet, when taken away from each other, both were calm and peaceful. They were actually quite likable. Both had bizarre senses of humor, they laughed at themselves as much as anything else. When I first met with them, they made fun of themselves. But all that changed. The consequences of their games were tragic.

My own Zelda was an accomplished game player. She pretended to be an expert at virtually anything she became interested in. When I met her, she was an expert in accounting. In fact, that's *how* I met her: She became my accountant. I later discovered that her mastery at accounting was similar to her mastery of everything else. She was actually a terrible accountant, and I paid dearly for trusting her with my finances. She played at being mentally stable. She played at being an accountant. And she failed miserably at both. But similar to all Zeldas, she wasn't willing to accept the consequences.

> *Men willingly believe what they wish.*
>
> —Julius Caesar

The games we play as adults have a great deal to do with the expectations we bring into our relationships. Expectations result from complex interactions that occur over time. From observation and direct learning, we develop deep beliefs about ourselves. From these spring our expectations. There is nothing simple about expectations. We develop them through early learning experiences. Further experience builds on these experiences and may alter our expectations in some minor way. Our personalities may even change as a result. Short of drastic circumstances, however, such as trauma from combat, chronic illness, or tragic accidents, beliefs and expectations remain pretty much the same.

Expectations are predominantly taught indirectly. From early childhood, we begin to think of ourselves in certain ways. These create our self-image, which, in turn, creates outcomes. If we have positive beliefs about ourselves, we expect positive outcomes. If our belief systems are on the low end of the scale, our expectations will correlate with that.

By observing my grandparents as a young child, I developed certain beliefs and expectations about life. They lived on a small farm in rural Piedmont, North Carolina, and both worked extremely hard. There was no such thing as men's work or women's work. There was just work. And everybody did it, regardless of gender or age. My grandmother would begin cooking supper in midafternoon. She would get a pan from the cabinet and pour flour into it. After blending flour and shortening, she would add homemade buttermilk—that's when the work began.

"Johnny," she'd call out. "Get yourself over here and help Granny work the biscuits."

Everyone helped cook unless they were working outside. Her biscuits were so delicious we would sometimes have them as dessert with straw-berries and milk on top. But all that occurred some three hours after she began making the biscuits and working the dough. If we wanted fried chicken, which was my favorite, someone had to go to the henhouse and convince a chicken to give up her life for our lunch. That took a great deal of time as well. If we wanted potatoes, that meant more work. We either dug them out of the garden, or crawled into the cellar and sifted through the lime until we found edible ones. The implied learning was that anything good takes work, cooperation, and time. This learning was transferred into a core belief about myself, and life in general. From this, I developed a set of expectations about work, and—more specifically—about life. Though my framework has changed somewhat, I still maintain the same set of beliefs and expectations.

A physician friend of mine has a daughter with a different set of expec-tations. She attends an exclusive private school where children are pam-pered, if not spoiled. For her sixteenth birthday, my friend gave her the used family Volvo and bought himself a new car. Rather than responding with gratitude, she was incensed. Her friends at school had received new cars for their birthdays, and none of them were Volvos. They had received brand-new Acuras, Infinitis, and one even had a brand-new Porsche. Her expectation was that she was entitled to a new sports car. My friend and I had a long discussion about the unrealistic expectations she was developing. I finally got through to him when I asked if he would like to be married to someone who had such expectations.

One of the vital steps toward overcoming the Zelda Complex is to examine the validity of your expectations. Most expectations are uncon-scious, uncommunicated, unrealistic, and unfair. You can end up feeling betrayed, or cheated, when you haven't been. Those feelings perpetuate the insecurity that fuels the Zelda Complex. Betrayal is when someone has made a commitment and broken it. But you can expect something without anyone else ever having agreed to give it. You may end up feeling *entitled* to regal treatment.

My friend's daughter would probably enter any relationship with grandiose expectations of how she should be treated. She'd feel entitled to plush treatment as a birthright. If her new husband didn't give her the car of choice, there would be hell to pay. After all, assuming her dad contin-ued to give in to her tendency toward entitlement, she would expect her husband to do the same. Before you get upset at the gift or the giver, there is an important question to ask: Is it the gift that is unreasonable, or my expectation?

Emotional expectations can get you into trouble. On one occasion, I saw a couple in therapy after they had a fist fight. The altercation started over her birthday celebration. On the morning of her birthday, he had pulled out a credit card, given it to her, and told her to buy herself five hundred dollars' worth of new clothes. To me, that sounded like a great gift. But to her, it was not only unromantic but unthoughtful. He had an expectation that she would be appreciative. She had an expectation that he would be romantic. When he asked me what I thought of the gift, I responded honestly. I told him I wished somebody would do that for me. As I did, I noticed she rolled her eyes and shook her head.

Then I explained, "You asked me what *I* thought. Now, can I tell you what most *women* would probably think?" He nodded, so I continued. "I bet they'd say you were a thoughtless jerk or something like that." They laughed out loud. She had actually described him as far worse. It wasn't the exchange of gifts that got them into trouble; it was the expectation.

I often get to speak at conferences and seminars. On many occasions, I am one of several speakers in concurrent sessions. I enjoy visiting other sessions and listening to other speakers. On one occasion I was speaking at a convention being held at the sprawling Xerox Conference Center in Leesburg, Virginia. One of the speakers was a John Madden look-alike named Chris. He happened to be speaking on the subject of performance, but ended up speaking about expectations. He strutted around the podium, jabbing his left forefinger while waving a ballpoint pen in his right hand like a symphony conductor's wand. His navy blue sport coat flew open as he gestured, revealing a maroon tie hanging loosely from his neck. Before long, his shirttail was hanging out.

"Here's the hot scoop," he continued. "The most important thing you will ever develop in your employees is their expectations. As long their expectations are in an alignment with yours, you won't have any problems with quality control. However, if your expectations are way up here—" He held his left hand above his head. "And your employees' expectations are way down here—" He held his right hand down at knee level. "Then you've got some problem. The distance between that gap *is* your quality-control problem. When it comes to performance, expectations are everything."

He took off his glasses and began cleaning them with his tie. "Gettin' steamed up," he mumbled. He was answered by a murmur of guarded laughter. He paced restlessly from one side of the room to the other, like a huge bear with one foot tied to a stake in the ground. "You see," he continued, jabbing again with his pen, "this is the thing. The problem doesn't start with the level of performance. It goes all the way back to your expectations. You can only understand the defects and loss by understanding the expectation. Now, that's not to say you adjust your performance, or that you adjust only your expectations. The deal is, you adjust the expectation level of the people that are working with you."

I never got to find out much about Chris. He is a consultant on quality control and human performance. What he had to say made a lot of sense to me. It is expectations that lead to difficulty. People who experience the Zelda Complex have expectations far out of line with reality.

> *Before we set our hearts too much upon anything,*
> *let us examine how happy those are who already possess it.*
> —Francois de La Rochefoucauld

In 1968, like many other young servicemen, I was getting ready to go to Vietnam. I was eating lunch at a bar outside of Camp LeJeune, North Carolina, at the time. Kenny Rogers and The First Edition were singing "Ruby Don't Take Your Love to Town" on the jukebox. "It wasn't me who started that old crazy Asian war, but I just thought I'd go and do my patriotic chore." It was one instance where music defined rather than described the mood. The bar was filled with several marines, a group of bikers from The Outlaws, and some of their girlfriends.

One of the ladies was standing behind her biker boyfriend. He was sitting at a table playing cards and drinking. As I watched, she wrapped her arms around his neck and whispered something in his ear. This occurred several times. Each time he waved her away with the back of his hand. She was extremely thin and had long stringy hair plastered to her back in an unkempt fashion. I was sitting facing them and could not help but notice their interactions as they escalated. She finally leaned over, wrapped her arms around her Outlaw, and whispered something in his ear. Without speaking, he frowned angrily while slapping his cards down on the table. Then he aggressively threw his forearm and balled up fist behind him. The back of his fist and forearm smashed into her nose. As blood flew everywhere, she collapsed to the floor. Then, like an animal, he turned to stand over her. He pointed his right finger at her and swore. "Love you? Love you?" he screamed. "Bitch! I love my 'dawg!' I love my motorcycle! I love my brother! But I sure as hell don't love you!"

It is predictable: you will someday experience difficulty with your expectations and definition of love. How you define love will determine the satisfaction you experience in relationships. The Outlaw had a particular approach to defining love. His girlfriend had another. His expectation probably led to satisfaction for him; her expectation, however, led to pain and serious injury. Expectations are inevitable. Everyone expects certain kinds of happiness. We expect certain kinds of struggle. And we certainly develop expectations when it comes to love, relationships, and sex.

The first year of any relationship goes goes a long way toward determining how the relationship will continue in the future. It is the most important year of any relationship and probably the one most people are least equipped to handle. People have totally different expectations of how difficult the adjustments will be. The changes some people go through when a marriage is formalized resemble a transformation from Dr. Jekyll to Mr. Hyde. Typically, it is in the first year that any potential for later abuse will show up.

Differences, personality quirks, and previously unnoticed differences in values surface during the first year. A lot of reality testing also occurs. People ask themselves, Is this really how I want to be living for the rest of my life? If the relationship has depth, most of these things can be overcome. But people who are naive, and not so fully committed to the relationship, can be alarmed by these signs. They feel disturbed and trapped. Rather than negotiate, they simply run.

One of many difficulties Zelda had in her relationship with Scott was the limits marriage placed on her freedom. In the Sayre household, Zelda's idiosyncrasies were tolerated, if not applauded. Scott held her more accountable, and after the birth of their child, there were even more limits imposed. She felt like she was losing her freedom, and later in their relationship Scott became the ogre she feared he would become. Neither Zelda nor Scott realized that the difficulties they had were normal in marriage and could be overcome. Zelda, especially, was so isolated, she didn't have a basis of comparison. She was alienated from most of her former friends. Her grandmother had committed suicide. Her mother and other extended family had histories of mental illness. Her older sister was in the throes of emotional and marriage difficulties. Her brother suffered from so-called nervous prostration and ultimately committed suicide. Talking to her family about problems was an exercise in futility.

Most people who suffer from the Zelda Complex experience isolation. My own Zelda had lived in the same city her entire life. I had only lived there a few years. She had been involved in the same church for more than thirty years. She had attended high school and college in the area. Yet she claimed her only friend lived four hundred miles away. As far as I could tell, she was right. Her personality was overwhelmingly extroverted. I, on the other hand, was a die-hard introvert. But I had more friends than she. When her troubles began with me, she felt there was no one to discuss them with. She probably did speak to her mother, but her mother had far more emotional problems than my Zelda. She kept her feelings inside and ultimately ran into major difficulty.

Like my friend's daughter, my Zelda felt a sense of entitlement. In her thinking, she deserved to be treated with deference. She had expectations of near grandiosity. She had attended the same exclusive school my friend's daughter now attends, and learned to expect similar treatment. When her expectations were not met, she exploded. The identical phenomenon happened with Gary and Katie, Walt and David, and Bob and Sam, and so on. The disappointment of not having expectations met most often leads to marked combativeness.

Combative couples bait each other constantly. Fights can start from something totally insignificant, and often culminate in passionate lovemaking. Bob and Sam continually teased, goaded, and prodded each other. They could agree on nothing and shouting matches were part of their lifestyle. But their combative rituals were also an essential prelude to sex. Fighting was, indirectly, stimulating foreplay. There are people who simply can't go a single day without some type of conflict in their lives. The disagreements and brawls get their adrenaline pump flowing and they can actually experience a high from the encounter. Some of these people begin to believe that if there's no fighting, there is no love. But the problem is, it can develop to dangerous levels.

These people feel they have to win. They keep score. They become competitive and find themselves trying to outdo the other. As with all Zelda situations, these individuals are very insecure and winning is just a way of making them feel safe. However, the toll it takes on a relationship will destroy it over time. The conflict can become a perverse glue that holds them together. Yet it can often lead to violence. There is little an outsider can do to resolve the conflict. If someone does attempt to intervene, he or she is seen as an enemy rather than a friend. It's usually not *content* that creates the problems, anyway, but rather *how* the couple relates to each other. The pace at which the conflicts escalate is phenomenal.

Statistics suggest close to six million wives and three million husbands have been severely beaten by their spouses. Another study found that more than two million of these experienced at least one episode in which a knife or a gun had been used. Nearly 25 percent of all murders occur between spouses or ex-spouses. Each year, thirty-two hundred husbands are convicted of murdering their wives. That statistic does not include reduced sentences such as manslaughter, or those cases that yield no conviction at all. Most, if not all, of these tragedies are the result of conflict over expectations that vastly differ from reality.

> *Blessed are those that nought expect, for they shall not be disappointed.*
> —Walcott, *Ode to Pitt*

Scott's expectations for marriage arose from his romantic notion of finding a damsel in distress whom he could rescue. Perhaps this was a result of his need to prove his masculinity, or just simply the gallant way he liked to see himself. Zelda was definitely in distress, but not the kind of distress Scott could rescue her from. Someone was quoted as saying that he was looking for a king's daughter. He found her. Zelda's father sat on the Supreme Court in the state of Alabama. In the South, it is not possible to be much closer to king than that. Throughout the course of their relationship, Scott tried to rescue Zelda from the dragon. But it didn't work.

Zelda's expectations were just as unrealistic. She dreamed of a big strong man who would make everything right for her. She fantasized of pilots flying her away. Or perhaps her football hero would score the victory in her life. Later, she thought the French naval aviator would rescue her from Scott, who by then had become the dragon. She fantasized her psychiatrist could slay the evil lord who prevented her from taking her rightful throne. But they all let her down. Zelda was looking for answers to her problems. Yet when she was offered help, she toyed with it, from all reports. She could have married one of the aviators. Her chosen football hero described himself as not being in love with her, but said his roommate was and had plans to marry Zelda.

Like people who struggle with the Zelda Complex today, the Fitzgeralds had intensely unrealistic expectations about what love could provide. You probably have struggled at one time or another with an expectation that something wonderful will happen to make everything better. We certainly believe fables that teach such lessons. As a child, you may have read about the knight on a white horse that whisked damsels away to a land where they lived happily ever after. It is a fantasy that leads to despair and hopelessness. There are escapes, such as those provided by alcohol and other drugs, but they are only temporary.

Jack had expectations that Sandra would be exclusively his, and his alone. He didn't even want to share her with children. He reluctantly admitted that this was one of the real reasons he had insisted Sandra never get pregnant. They didn't have intimacy, or sex. Regardless, his biggest complaint was that she had friends besides him. He simply couldn't understand why she needed to spend time with her friends when she could be at home with him. Admittedly, Charles did become a romantic interest. But that had occurred more as a result of the lack of intimacy she had with Jack than of any sexual feelings.

Both Walt and David had developed expectations at an early age that life would be easy. They saw themselves as the crown princes awaiting their rightful throne at the head of the family business. This, too, was a sense of entitlement, and led to great disappointment later on. They each felt they should be running the business individually as president. They easily saw the flaws of each other, but glossed over their own, individual problems. In all honesty, they were a good team. It was their intense competitiveness and hostility that led to the near downfall of the company.

Gary and Katie had unrealistic expectations for marriage. Gary expected Katie to ignore her own talent and potential. He expected her to delay gratification virtually forever. He had no understanding of why having achievements and a career of her own it would be more satisfying to Katie than simply being Mrs. Gary. Actually, Katie had unrealistic expectations of Gary. Considering who Gary was, her expectation that he would be understanding and supportive was not only unrealistic, but naive. Gary was so incredibly narcissistic, it was sickening.

Once I asked Katie if she thought Gary could possibly be having an affair. She laughed at my question and responded, "Are you kidding?

He's so in love with himself. There's simply not enough room in there for anyone else." She was probably right. Even his personal grooming was done to a fault. He spent more time primping in the morning than she did. He went to a tanning bed. He colored his hair. He had his nails manicured weekly. He even admitted to suffering a bout with anorexia because of his concern about gaining weight. Gary's problems went beyond simple vanity.

Each of these couples likely got together for quite functional reasons. But people change over time. The kind of things needed at one point in a relationship are not necessarily the same things needed later. One couple I worked with illustrated this quite clearly. She had been a physical therapist working at a military hospital in South Carolina. The man of her dreams was a returning Gulf War veteran who had been wounded severely and was in the hospital for rehabilitation. He was learning to walk after having most of the muscles in his hips and thigh severed by an explosion. They were both young and single at the time. He needed somebody to help him learn to walk again. She needed somebody she could fix, and who needed her. They got along quite well, as long as he was sick and she was strong.

Within months, they were married. But, as could be predicted, things changed. He started getting well. He didn't need a crutch anymore. In fact, he became quite an athlete and started running in marathons. Understandably, problems began in the marriage. They had entered the relationship with unspoken, unconscious, and unrealized expectations. Had those expectations been articulated, they would have sounded something like this:

"I'll be strong and confident and you can lean on me."

"Yeah. I'll be crippled and sick, and you can be my helper and my crutch. Okay?"

"It's a deal."

Actually, those were the unspoken terms of the contract, which set up expectations for the relationship. They were probably unaware of them at the time because of the intensity they felt and their lack of maturity. Nevertheless, the expectations existed. Most long-term relationships have similar thematic agreements. Once this couple entered therapy, it wasn't long before they realized what they had done. They were able to renegotiate the terms of their contract and continue their relationship. It took tremendous adjustment, but they were eventually successful. This process is normal. When you're crippled, you may need to use a crutch; when you're not, you don't want to use one. It is typical, and healthy, for needs to change. Occasionally the way you treat each other needs to change as well.

Yet people fail to admit these things to each other. They hesitate to rock the marital boat for fear they'll lose the other partner in the process. What they fail to realize is they *will* lose each other if they don't make the necessary changes to stay together. This is true with each of the four couples discussed in this book. It was painfully true with Scott and Zelda Fitzgerald as well. Their failure to renegotiate the terms of their relationship led to Scott's and Zelda's deaths. It has also led to many others.

Expectations result primarily from previous experience. Experiences leave what is seen, at first glance, as unforgivable programming in the computer-like subconscious mind. That programming helps people develop a core set of beliefs about themselves, beliefs that mold self-worth. Upon those beliefs are built expectations about life in general, and relationships in particular. And choices later reflect them. Most people's computers were programmed inaccurately. As a result, they make bad choices about relationships early in life. Such choices can affect one's entire life, and sometimes destroy it. The good news is, this programming can also be changed. The bad news, most people don't know how to change it. Or, on the occasions when they do know, as with Jack and Sandra, they are scared to make changes because of the potential consequences.

You mustn't force sex to do the work of love or love to do the work of sex.
— Mary McCarthy

People who experience the Zelda Complex are usually highly sexual. For a number of reasons, this is the arena in which expectations are most confused, and potentially explosive. There is tremendous repression and denial when it comes to sex. There is more misinformation than helpful discussion, misinformation that is frequently passed down from parent to child. A friend of mine was approached by his mother three days before his wedding. She informed him there was something she needed to tell him about sex. After some awkward shuffling, she handed him a shoe box with a douche in it and counseled her son to make sure his wife used it. That was all he was ever told about sex by any adult.

Another friend was told not to have sex during his new wife's menstrual cycle, because it would cause acne. A woman friend of mine was told that turning down her husband for sex would cause him to be impotent. Another woman was told to make her husband happy and not to worry about enjoying it herself. A relatively recent phenomenon has added to the collection of bizarre expectations about sex. Tabloid talk shows and soap operas have raised sexual expectations to an unrealistic level. This is further complicated by some people knowing how to show love only through sex. When I was in graduate school, I saw this illustrated in a very helpful, and dramatic, way.

Len, one of the clinical instructors, was a very charismatic communicator and teacher. He supervised a small group of graduate students who were doing internships. During the course of the year, we had all become quite close. In the last several weeks, when we were assured of graduation, people relaxed and started being more authentic. One very attractive female student was attracted to Len. She had dropped hints on several occasions, and during one of our last class reviews, she said that Len was quite sexually attractive. Len overheard her and interrupted the conversation.

"What do you mean by sexually attractive?" he asked.

She broke eye contact and acted embarrassed. Finally, she stammered, "You know, I just find you to be a very sexually attractive man."

Len continued to question her, but gently. "Okay, tell me what it is that you find attractive. Tell me specifically what it is that attracts you to me."

"Well," she stuttered, "I think your eyes are sexually attractive."

"So, compliment my eyes," Len responded.

"What?" she gasped. "Compliment your eyes?"

"Yeah." Len continued, "Tell me you like my eyes. If you think I've got nice eyes, tell me I've got nice eyes."

"Okay." She continued uncomfortably, "Um . . . well . . . um . . . I really . . . I really like your eyes."

"Thank you very much," he answered. "I like my eyes too. What else do you find attractive? What else do you like about me?"

"Well," she began. "I like the . . . um . . . I like the way you communicate."

"So compliment the way I communicate. Tell me you like the way I communicate." Len edged closer as he continued to goad her. The process continued for more than an hour. She ended up complimenting every single thing she found attractive about him. When she could think of nothing else, Len summarized the conversation in a way I've never forgotten.

"Thus far, I've counted twenty-seven compliments you have given me." He turned to the class and explained, "Yet none of them have to do with sex. She didn't compliment my penis. She didn't compliment my butt. She didn't compliment the way I kiss her. She didn't compliment the way I touch her. I've never done any of those things. You see, we live in a society that has grown to interpret anything friendly, admirable, or attractive as sexual.

"For God's sake! We call *cigarettes* sexy. We call *cars* sexy. We assign sexual interpretations to things and events which are absolutely asexual. I'm not trying to make fun of her. We all do it. I'm trying to create a learning experience for all of you. Don't confuse sex with admiration. And don't let your clients do the same. Don't confuse sex with a hamburger." Everyone laughed.

"Well you do!" he exclaimed. "Listen, ad agencies have created a reaction in society such that we think of a cigarette or a glass of beer as a sexual experience. They can make a hamburger sexual as well. What about a hot dog?" Everyone laughed again, louder.

Len was making a point that illustrates the misunderstandings created in our society about sex. Part of it, certainly, is the marketing strategy used by advertising agencies to convince us that their products are sexually arousing. They've done a great job! Sex sells. But every time it sells, it creates additional problems. It creates a set of expectations associated with sex that are not only unrealistic, but also unfair. It leads to mass misunderstanding, and ultimately disappointment. Real life cannot match the expectations that marketing has offered as reality.

Unrealistic expectations of love and sex are largely caused by unrealistic representations found in movies, television talk shows, and soap operas. The impact on those who are watching is problematic. People compare the reality of their primary relationship with some of the stories they hear on these shows. You can find yourself woefully inadequate in your relationship and, frankly, somewhat boring if you believe what you see on TV.

At the extreme are people who compare the reality of their relationship to the fantasy of what they see on television, grow disappointed, and exit. Others develop a type of performance anxiety. They begin to develop feelings of inadequacy. Occasionally, these feelings can become so deeply rooted they render people sexually ineffective or impotent.

In chapter 4, Jack and Sandra illustrated the power of what they called the do/do pattern. This "damned if you do, and damned if you don't" pattern occurs in sexual relationships when partners use sex as a tool. It's common for one partner to give off sexual messages and then act offended, whether the other partner responds or not. This leads to arguments, because it is a no-win proposition. If the partner responds, the instigator throws it back in the partner's face, saying he or she is wrong or perverted. If the partner doesn't respond, he or she is frigid or impotent, and wrong as well. For Bob and Sam this took a twisted turn. On one occasion, Sam had purchased exotic underwear and negligees. Later that evening, when she and Bob had been drinking heavily, Sam flirted with him in a very seductive way. When he finally responded, she objected vigorously. She slapped him, and he slapped her back. She ran away and Bob chased her down the interstate at 130 mph. This was the occasion mentioned in chapter 1, when Bob was shooting his pistol at Sam, and Deb was chasing them both.

When one person develops a set of expectations that is inconsistent with his or her partner's, misunderstanding is inevitable. Additionally, sexual relationships multiply the opportunity for misunderstanding. Because sex is passionate, disagreements can become passionate. This is one of the reasons it is so important to continually clarify sexual expectations in any relationship. The more intense the relationship, the more important clarification becomes.

But did thee feel the earth move?
— Ernest Hemingway, *For Whom the Bell Tolls*

By changing expectations, you can change the character of a relationship. This is not an extremely complicated process. Superficial expectations can be changed rather easily. Deep expectations need to be addressed at a deep level. Yet the path is similar, however deeply rooted the expectations.

To initiate change, you must first clearly and precisely define your expectations. This was extremely difficult for Jack and Sandra. They feared that facing their expectations meant facing the barren reality of their relationship. The sheer reality of looking at their relationship on paper meant admitting that possibly something was deeply wrong or unquestionably missing. They didn't want to face that possibility. Accurately and honestly assessing your expectations about the relationship is the first phase of overcoming the Zelda Complex.

There are specific steps to help you accomplish this. For some people, it's very easy to recognize expectations. For others, it's more difficult and requires a great deal of thought. The simplest way to begin is by writing down the phrase: "I expect from my partner . . . " Write it twenty-five to forty times. Then, complete the sentence fragments. Write freely, until you're unable to think of anything else. For most people, between two and five handwritten pages are necessary. The more you write, the better. Interestingly enough, the first thing you come up with is rarely the most important. Keep writing. When you've gotten it all down, you should feel purged.

The second step is to begin writing things you remember your parents telling you about this particular type of relationship. For example, if you are engaged in the Zelda Complex with your spouse, write about things you remember your father or mother saying about marriage, the opposite sex, or closeness in general. You may recall your father's exasperation as he said, "Women! You can't live with 'em and you can't live without 'em!" If you heard that repeatedly, you may carry a certain set of expectations about women and marriage. Similar sentiments may have come from other authority figures such as teachers and priests. Write down those things you remember hearing that would generally categorize or label members of the opposite sex, that could have contributed to expectations you have developed for your spouse. From that list you can evaluate the usefulness or worthlessness of each.

The next step is to recall any myths, stories, or fantasies you believed as a child that represented the way things are supposed to be. Perhaps your mother perpetuated some myth of living happily ever after. If you were ever told that if you married the "right" man you would live happily ever after, that's significant. Maybe you were misled to believe that If you have to work at a relationship, it wasn't meant to be. Anything you were told or believed as a child that has contributed to unrealistic fantasies about your future is important. This is especially true if it contributed to a sense of entitlement. Some of the people mentioned in this book really thought they were entitled to success without the labor that went along with it. My friend's daughter who thought the four-year-old Volvo was not good enough for her birthday present is an example of a Zelda waiting to happen. If she were to honestly complete this analysis, it would include the belief that she felt like she was entitled.

It may be difficult to compose these expectations on paper.

Nevertheless, it is extremely important to do so. Once you have accomplished this segment of the analysis you can proceed to the next step. However, be certain you have definitively characterized the essence of your expectations. It takes most people several days to accomplish this step adequately.

The fourth step is to ascertain a set of *realistic* expectations. This can be done in a variety of ways. One is to discuss the expectations with your partner. If you were my friend's daughter, you might list the following: "I expect you to buy a brand-new car for me on my birthday." Then, you would need to discuss that expectation with your father or husband to see how realistic it was. It could also be discussed with an accountant, financial advisor, or anyone else you trusted with financial matters. You might also discuss it with a marriage or family counselor. The purpose of these discussions is to produce a "reality check." After receiving feedback, you should ask yourself, Where did this expectation come from? If the expectation is unrealistic, it's important to realize where it originated. There are probably other expectations that originated from a similar source.

Many men today have unrealistic expectations about domestic responsibilities. Sometimes a man feels entitled to a maid service, instead of a wife. I've seen it often. When the issue is discussed objectively, however, he often realizes how unrealistic his expectations are. Occasionally his mother performed domestic responsibilities his current wife or partner doesn't. But when he realizes, as an example, his mother didn't work outside the home, he usually begins to understand the problem. Times may have changed. Circumstances may have changed. But the man's expectations have not. It is very important to go through this process. When you sit down and renegotiate your expectations, the most important person may be the third party whom you invite to act as a reality tester. Testing reality is the key here. Most couples are not able to be objective enough on their own.

> *Sometimes I wonder if men and women suit each other.*
> *Perhaps they should live next door and just visit now and then.*
> —Katherine Hepburn

After many years in a relationship, negotiating new expectations can be frightening. Sometimes it results in loss. Occasionally that loss is necessary—delusions of absorbing or taking over your partner's success, for example. It's equally important to let go of any fantasies that you'll be taken care of, or meet the right person and live happily ever after.

An alarming number of people enter relationships based on Stage Three delusions. A woman who came to see me for therapy had such an experience. She and her husband were both members of a conservative religious denomination. Unfortunately, churches often raise among their members unrealistic expectations of how life should be. One of the unrealistic expectations she had espoused was that marriage would be comparatively trouble free if she married the *right* person in the *right* place at the *right* time. Each one of those *rights*—person, place and time—were prescribed by the church. She followed the prescription carefully and expected "happily ever after" results.

They weren't forthcoming. She found her husband to be controlling and violent. He dictated where she could go, who she could be with, and when she had to return home. She frequently was left to find transportation for herself—even to church—since he took their only car or required that she not use it, "in case he should need it." Likewise, he described who she could talk to on the telephone, or if they even had a telephone. When they did have one, he put a limit on the length of her calls. Calling her parents long-distance was out of the question, even when it was collect. Meal preparation, clothing, hair style, hobbies—all were subject to his approval. Their children could not participate in any extracurricular activities, because she was to be home whenever he was. If she went against his wishes he grew angry, and sometimes violent.

Rather than realizing it was the relationship that needed work, she decided her unhappiness must be her own fault. Part of her religious upbringing included the belief that if you kept the commandments you would be happy. Also included was the idea her husband was in charge. He told her he wouldn't get violent if she would just do things the way he told her to. So she redoubled her efforts many times over the years, to keep the commandments as well as be the perfect wife and mother.

After fifteen years of marriage and four children, however, she realized she had more self-determination as a child than she did in her marriage. She went into counseling and tried to renegotiate expectations with her husband. He refused to go with her, suggesting it was a waste of time. One evening, she talked to a girlfriend on the phone without his permission. That same afternoon, she had gone to a codependency meeting. Most of the changes she had made were fairly minor, but he felt threatened nonetheless. The following morning, he calmly walked into their bedroom and announced he would either divorce her or kill her if she didn't change back to the way she had been. She left that afternoon.

They're divorced now. He refused to renegotiate. He had totally unrealistic expectations for marriage. Those expectations were compounded as a result of having his way for so many years. He had never experienced any type of reality check. His wife had worked so hard to make everything perfect that, for the most part, his expectations were met. He saw no reason to change. As a result, the marriage ended.

Losing a relationship is a risk of renegotiation. But without it, loss of that relationship is inevitable. Such was this woman's experience. It was the same for the Fitzgeralds. The alternative is to work through the steps above and formalize a new list of expectations. Write them down. Agree to them. Practice them. And be patient. This is new learning. Be kind to your partner and yourself during the process. If you have successfully renegotiated expectations, you have come a long way. Incorporating them will often take time.

CHECKLIST

Instructions: Check those statements that apply.

_____ 1. I have no friends with whom I can be totally honest.

_____ 2. I feel I deserve better treatment than I receive.

_____ 3. My partner ignores me, even though I have requested more attention.

_____ 4. I believe the "right" relationship can make me happy.

_____ 5. I need to feel needed in a relationship.

_____ 6. If a relationship takes a lot of work, it's not meant to be.

_____ 7. My partner has accused me of being too romantic and not practical enough.

_____ 8. My partner has told me that if I talk to friends or relatives about our relationship, I am violating a trust.

_____ 9. There are times when I feel my partner has gone out of his or her way to make me feel badly.

_____ 10. I would like to develop my talents, but don't have enough time, money, or emotional support from my partner.

_____ 11. I am tired of being Mr. or Mrs. So-and-so.

_____12. I have been told by my friends or parents that my current partner is not good enough for me.

_____13. My past relationships haven't worked out because my partner wasn't "right" for me.

_____14. There are some changes I would like to make in our relationship, but I don't know whether my partner would be willing.

_____15. Even when I am around people, I am terribly lonely.

Scoring: Total the number of check marks. Less than five checks indicates little problem with isolation or unrealistic expectations. Scores between five and seven suggest you are isolated from others. Consider choosing someone with whom you can be honest. From time to time, feedback from an independent observer is necessary to give yourself a reality check. If you have more than seven checks, you may need to evaluate your expectations to make sure they are realistic. Again, sharing this checklist with a friend would probably be helpful.

JOURNAL SESSION

1. Defining Expectations — Partner Along the left-hand side of a sheet of lined paper, number each line one through thirty. Next to each numeral, write the following statement: "I expect my partner to . . ." Now, go back and complete each statement with an expectation you have for your partner. For example, " . . . keep the cars maintained." If you run out of lines, add more. Add to the list over a period of days. Usually, the more you list, the more thorough you have been.

2. Defining Expectations — Role Model Write down things you remember your parents telling you about relationships. Include any instructions that concern your gender. For example: "Women should never say no." Afterwards, list similar statements made by relatives, teachers, coaches, scout leaders, and so on. Especially important are role expectations described by religious leaders, past and present.

3. Defining Expectations — Myths and Folklore Record any myths or stories you believed as a child that represented the way things are supposed to be. Include any romantic notions you may have had concerning falling in love, and what determines whether or not a relationship is "right."

4. Defining Expectations — Reality Check Review the list of expectations from Step One. Share them with your partner, a close friend, or a counselor. The purpose of sharing is to determine whether or not your expectations are realistic. Your expectations may be realistic under some circumstances, but unfair in present ones. More than likely, many of your expectations may need to be renegotiated because of added responsibilities for both partners.

Chapter 9

RENEGOTIATION
GETTING OUT OF THE
ZELDA SPIRAL

Well I know someone who just heads for the sun
She says "I don't wanna be wise, I just wanna stay young.
— Daryl Hall and George Green "So Close"

One of my early heroes was the late anthropologist and philosopher Dr. Margaret Mead. She was a gifted speaker, whom I had the honor of hearing on several occasions. I am not quoting her directly, but I recall Dr. Mead saying something similar to this: Considering the differences between men and women in the world today, it's no surprise the divorce rate is so high. What's surprising is that couples can actually stay together long enough to perpetuate the species.

Relationships are truly difficult in today's world. There are a variety of factors contributing to those difficulties. The incredible pace of change in gender roles over the past thirty years has greatly contributed to the problem. Times change. People change. Responsibilities change. Yet expectations have remained pretty much the same. People today expect a great deal out of marriage. In fact, they expect far too much, considering the responsibilities we all face.

At a minimum, today's couples expect romance, empathy, excitement, and security. They expect to be taken care of, nurtured, provided for, and stimulated. Additionally, they expect their partner to be a teacher, lover, provider, therapist, protector, priest, policemen, and domestic. On top of all that, they expect their partner to stay in excellent physical condition as well as look like a million bucks in the morning. No wonder people are still looking for the perfect relationship.

One of the keys to overcoming the Zelda Complex is to successfully negotiate both partners' expectations into a mutually satisfying contract. This requires two partners who are not only mature enough to negotiate, but also willing to enter into the process. There are few examples available of Scott and Zelda negotiating or compromising. This is simply because neither of them were willing to do so. Scott's idea of negotiation was browbeating and intimidation; Zelda's was withdrawal. Her strategy of negotiation was to throw a tantrum until she found out she wasn't going to get her way, and then return to her bedroom to sulk. The bedroom later became a psychiatric institution. As a means of escape, the pattern remained the same. It was her palace to pout. The tantrums were translated into affairs and suicide attempts. My own Zelda was similarly unwilling to negotiate or compromise. Her strategy was to blackmail or bribe her partner into submission, then to pretend it was his idea. She spent a great deal of energy trying to accomplish it.

Most people are capable of compromise. As the Zelda Complex progresses, however, it seems less likely. As people grow more out of touch with reality, their expectations become increasingly unrealistic. In the earlier stages of the Zelda Complex, the skills and sensitivity necessary to negotiate remain intact. As a couple moves toward Stage Four, however, the likelihood of compromise lessens.

To successfully negotiate your way out of a full-blown Zelda Complex it's important to look at your alternatives. There are actually a limited number. Occasionally, the only healthy alternative is to save your life by getting out of the relationship. Because many people in Stage Four have already lost contact with reality, however, this option is often forfeited. Another alternative, as Zelda and Scott Fitzgerald demonstrated, is death. This can drag on insidiously, as it did with Scott; or it can progress quickly and dramatically, as it has for literally thousands of people who commit suicide annually. Zelda's death was suicide, although of a different type. Initially, she died psychologically, then spiritually, and finally physically. Hers was an alternative many people choose.

Sometimes, as in Zelda Fitzgerald's case, suicide looks accidental. It's difficult to determine if a traffic accident is actually an accident. The woman mentioned at the end of chapter 8 had a near-miss, head-on collision. Trapped in a marriage of control, she had been considering suicide that week. On a subconscious level, she was acting on that impulse. To her credit, the collision was a wake-up call and she entered counseling.

Many accidental drownings are actually people going through the same thing. Drug overdoses, in my opinion, are seldom accidental. The same is true for many of the people killed in gun battles with police. It's the ultimate suicide; it's just done in the line of duty, or in the line of "misduty," whichever applies.

Insanity is also an outcome of the Zelda Complex. This has been illustrated repeatedly in marriages. Gary tried to prove Katie was insane. Scott tried to prove Zelda was insane. My own Zelda claimed I was insane, then alternately claimed she was.

Other people simply stay in Stage One or Two relationships and never go beyond that. However it is rare for someone to remain at Stage Three without eventually advancing to Stage Four. Anyone who ends up at Stage Four risks the possibility of losing control and touch with reality. When that happens, the alternatives are few, and uncomfortable.

Jack and Sandra, through our formal process of negotiation simply decided to remain at Stage One. It was their conclusion that it was better to waltz around the obstacles than to risk the ultimate pain and discomfort of resolving them. For them, simply admitting their problems was barrier enough. We went through three psychotherapy sessions of actually analyzing their expectations and unspoken marital contract. In the end, they decided to stay where they were. Sometimes that option is probably best. "It's not that I don't want a better marriage with Jack," Sandra explained stoically. "It's just that I don't know if I want to risk the unexpected. Right now, I know what I've got. I can predict exactly what's going to happen and that makes me feel safe."

She continued, "What was it I heard someone say one time? Something like, The devil you know is a heck of a lot better than the devil you don't. Maybe . . . maybe that's better for me. And besides, if we really confront the truth, he may not want to be around me. He may not be able to stand me. If I made the same kind of demands on him that I make on Charles, Jack would go crazy. We would argue all the time. I really do believe it would be the end of our relationship. So, really, isn't it better to stay where we are, John?" she asked.

I thought a few minutes before responding and then leaned toward her. "You have to decide for yourself what you are willing to risk, Sandra." I nodded my head. "I'm really not sure the payoff is worth the risk. First of all, I don't think Jack would ever be able to handle *real* intimacy. Things have gone pretty well just staying at Stage One. If it were me, I probably wouldn't risk it. But you have to decide for yourself. Personally, I don't think I would take that chance."

Honest discussions such as these help people make the difficult decision of how to continue, once locked in the throes of the Complex. There are always secondary gains to be had by remaining in a dysfunctional pattern. If Zelda had given up her revolving door approach to psychiatric hospitalization she would have been forced to become a responsible wife and mother. Even as a child, she had never really been held responsible for her actions. I simply don't think she was willing to take responsibility. The secondary gain for her illness was, she got to be taken care of. Permission to be irresponsible and the opportunity to be taken care of— both were important to Zelda.

Scott received similar secondary gains for his dysfunction: He was able to miss book deadlines. He was able to remain intoxicated. He was allowed to continue using his drug of choice. He got to feel sorry for himself. In most of these cases, people find the secondary gain more rewarding than the risk of change. As a result, they are unwilling to pay the price of improving their lives. This is especially true in the advanced stages of the Complex, when the lines between reality and fantasy blur. At this point, they are intoxicated by the relationship. Their state of mind has been altered. It is better to renegotiate the contract much earlier in the relationship, than to be consumed later.

> *Nothing is permanent but change.*
> —Heraclitus, *Lives of Eminent Philosophers*

The silent pause seemed even more profound than her previous screaming. Yet I sat motionless in the rocker, my eyes fixed somewhere to the right of Katie's downcast face. Traffic passed silently on the highway, a hundred yards away. I squinted at the blue van in the distance, trying to read the illegible inscription on its side. I respected her silence, and waited for Katie to look up before I responded.

I had known Gary and Katie for several years by this time, though I had seen them in psychotherapy fewer than ten times. They had remained in the relationship, though it was unrewarding for both. Gary had accomplished his goals. He had kept Katie beaten down, and was subsequently elected to the district attorney's office. To me, it was time to progress beyond the superficial work of initial psychotherapy. I wanted to achieve a deeper, more serious level of change. After all, such was the inevitable goal of all good marital psychotherapy. By this time, all facades had been dropped. We knew each other well. Gary didn't have to worry about me voting for him. In many ways, today's session was the culmination of what we had been building toward for some time. I finally broke the silence and directed my attention away from Katie, and toward Gary.

"Gary," I gestured toward him. "To me, the bottom line is this: Are you willing to give up the control you have over her, or not? Now I'm going to say some things you're probably not going to like. I'm going to ask some tough questions. But I'm objective. The only side I'm on is the side of the marriage. Is that okay with you?" I waited for Gary to answer. He nodded his head silently.

"Okay, here goes." I rubbed my hands together and leaned forward, my elbows on my knees. "I get the impression at times that it's more important for you to have *control* of this relationship than it is for you to have *the relationship*. Does that make sense?" I continued without waiting for a response. "I mean, it sounds to me like the number one thing that's important for you is to stay in control of this woman. She's intelligent. She's gorgeous. She's got a tremendous personality. But you guys keep fighting the same battles over and over again. That's because the battles are not about the issues you are fighting. The battles are about control.

"Ninety percent of the conflicts you are having are pure control. You have to be willing to give it up, if you want any semblance of a happy marriage. You guys can focus on images for the rest of your lives. You can focus on the external. You can try to look good and die that way. I mean, you can die looking good, if that's what you want. But what the hell is that going to accomplish? It comes down to what I said the other day. Do you want to be right, or do you want to be happy? I just don't believe you can have both, in this situation.

"Let's face it. This is really sick. After I get through talking about this, you may never come back again. And if that's the way it is, that's the way it is. We've been through a lot together and, as far as I'm concerned, you are still playing the same stupid games. But Gary, let's just take a look at this.

"You thought Katie was having an affair because all of a sudden she became happy. Now just think about that for a moment. As long as she is miserable, as long as she is beaten down, as long as she is unhappy, depressed, or thinks she is crazy, you act like everything is okay." I emphasized each phrase by beating my fist on the rocking chair in rhythm. I was becoming more and more incensed as I went along.

"I mean, as long as she's depressed and beaten up, you're happy. The moment she makes a little progress and her self-esteem improves a little bit and she smiles, you become suspicious. She *must* be involved with another man. Do you realize the absurdity of that? It's almost like you're saying she's incapable of being happy by herself without a man screwing her. I mean, is happiness for a woman at the end of a penis? Is that the idea?"

I was irate. I was probably unloading on Gary, yet I was doing it purposefully. Sometimes the only way to penetrate a facade of defensiveness is by being aggressive. This is especially true in Stages Three and Four of the Zelda Complex. I glanced toward Katie. She had raised her head and was staring at me with a look of horror on her face. Perhaps she had never heard anyone speak to her husband that way, although I doubt it. More likely, her shock was that anyone would see reality for what it was, and confront it.

At this point, I felt there was literally nothing to lose. Gary had told Katie he wasn't going to come back to marriage therapy. He had explained that it would be bad for his career if anyone found out he was "seeing a shrink." He had also said this was the last time he'd pay for her counseling. They were permanently locked into Stage Three of the Zelda Complex, and had even crossed the line into violence on a few occasions. I felt like I had one shot with Gary, and I was doing my best to break through his defenses. If nothing else, I wanted him to see reality.

The reality was, their relationship contract focused on control. Nothing else mattered. Control is a common contractual theme, found most often between insecure partners. Both Gary and Katie had experienced extreme periods of insecurity. In the past, control of the relationship had flip-flopped. While Gary was in college and law school, Katie had been in control. Since then, Gary had grown increasingly in charge of the relationship. There were times when Katie had been satisfied. But now, her needs were no longer being met by Gary. She was getting nothing from the relationship, except the security of a common misery. With her recent increase in self-esteem, this was insufficient. Gary's accusation of an affair was simply an attempt at escalating his leverage. He was trying to regain the control he had lost.

Another common contractual theme is one of escape. Some people marry to escape abusive parents. Oftentimes, these people—usually women—marry someone even more aggressive and more dominant than the abusive parent. Women have frequently left an abusive father or step-father only to end up with an abusive husband. Pressured relationships of any sort often revolve around the theme of escape as well. In one marriage, as an example, the husband married his wife literally to "get her off his back." She had been pressing for marriage for several years. He finally gave in simply to escape the pressure she was placing on him. Such contracts are seldom functional in the long run. As a result, the marriages are not functional either.

A third, common contractual theme centers around completeness. In this context, *completing* is different than *control*. Basically, one partner feels there is something he or she needs from the relationship to be complete. Marrying for money is one example. Oftentimes, completeness contracts look almost like business propositions.

One couple I worked with had a tremendous "working relationship." Household duties and expenses were distributed equitably. Both partners benefited from this contract, but the relationship was void of intimacy, physical affection, and sexual expression. The couple entered counseling in an attempt to fill the void. Other people who marry to become complete marry for legitimacy. This includes marrying for the sake of having children. Another example of this is gay men or lesbian women marrying so they can appear together and legitimate to others. Others marry simply out of religious beliefs. Each of these scenarios revolves around the need to feel complete.

A fourth contractual theme, although less common, is stimulation. Stimulation is the basis for many relationships between people who are more intense than the norm. This can be physical or sexual attraction. It can also be an addictive relationship whose purpose is simply maintain the intensity level of those involved. Often, however, these contracts last only as long as the feeling or the charm. They are almost always temporary.

> *Quarrels would not last long if the fault were only on one side.*
> —La Rochefoucauld, *Maxims*

There are also several healthy contractual themes—themes that revolve around two people who see themselves as changing on a continuous basis.

They don't get hung up in the inevitable shifts that occur over time. They are not continuously evaluated based on the past. Instead, there is an implied agreement that both partners will do their best, realizing change will occur and problems will occasionally result.

The primary difference in healthy contractual themes is that agendas, needs, and expectations are discussed perpetually. Both partners understand and agree to the terms and no manipulation is allowed. Another difference is depth. The healthy contract is based not on image, but on the substance of both people involved. It includes two people, becoming healthy, and growing through life together. Unfortunately, Gary was preoccupied with appearances. To him, image was vastly more important than reality. There eventually came a time when he lost his identity to the facade he had created. He pretended for so long, he forgot who he really was. He knew about his career. He knew about his goals. But he didn't know about himself. As a result, his marriage suffered substantially. Rather than accept responsibility himself, he blamed his wife. He assumed it was her problems that were preventing them from having a happy marriage.

As Walt and David eventually found out, there are constructive ways to negotiate. You can learn to do this without losing your identity. In a skilled negotiation, both sides can win by not only resolving the issues, but resolving the painful feelings between them. Before getting involved in a negotiation, the first thing you must do is understand your partner's position. This is the point at which most negotiation fails. It is very important to know when to be quiet and when to speak up. Trying to prove the viability of your position without listening first will block communication. That is exactly what you want to avoid. If you are not willing to understand your partner's position first, don't negotiate. Furthermore, don't discuss anything about the relationship of which you are unsure during negotiation. It's important to be certain of the basics before you get into areas of conflict. Successful negotiators realize that conflict, though it usually has a bitter interpretation, is an important element in any relationship.

Healthy couples negotiate about money, children, recreation, personalities, in-laws, roles, religion, politics, and sex. The first five areas are frequent sources of friction. Problems with role, on the other hand, impact an increasing number of people as more women enter the workforce. It's typical for women working outside of the home to also be responsible for household responsibilities and children. In most relationships, this is something that must be negotiated. But the same problems of role occur in the workplace. People may be playing mixed roles in the office or on the factory floor as well. Conflicts about who does what around the house and in the workplace affect an increasing number of women and men.

There is another issue to understand before attempting negotiation. You must be willing to admit there are probably some flaws in your position. Trying to prove you are right, or perfect, will destroy any progress you potentially make. It's important to remember that the relationship is more important than anything you're discussing. Although you're part of the relationship, you are only one part. Your partner has his or her own set of expectations.

The problems healthy couples experience are occasionally the same as those in the Zelda Complex. What makes healthy relationships different is their awareness of how important it is to confront problems. Fleeing or ignoring difficulty does not help. Facing and resolving it does. By facing problems, a buildup of resentments that could destroy the relationship is avoided. Contrary to conventional wisdom, avoiding conflict doesn't strengthen a relationship. It weakens it.

On the other hand, any win-lose or lose-lose fight will have a negative effect on the relationship as well. A healthier approach is to seek a resolution where both people are allowed to win, at least to a small degree. This may call for some creative problem solving that will allow both people to feel victorious. This is one of the reasons it is important to understand your partner's position before entering negotiation. It is sometimes best to take one day just to understand your partner's position; work on a resolution the next day. In most cases, simply understanding your partner's position will solve much of the difficulty. Good negotiation involves listening first, and then speaking.

Always define negotiation in terms of a particular *issue*, rather than a particular *person*. Talk about *things*, not *people*. It's important to look at the negotiation process as one of mutual cooperation, rather than mutual combat. Resist the temptation to belittle or criticize your partner. The healthy approach is to understand, not criticize. By doing this, you will keep your partner's well-being in mind, and avoid difficulty in the long run.

In marriage, negotiation needs to occur as the relationship changes. People enter marriage with one set of understandings, but conditions inevitably change. One of the most dramatic places a renegotiation may be required is after children are born. In a study done many years ago, marital satisfaction dropped sharply for new parents, while it stayed stable for childless couples. This occurs because demands of work, child care, and in-laws zoom exponentially when children arrive. The study's results were even more true when the first child was born, and when the grandparents had relatively few grandchildren. The demands of career, housework, cooking, and childcare usually receive the preponderance of attention. What is usually placed on the backburner is marriage. Women usually end up feeling victimized as a result, leading to tremendous resentment and sometimes overt anger.

Occasionally, I say things on television or radio I later regret. I once said it was my opinion that children were the biggest cause of divorce. Actually, that puts the blame where it doesn't belong. Children don't cause divorce. It is the parents' inability to cope with the added stress of children. In my opinion, the stress of parenting has created more divorces than any other single cause. The biggest problem is that after the birth of children, couples fail to renegotiate their contract. The dynamics of a family and marriage are undeniably altered due to childbirth. The old contract should be null and void.

It was Susan Smith's inability to cope with a divorce, single parenthood, and a new boyfriend, that led to murder. The burden of parenting is, unfortunately, often placed on unequipped and immature mothers. There's nothing about being a woman that necessarily qualifies her to be a good parent. Yet the expectation is that a woman will not only be a good mother, but continue to keep up with other responsibilities. Most often in today's world, that includes employment. Obviously, this is not always the case. However, in each of the couples discussed thus far, except for Walt and David, this was definitely true.

Occasionally this leads to one person developing a hair-trigger personality. Partners must put tremendous energy into coping with the necessities. As a result, they have little opportunity to focus on a relationship. This is especially true if those involved have classic Zelda personalities. In long-term relationships, couples report greater satisfaction when both partners embody cross-sex characteristics. Couples in which each partner displays traditionally defined characteristics of gender rate lower on happiness. It's very important in the health and happiness of relationships for men to develop more androgynous communication skills. This is especially true when it comes to listening. If marriage is going to survive, men must begin communicating more like women, rather than vice versa.

In Gary and Katie's case, this became extremely significant. He was so preoccupied with political ambitions that he didn't have time for Katie. When she complained about their relationship, he responded by listing all the things he had given her. When she said he never listened, he responded by describing her opulent lifestyle. If the complaint continued, he would suggest that perhaps she needed to consider hospitalizing herself again. This became the couple's do/do pattern. If she verbalized what was bothering her, Gary would ultimately respond by threatening hospitalization. Unable to express her feelings, she became resentful, and either imploded into depression or exploded into rage. Unfortunately for her, the cycle continued. Unfortunately for Gary, he was too stubborn to get help.

> *Always refuse the advice that passion gives.*
>
> —English proverb

It's easy to get stuck in a pattern within a relationship. To negotiate your way out is obviously a difficult process. Relationships develop themes that resemble contracts. They are usually unspoken, and even unknown, agreements made and perpetuated throughout the history of a relationship. These contracts can be changed. But change requires two people who are capable and willing to negotiate. Scott and Zelda were neither capable nor willing to do so. In the Fitzgeralds' case, both had a tremendous investment in remaining the way they were.

In Gary and Katie's case, the relationship contract was based on her helping him. An additional clause was implied that once Katie had done her part, Gary would help her. That clause, however, was ignored. She was ready for Gary to fulfill his contract, but Gary was not. Then, they unconsciously negotiated another contract, this one based on parenting. Once again, Katie fulfilled her end of the agreement. Finally, they agreed on another one. It implied Gary would be healthy and Katie would be sick. As long as she was miserable, unhappy, and overweight, everything was fine. After giving up on marital therapy and entering individual therapy, she began to change. She lost weight. She started to become happy. She began dressing nicely and entered an intense exercise program. At this point, she was in direct violation of their final relationship contract, and Gary escalated. He accused her of having an affair.

There is a sick security in remaining miserable. One of the foundations of a good relationship is security. Nothing can make you feel more secure than knowing exactly what your partner is going to say or do at any given time. Gary found security in knowing Katie was miserable. It was even more relevant to him that he had made her that way. She found security in knowing he was domineering and narcissistic. I once told her she would become so accustomed to this type of treatment that she would run from anyone who treated her pleasantly. Her response was laughter, but there was no smile or humor in it. This pattern can become so sick that the familiar, the predictable, is redefined as normal or healthy. Insults grow to be expected. Apathy becomes a friend. Boredom, or chaos, becomes a way of life. For many people, the pattern becomes so routine they only grow suspicious when something seems to be going right!

Scott and Zelda grew accustomed to the continuous uproar in their relationship. Bob, Sam, and Debbie became addicted to the intensity and passion of their triangle. Walt and David had competed for their father's attention for so long, it seemed abnormal to cooperate, even for the sake of their own company and future. Jack and Sandra grew so accustomed to waltzing that it became the pattern that defined their relationship.

When Katie began developing different beliefs about herself, the relationship began to change. Gary's investment was in keeping her as she had been, so he responded adversely. Yet the relationship was permanently changed, regardless of the outcome. As long as Katie saw herself as overweight, worthless, and miserable, the relationship was a cooperative agreement. When she changed her self-image, however, the relationship required renegotiation at some level.

In some cases, renegotiation may not result in a totally different contract. Initially, Gary was unwilling to give up his control over Katie. Yet once she changed, even to a small degree, the balance of the relationship was permanently altered. If nothing else, *she* knew she was no longer fat, miserable, and unhappy. That alone was enough to shift the balance. By accusing her of having an affair, Gary shifted the balance further. Gary's intensity was no longer spread only between the two of them. A mythical third person was now factored in. This created a dramatic shift in power.

Usually the balance of power changes to the smallest extent possible that will accommodate each party. Gary was unwilling to give up total dominance and control in his relationship with Katie. Katie was unwilling to walk away from the relationship as a gambit to create change. So, they arrived at a mediated level of acceptable change which then became the new status quo. A couple will usually remain at this level until another crisis occurs. At that point, one or both partners will shift again to accommodate the new balance of power in the relationship. If they fail at this process various things can occur.

Often a third person is triangled in. Sandra triangled in Charles as a way of balancing the power in her relationship with Jack. Katie and Gary brought in a therapist. Walt and David triangled their father, and then me. Bob and Debbie triangled Sam, and then me. Basically, when anxiety rises in a two-person relationship, the partners often resolve it by bringing in a third person. This opens up a wide variety of interactive responses, but the immediate reaction is to reduce the anxiety by about 33 percent.

The number of these triangles that become sexual affairs is unknown. Some estimates have gone as high as 60 percent. In some of these cases, an affair actually stabilized and prolonged the marriage. It can also be the beginning of the end. Affairs begin for a variety of reasons. It's my belief that few of them have to do with sex. The reasons can be as varied as getting attention, medicating an emotional illness, seeking or revenge. It may also have to do with acceptance, affection, or finding someone who listens.

In my years as a psychotherapist, I have never seen one partner enter a sexual affair without some sense of provocation from the other. It may be popular in court to look at one person in a marriage as the victim and the other as the evil perpetrator. Yet the reality differs dramatically. Sandra had what amounted to an affair, though it may not have met the legal definition. I saw it as having more to do with Jack than with her. To my knowledge, Katie did not have an affair. She did have a relationship with someone who helped her believe in herself. In Gary's eyes, that was probably the worst kind of adultery.

An affair is not something that happens to or against one partner. It is a phenomenon that usually occurs within the triangle. The purpose of an affair is rarely about orgasm or sexual stimulation. More than anything else, it is a message that something is terribly wrong within the marriage. If this message is received, it can be the beginning of a new and healthier balance of power; if ignored, the problems have only begun.

The reason why lovers and their mistresses never tire of being together is that they are always talking of themselves.

—La Rochefoucauld

At this point, you may wonder where to begin. If you recognize yourself as being in Stage Three or Stage Four of the Zelda Complex, it's probably necessary to bring in a third party to discuss your problems. There may be occasions, especially in Stage Three, when the relationship is stable and the two individuals are calm enough to discuss things privately. This is typically not the case, however. A counselor, minister, or someone who specializes in negotiating, such as a conciliation counselor, can often be helpful.

If you see a relationship in turmoil, the first thing to negotiate is how to solve the particular problem. Then you go beyond it, to discuss how it started in the first place. If a fire is burning you need to put it out first. Once the fire is extinguished, you turn to the factors listed in chapter 1. The basic factors lay the foundation. They usually require little negotiation. Factor Three, self-esteem, occasionally leads to difficulty. The way to resolve it is for both people to talk to a therapist. If you have problems with self-esteem or emotional problems that existed before entering the relationship, you need to get individual counseling. If one partner is acting out, as discussed in Factor Four, it is necessary to address that as well. This can also be done in individual counseling.

Factors involving family background are most often found in Stage One of the Zelda Complex. Some people can negotiate this area on their own, without getting someone else involved. I have known couples who have recognized these factors as problematic and proceeded to handle them legitimately as a couple. One person in the relationship often needs approval more than the other. This need may shift back and forth from time to time. The best time to negotiate this area successfully is when both partners are feeling rational and in a good mood. Ways can be found to help the other person feel appreciated and loved, Factor Five. A simple discussion focused on what one can do to help the other can stimulate improvement on many levels. Factor Six often leads up to those unrealistic expectations discussed elsewhere. If one person feels entitled to some sort of special treatment, psychotherapy may be helpful. If both partners are willing to discuss it fairly, this can usually be resolved in a period of hours.

If one or both partners came from families with marked histories of mental illness, Factor Seven, the relationship is not necessarily doomed to failure. Individual psychotherapy can usually help people cope with any scars they received from their families of origin. Those copping mechanisms can be negotiated into the basic agreement in a relationship.

Factors of achievement usually show up in Stages Two and Three of the Zelda Complex. It's important to understand that both partners in a Zelda Complex are usually competent and capable. It's also true that one of them is usually a chronic underachiever. Finding some avenue where the underachieving partner can begin to excel will often create the necessary change to balance the relationship. This is especially true if the intelligence level of those involved is in the higher range. If the underachiever is allowed to achieve on his or her own, this will usually diminish the need for competition. The competitiveness inherent in the Zelda Complex most often results from the underachieving partner feeling inadequate and unhappy.

The remaining factors of achievement are difficult to negotiate without professional help. Yet, in some cases it can be done. If the more powerful partner receives a wake-up call, he or she may be willing to negotiate. If the couple can affect a negotiation at this time, the relationship will often work out. With the absence of that wake-up call, however, a professional must be involved at this level.

Factor Thirteen is easy to discuss, but frequently difficult to change. Research has adequately proven the importance of partners sharing gender characteristics. Men who are testosterone saturated rarely have successful marriages. The same is true of women who are void of any traditionally male characteristics. It is the man who has predominately traditionally male traits, but who can communicate and show sensitivity that will usually be able to have a satisfying marriage.

Factor Fourteen is something that can usually be dealt with in individual psychotherapy. It becomes a relationship problem when one of the partners has suffered substantially as a result of bold misrepresentations by the other. Such fantastic lying can lead to vast difficulty in any relationship. In my own Zelda relationship, this resulted in legal problems as well. Bold misrepresentation goes one step beyond pretending, and it will occasionally be necessary to seek intensive psychotherapy to overcome it. The same type of intervention may be required to overcome marked narcissism. This is something that can rarely be negotiated within the context of a relationship.

The advanced factors, beginning with Factor Seventeen, are usually not able to be negotiated successfully by the couple alone. Resolution requires intervention by a professional. The real question to settle is, Is the relationship worth it?

It is only the wisest and the very stupidest who cannot change.

—Confucius

It is inevitable: a Stage Three Zelda Complex will ultimately bloom into Stage Four if negotiation does not occur. Yet this is one of the most frightening times for people to successfully conduct a negotiation. It requires incredible maturity to face these problems honestly, especially if traditional gender roles turn out to be reversed. It can be accomplished, however. I was part of one such successful negotiation.

The couple came to see me as a way of negotiating a successful conclusion to their relationship. They had been married for fifteen years and the wife had recently decided to leave the marriage. Her husband was intensely against the divorce, but was, at least, somewhat rational about it. Understandably, he felt rejected and abandoned. But he also saw the value in calmly negotiating a settlement when the marriage was so obviously beyond salvaging.

Both parties were highly educated and talented individuals. They had chosen similar careers, but the results had been vastly different financially. She was earning in excess of $500,000 a year and was considered quite successful in her field. He was also considered successful in a similar and quite prestigious field. Yet he had topped out in earning potential and was making a respectable $50,000 a year. Over the course of their marriage, their lifestyle had risen to match her level of income. In the years to come, she would likely earn a bit less and he would probably earn a bit more. Yet they both agreed that the disparity would never be overcome.

There are a lot of jokes made about unscrupulous attorneys. The truth is, there are probably no more unscrupulous attorneys than there are unscrupulous mechanics, unscrupulous psychotherapists, or unscrupulous ministers. For some reason, attorneys get more press. Perhaps it's because they outnumber those other professions. Regardless, this is one of those cases in which an unscrupulous attorney would have licked his or her chops. I've been involved in several dissolution counseling sessions with people of substantial income. By my estimations, this was a divorce that would have cost the couple in the neighborhood of $50,000 in attorney's fees, had it gone in that direction. Instead, they were making a sincere attempt at remaining amiable and keeping the lines of communication open. Their good will toward each other seemed sincere. I wanted to keep it that way.

During the course of our discussions, it became apparent that for the past seven to eight years they had been living in a Stage Three Zelda Complex. However, the roles were reversed. At this point in their relationship, he was having difficulty with her level of success. He was also having problems with the disparity in their income. Most of all, he was worried about the future. He felt certain his income and lifestyle would never be equal to what it had been during the marriage. To his credit, however, he didn't want to be supported by her and preferred not to accept alimony. He did wish to be treated fairly.

In addition, there was the delicate matter of informing their young children of the upcoming divorce. Because of their sensitivity, this was accomplished successfully. The financial settlement required more effort. Occasionally, there's a tremendous difference between what's legal, what makes sense, and what's fair. Sometimes the three are similar. Usually, however, they are vastly different. With this particular couple, it became readily apparent that the legal alternatives neither were fair nor made sense. Legally the man was obligated to pay 32 percent of his income for child support. In reality, his wife made ten times what he did. This was especially significant, given the tremendous drop in lifestyle and total income he would experience after the divorce. During the marriage, they had combined their incomes. On a base income of $50,000 a year, he was able to live the lifestyle of someone making $550,000 a year.

The children were going to remain with their mother, and would also benefit from her earnings and lifestyle. To their credit, what the couple eventually did was fair, and made tremendous sense. With the help of an accountant they figured the actual annual cost required to provide for the children and they arrived at a percentage for which he'd be responsible. It turned out to be much less than the legally enforceable 32 percent. By negotiating fairly and reasonably, they were able to avoid tremendous attorney's expenses.

For me, it was an opportunity to see a Stage Three Zelda relationship that did not have disastrous results. It's important to understand the reasons this one worked out positively. First and foremost, the husband did not allow himself to become enmeshed with his wife's success. She used her maiden name professionally. She was known for her talent, not for being Mrs. So-and-so. He was known for his own substantial career accomplishments, not for being her husband. In fact, few people even knew they were husband and wife.

He also had tremendous passion for his hobbies. He was an avid runner, an accomplished pilot, and a creative talent. Fascinatingly enough, his Stage Three feelings only surfaced after he dropped running and flying. During the process of our negotiation I encouraged him to pick up his old hobbies. Once he did, he felt better about his own life and became easier to negotiate with during the sessions. Furthermore, he had not become addicted to the lifestyle. While his wife was a rather extravagant dresser and had expensive tastes in automobiles, his appearance was commensurate with his own income. He drove a low-cost automobile and dressed in a fashion less expensive than he could have actually afforded. He was not much of a socializer and his identity certainly did not revolve around the opulence with which he could have lived.

Equally important, both valued their children. As a result, they were not prone to narcissistic impulses. Admittedly, they did have domestic help for their children, but they were both actively involved as nurturing parents. It may be that they simply wanted to maintain a sense of peace for the sake of the children. Regardless, both their negotiation and exit from the Zelda Complex were a success. I wish the same were true for Katie and Gary, and for Bob, Sam, and Deb. But it wasn't.

Full of wiles, full of guile, at alltimes, in all ways, are the children of men.
—Aristophanes, *The Birds*

At best, relationships are very confusing. Like any chemical combination, a relationship can take on a different nature than that of its parts. Hydrogen and oxygen, alone, are hydrogen and oxygen. When chemically combined, hydrogen and oxygen become water. The difference is only in the bond between the two chemicals. When I conduct marriage counseling, I tell people that the marriage is totally different than the sum of its parts. I tell them my contract is with the marriage, not with one of them. I see it as a phenomenon with a life of its own.

When a person applies for a job, one would hope, they are given an opportunity to read the job description. Marriage is similar. If couples would write job descriptions for themselves and their partner, many things would be clarified. When expectations become blurred, partners in the relationship can only react. The problem is, they are reacting to the unknown. If expectations are discussed openly, individuals can at least measure their progress against their expectations. The expectations are the job description. And just as job requirements change, so do people. The importance of this cannot overemphasized. The contract must be renegotiated periodically, either to update it or to match the changed requirements.

Jack and Sandra did this and made a decision to continue their relationship, though it was less than what they had originally hoped for. They decided between themselves not to risk the necessary improvements. Partly as result of their business background, Walt and David embarked on a thorough negotiation process. The other reason, their father required it. Their negotiation resulted in substantial savings for them and their company, and the hundreds of people who worked for and with them. Gary and Katie were unable to negotiate, primarily because of Gary. And the triangle of Bob, Sam, and Debbie was simply out of control; the momentum generated by the massive confusion was now in charge of the relationship and its members.

At Stage Four, many people find themselves in situations so out of control that the possibility of choice is removed. As mentioned in chapter 1, the mixture of water and sodium is combustible. In April 1995 an incredible combustible reaction decimated a government building and killed 165 people in Oklahoma City. The combination was simply fertilizer and fuel oil, ignited by a simple blasting device available to almost anyone. The consequences were not only severe for Oklahoma City and the people in the building, but for the entire country as well. In the future, it will probably be looked on as a world-changing event. This explosion will likely change forever the way laws are enforced in our country. The series of events following the Oklahoma tragedy may in fact change the course of history.

Ordinarily, fertilizer can be stored side by side with fuel with little or no risk. In the Oklahoma City disaster, the ignition device was the key. It was a combination like sodium and water that caused combustibility. Once that combustion occurs, there is simply no way to stop the reaction. The same is true in some relationships. Katie and Gary were about to find this out in one manner. Bob, Sam, and Debbie discovered it in a ghastly, alternate way.

CHECKLIST

Instructions: Check each statement that applies.

CONTROL

_____1. There are few areas in my life over which I have control.

_____2. My partner complains about me talking on the telephone.

_____3. If I change the furniture, I hear about it the next day and frequently have to change it back if my partner doesn't like it.

_____4. I wear my clothes, makeup, and hair the way my partner likes them best.

_____5. If we disagree—on paint color, for instance—my partner has the last word.

_____6. My partner does the finances and I must account for every cent I spend.

_____7. When my partner is home he or she expects me not to go out.

_____8. Mealtimes are scheduled for my partner's convenience.

_____9. Bank accounts and property (including cars and insurance) acquired since the beginning of the relationship, do not have my name on them.

_____10. I have participated in sex acts with which I am uncomfortable to make my partner happy.

ESCAPE

_____1. I married to escape an unhappy home life.

_____2. My partner was "bugging" me to get married, so I finally gave in.

_____3. My partner is a citizen of the United States and I am not. I married him or her to escape from my country.

_____4. I was tired of going to school and/or working. I got married so I could have a reason to stay home.

COMPLETENESS

_____1. I married because I was pregnant.

_____2. I married so that my partner and I would appear legitimate.

_____3. Because my partner is wealthy, I couldn't resist marrying him or her.

_____4. Marriage is important in my church. I married my partner because I was afraid no one else would ask me.

_____5. To be honest, I married my partner because of his or her notoriety or career status.

_____6. My partner has the talents I need in business. Since we have to spend so much time together, marriage seemed the appropriate route to take.

_____7. I always wanted to do what my partner does (job, hobby, education, and so on). I admire my partner. Deep inside, I thought that maybe my partner's talent would rub off on me.

STIMULATION

_____1. Sex was the best. I decided my partner had to be the right person for me.

_____2. I feel alive when I'm with my partner.

_____3. My partner makes me feel younger than I really am.

_____4. I married my partner because of his or her looks. He or she is the best-looking person I knew.

_____5. I only have fun when my partner is with me.

Scoring:

Control: Total the number of check marks. Scores less than three suggest this relationship is not focused on control. Totals between three and seven indicate control is a possible contract theme in the relationship. More than seven check marks signify trouble and indicate that control is a major contract theme. Without professional assistance it is doubtful negotiation is possible, but confiding in a counselor or member of the clergy without your partner's permission may have serious consequences you may need to consider as well.

Escape, Completeness, and Stimulation: Check marks beside any of the statements in these three categories suggest unhealthy contract themes for the relationship. Renegotiation probably needs to be encouraged. Healthy contract themes are discussed in the following chapter.

Chapter 10

ILLUSIONS OF LOVE
ATTEMPTING TO MAKE PEACE WITH THE ZELDA COMPLEX

So close
Yet so far way
We believe in tomorrow and a better day
We lie down to sleep so close
Yet so far away.
—Daryl Hall and George Green, "So Close"

A s my fascination with the Zelda Complex grew, I spoke about it on a regular basis. During one question-and- answer period at a women's club meeting, someone asked if I thought the Zelda Complex was more common among southern women. I had never thought about it in that context. I suggested that initially it was probably more common among women than men. I also said it was more frequent among the wives of type A male personalities. I had never considered the Zelda Complex as a regional phenomenon, but rather a cultural one. To the degree that a woman fills a traditional subservient role, she is more susceptible to the Zelda Complex. That was certainly true of southern women in Zelda's lifetime. It is also true today, although to a lesser degree.

To truly understand the Zelda Complex, you must first understand its roots. Montgomery belles of the 1920s were vastly different women than those today. Zelda's family was extremely well connected politically, and wealthy by any standard. In some ways, the South of that era resembled the caste system of India today. People were divided into classes which were rarely, if ever, penetrated. Zelda originated from a gentrified class in which women played a well-defined and almost privileged role. She was a belle, a debutante. Her place in society was to marry a rich man and be his trophy. Her primary responsibility would be to supervise servants, housekeepers, and other domestic help. It's not that all women reared in the South back then were socialized to be Scarlett O'Hara. Zelda simply belonged to that caste of young ladies who were. Others not of her social standing probably wished they were as well.

Times have changed, even in the South. Yet there still remains a strong tradition of the southern male and female role. To the degree women or men subscribe to that stereotype, they probably are more susceptible to the Zelda Complex. Dan Broderick worshiped Rhett Butler as his hero. Hanging in his girlfriend's office was a four-foot mural of Dan sitting astride a white stallion rearing into the air on its hind legs. It was certainly a Rhett Butler pose. This stereotypical fantasy led to difficulty for him. His wife Betty had similar gender-appropriate fantasies and perceptions that led to difficulty for her as well. Yet neither Dan nor Betty were raised in the South. It's not necessarily the region where someone grows up that creates the problem. It's the traditions and stereotypes they accept that lead to difficulty.

Anyone who assumes her primary and exclusive role is to support her spouse's career may be headed for the Zelda Complex. If you receive self-esteem or identity from your spouse's successes you are a candidate as well. And if you subscribe to the fantasy that you are going to meet the perfect mate and live happily ever after, you are deluded.

Some time ago I was a guest on a radio talk show. During my segment, the station was giving tickets away to *Fiddler on the Roof*. To win, callers had to sing a number from the play. One woman called in with her three young daughters and sang "Matchmaker, Matchmaker." It was a talented rendition, but the narrative she gave fascinated me. The woman said that she talked to her daughters about this frequently and that they were all awaiting the perfect match. I kept my mouth shut, but privately predicted disaster for any young person who buys into such a fantasy. Amazingly, people do this on a regular basis. The reality is, there is no perfect match. There are no perfect relationships. And there is certainly no way someone is going to come into your life and make you better.

Gender roles are changing rapidly. Women today are treated more equitably and educated more competently. Yet they still find themselves in Zelda roles far more often than men. Over the last twenty years, society has been redefining roles for men and women alike, resulting in an androgynous chaos of sorts. The transition has been an abrupt and difficult one for both genders.

In the South of the 1920s, things were far more dramatically proscribed. Zelda had her own ideas, but roles were well-defined. Had she not met Scott, Zelda would probably have gone through another few years of hysterics. Then she would have married an Auburn football player, or naval aviator, and faded into southern lore. However, there was one element missing that prevented Zelda from accepting the traditional, southern female role. This was probably the critical factor leading to the combustible relationship she had with Scott.

Southern women were traditionally caretakers. They took care of their children, their husbands, and their homes. Zelda was never socialized to play such a role. Instead, she continuously searched for someone to take care of her. When her marriage and daughter thrust her into a caretaking role, Zelda collapsed. She was woefully unprepared for the responsibility, and had no concept of how to fill the role. Instead, she reverted to multiple hospitalizations, attempting to find someone who would take care of her. This was a role her mother filled nicely. Zelda rotated between hospitals and her mother's home until her death.

This brings to the surface another point of conflict. As long as there is someone needing a caretaker, women who are socialized to fill that role do extremely well. It's only when caretaking responsibilities are removed that many realize they are in the throes of the Zelda Complex. Katie is a good example. She did quite well, as long as Gary's career was in its infancy and her children were quite young. She was perfectly willing to bury her own potential during this period. When those areas began to collapse, however, she quickly found herself in the middle of a Zelda Complex. If one of her children had been willing to play a role of helplessness, as Zelda did with her mother, Katie would have delayed her problems. She would not have solved them, but they would have been put off temporarily. The fact that she was needed by neither husband nor children resulted in Katie examining her inner self. She realized there was something missing. This was the critical period for the onset of her Zelda Complex.

"Just because you are biologically female and capable of bearing children and nurturing them, does not mean your dreams have to die and your life has to end," Katie suggested to me one evening on the telephone.

"It's difficult to have a life and three children, and do both things well. I did make the decision to be a wife and mother and career woman. It exhausted me. It ran me ragged. And it depleted me. I eventually gave up on the career. Frankly, I made the decision for the wrong reason. I made it for Gary, who is obviously unable to reciprocate, though I believed he would."

At this point, Gary and Katie began nearly a roller-coaster cycle of demands, changing expectations, and conflicts. During one of their multiple separations, Katie telephoned me and complained Gary had kicked her out of the house. My first reaction was to tell her it was impossible for him to kick her out of the house. We'd had this discussion before. He could ask her to leave, but I had encouraged her not to do so. To me, it set a dangerous legal precedent that could come back to haunt her if they ever did divorce.

"Why can't we just have a normal relationship?" she pleaded. "Why is it this has continued to happen?"

"This *is* normal, for you guys," I responded. "That is what your relationship has become. This is typical. You have defined your relationship as a roller-coaster ride. It's going to have these multiple ups and downs for the rest of your life. I'm not saying it's what you want. I'm not saying it's healthy or desirable. But this is your pattern, and you may as well get used to it. If you want a healthy relationship, now, that's a different thing. You are probably going to have to get out of this one to find someone healthy."

"John, I simply don't understand." She continued aggressively, "I have done everything I was supposed to. I have been an obedient wife. I have done a good job as a mother. Don't you agree?"

"Sure I do," I responded. "You've done a great job in both of those roles. If you're judging by the way you've been a mom or wife, then I'd have to agree. But what you don't seem to understand is, the expectations have changed. You subjugated your talent, your creativity, and your intelligence. You put a lid on all that for him. And he doesn't need it anymore. He's so narcissistic, I don't know that he needs anybody or anything but a mirror.

"Mainly, he doesn't need what you offered him in the past. Frankly, you don't need it either. What's the big deal? Don't you think it's time for you to live your own life? Your children don't need a martyr anymore. Your husband doesn't want a partner, he wants a housemaid. If you're willing to play that role, you're going to be fine. If you're not, you're going to live through absolute hell until you conform, get out, or go crazy. Believe me, I've seen it many, many times before."

"I know. I know." She began to cry softly. "I have thought seriously about this since you first brought it up. John, I hate to admit it, but I am just in love with my lifestyle. The cars, the house, the club, my friends, the money to travel. I just don't want to lose all those things. If I divorced Gary, I would have to give up everything. I have devoted my entire life to helping this man. If I leave now, you and I both know that I wouldn't get anything. I would lose everything I've got. I would lose the children. I would lose my identity. Then what would I be? What would I do? My life would be empty. It would be absolutely boring."

I waited for a few moments. I could hear her crying softly over the phone. "Well," I began, "sometimes boredom is better than death or insanity. Maybe that will be the decision for you. Maybe you will have to decide which is worse. The choice may be between giving up your lifestyle or giving up your life." I hoped it wouldn't come to that point.

It doesn't much signify whom one marries,
for one is sure to find [the] next morning that it was someone else.
—Samuael Rogers, Table Talk

At the women's club where I spoke about the Zelda Complex, there were many other fascinating questions that arose. One lady asked me if it was even remotely possible for a woman to be successfully married to a type A, obsessive-compulsive workaholic. I suggested it was entirely possible to remain married, but probably impossible for them to have a healthy marriage. Another lady raised her hand and asked the following: "Just what is a healthy marriage? The only people I know who are happy are the ones lying to each other. I'm not even sure I know anyone who has a healthy marriage. What is one, or is there such a thing? Do you know of any?"

Thus far, I have been describing the Zelda Complex and focusing primarily on toxic relationships. Her question was a relevant one and deserved a good answer. A healthy relationship is more than an absence of the twenty-five factors. It includes the presence of other important factors as well.

The first factor has nothing to do directly with the relationship.

Instead, it has to do with you as an individual. Self-confidence, including a belief you are neither inadequate nor a victim, is a major component of satisfaction in a relationship. Dependency, in any form, will always produce hostility. Independence, another term for self-confidence within a relationship, is vital if the relationship is going to be healthy. If you or your partner are dependent, one of you will ultimately feel inadequate or victimized. The best combination for a healthy relationship is two people who are friends and like each other. This prevents a one-up, one-down imbalance that will always lead to dependency, and ultimately hostility. Dependency and hostility always go together. Developing confidence in yourself reduces the chance of hostile dependency and improves your relationships.

The second quality of a healthy relationship is the ability to openly communicate feelings, beliefs, and thoughts, and have them accepted. This is usually much easier for women than for men. Some men can communicate their thoughts. Few, however, are able to communicate feelings. There is an even smaller number willing to listen closely, and accept what they hear. This leaves many women feeling emotionally empty within their marriage.

What men don't realize is, women communicate as a way of building closeness. Men communicate more as a tool for problem solving. When wives attempt to communicate, husbands often react as if they're being presented with a problem. As a result, they simply close up. Men don't understand that communication is her way of developing the friendship. Of all the components of communication, listening and accepting are by far the most important. If both people feel accepted, they are then capable of experiencing the third vital characteristic of a positive relationship.

Commitment, or a desire to maintain the relationship, is strongly related to stability. It directly affects whether or not the relationship survives. This concept has little to do with legal status. Whether someone is formally married is irrelevant. Commitment is an emotional concept. It's a cohesiveness that binds you together even when difficulty arises. Though it's emotional in nature, it must be verbalized or otherwise expressed for you to experience it. It's important that both partners realize a commitment exists, because it can free each of you from the pressure of perfectionism. You are able to relax and realize that even if you make a mistake your partner is still committed to the relationship.

The next characteristic of a healthy relationship is a feeling of equity. If one or both partners feels they are treated unfairly, they will do one of three things. And most often, they will do them in the following order. Initially, they attempt to restore a sense of equity. If that fails, they will usually attempt to get even. If this is not sufficient, they will eventually end the relationship. People who feel they benefit least often have the most complaints. If one partner thinks he or she is receiving fewer benefits than his or her partner, this will most likely be a problem. In a healthy relationship, both partners feel the distribution of power is equal. Realistically, all treatment can't be totally equal, yet there needs to be trade-off. It's when the balance of power has shifted dramatically, in one direction or another, that the feeling of inequity arises. After this feeling occurs, well-intentioned people will usually attempt to restore equity. It is only after repeated failures that the second or third alternatives are pursued.

The fifth characteristic of a happy relationship is a heavy investment. This occasionally includes financial investment, but it's far more than that. It is emotional investment. Investments are resources that are put into a relationship and not easily retrieved if the relationship ends. Most financial investments can be distributed. Emotional attachment, children, traditions, and rituals incurred during the relationship cannot be replaced. They are also not easily distributed if the relationship ends. The more invested the two people are, the more stable the relationship usually becomes. This is distinguished from emotional dependence, where one person leans on another. Investing means two people give equally and create a phenomenon—the relationship—that is different and more important than the two of them individually.

The sixth factor is a sense of couple identity. Partners create couple identity similar to the way each individual forms his or her self-identity. A couple's identity comes from social relationships, or reactions of significant others. A strong sense of couple identity develops amid social support, and can create stability and strength. In some ways, couple identity creates accountability. If you have other couples as friends, you look to them for support and approval. One of the adverse aspects of this factor occurs when people with a strong couple identity separate. When that happens, other couples within their network that are experiencing difficulty are far more likely to separate as well. Somehow, it appears to give borderline couples an unspoken permission to do the same thing. Perhaps another separation is perceived as less of a violation of the group identity because someone else has already done it.

People with high self-esteem are more successful at forming relationships, if for no other reason than they choose well. This is also a characteristic of healthy relationships. Good relationships are composed of people who, taken independently, have high self-esteem. They simply like themselves. As a result, they create an environment where it's easy to be authentic. If both partners are able to relax and be themselves within the relationship, the couple is far more likely to remain together.

The eighth quality found in healthy relationships is the ability to resolve conflict. Even in the best relationships, conflict will arise. Regardless of self-confidence, self-esteem, or communication skills, there will eventually be some sort of disagreement. If you blame, criticize, and call each other names, you will eventually experience trouble. If you can rationally resolve your differences, odds are greater your relationship will be more satisfying.

Another important quality of a good relationship is that physical and sexual needs are communicated and met. In nonromantic relationships, this applies only to physical affection. This factor increases in importance as the romantic intensity grows, however. In romantic relationships, sexual involvement is both significant and positive. If the sexual relationship is not equitable and rewarding for both partners, conflict will eventually surface. When each partner is mutually satisfied with the sexual relationship, it usually contributes to overall well-being.

The final quality of a good relationship is both partners feel compatible, working and playing together. The more time you spend together, the more closely your lives become intertwined. This usually increases the motivation to remain together. The more you interact, the more you will either like each other or recognize your problems and get out. This is especially true if you play together. Spontaneous play and a good sense of humor can help stabilize a relationship. It helps to balance the intensity of intimacy and is a means of defusing conflict. A healthy sense of humor within a marriage can be the strongest kind of glue. It serves as a type of self-directed therapy and helps both partners discuss sensitive subjects without risking loss of dignity or creating conflict.

At the time I was asked the question about healthy relationships, I'm sure I didn't volunteer all this material. If I had given a *comprehensive* answer, however, I would have. I would have added that I've seen few marriages I consider truly healthy. At one point in my life, I thought I had a healthy marriage. But I found out, only too soon, that the frailties of a relationship cannot be appreciated by one person alone. I quickly realized that it takes two willing people to create a healthy bond. But one person can destroy it. As long as two people are willing to be open and work with one another, a good relationship is possible.

Being open can also lead to pain. They are two sides of the same coin. You must be willing to accept the possibility of one, to find the other. Once you accept that your openness will bring some pain, the rest is easy.

Discuss it with your partner and suggest that you attempt to avoid intentionally damaging each other. Create an atmosphere where mistakes and frailties, along with some degree of pain, are allowed.

To have any other expectation can lead only to the Zelda Complex.

> *Perspective, I soon realized, was a fine commodity,*
> *but utterly useless when I was in the thick of things.*
> —Ingrid Bengris

The relationships mentioned in this book reflect both healthy and unhealthy traits. By reviewing them and your own relationship simultaneously, you can get an idea of your current relationship GPA. You can also discover where you need to work. Based on my observation and the information available, I have graded each couple's relationship. In each of the ten healthy relationship factors, the couples are graded as one unit, rather than as separate individuals. The grade is an average of the two people's individual grades.

Scott and Zelda Fitzgerald

Self-confidence (not feeling victimized or used) ....F
Communication (ability to openly communicate thoughts, feelings, and
    beliefs and have them accepted)..F
Commitment...C
Equitability..F
Investment...B-
Couple identity..A
Self-esteem (including the ease of being oneself) ....F
Conflict resolution.. F
Affection (physical and sexual needs communicated and met)................F
Compatibility (the ability to work and play together) C
Overall GPA... 1.05 [D]

My own Zelda relationship

Self-confidence	C
Communication	D
Commitment	D
Equitability	C
Investment	D
Couple identity	F
Self-esteem	C
Conflict resolution	C-
Affection	A-
Compatibility	D
Overall GPA	1.52 [D+]

Jack and Sandra

Self-confidence	C
Communication	C-
Commitment	A-
Equitability	F
Investment	A
Couple identity	B-
Self-esteem	D
Conflict resolution	F
Affection	F
Compatibility	C-
Overall GPA	1.54 [D+]

Walt and David

Self-confidence	C+
Communication	F
Commitment (forced by their father.)	C
Equitability	B-
Investment	A
Couple identity	A
Self-esteem	C
Conflict resolution	F
Affection	N.A.
Compatibility	D+
Overall GPA	2.26 [C+]

Katie and Gary

Self-confidence ....F
Communication ....F
Commitment C
Equitability ....F
Investment ....A
Couple identity ....B
Self-esteem ....D-
Conflict resolution ....F
Affection ....D-
Compatibility ....F
Overall GPA .... 1.12 [D]

Bob, Sam, and Debbie

Self-confidence ....D
Communication ....F
Commitment ....D
Equitability ....D
Investment ....D-
Couple identity (a triangle identity in this case) ......D-
Self-esteem ....C-
Conflict resolution ....F
Affection ....D
Compatibility ....D
Overall GPA .... .84 [D-]

For the factors that characterize the Zelda Complex I have given each couple another set of grades. These grades reflect the degree to which each couple identified with the series of factors. The lower the grade, the more problems the couple experienced with that set of factors. The higher the grade, the fewer problems they experienced.

Scott and Zelda Fitzgerald

Family background ....D
Achievement ....D-
Role playing ....F
Unrealistic expectations ....F
High risk ....F
Overall GPA .... .52 [F]

My own Zelda relationship

Family background ....C-
Achievement C
Role playing C
Unrealistic expectations...............................C-
High risk ....D
Overall GPA................................. 1.64 [C-]

Jack and Sandra

Family background ....D-
Achievement ....D
Role playing C
Unrealistic expectations...............................C
High risk C
Overall GPA................................. 1.52 [D+]

Walt and David

Family background ....F
Achievement ....F
Role playing ....C-
Unrealistic expectations...............................D
High risk factors...D
Overall GPA................................. .72 [D-]

Katie and Gary

Family background ....C-
Achievement ....D-
Role playing ....F
Unrealistic expectations...............................F
High risk ....F
Overall GPA................................. .44 [F]

Bob, Sam, and Debbie

Family background ....D
Achievement ....D
Role playing factors ....F
Unrealistic expectations...............................F
High risk ....F
Overall GPA................................. .40 [F]

I have effectively used this report-card system both descriptively and prescriptively. Couples find it extremely useful to describe where they are having difficulty. As a therapist, I also use the system to help prescribe for myself the areas on which I need to focus to help couples overcome the Zelda Complex. You can accomplish the same thing for yourself. This system can help you prevent the Zelda Complex. It can also help you locate problem areas in your relationship and negotiate steps to overcome them.

What we must try to be, of course, is ourselves . . . and wholeheartedly. We must find out what we really are and what we really want.

—Nelson Boswell

One of the goals of this book is to give you the opportunity to learn through the mistakes others have made. Odds are, you have already made some of these mistakes yourself. It's possible to reverse the momentum of a Zelda Complex at any stage. It is better to avoid it altogether. Each time I have spoken about this subject, people ask, What can you do to prevent it? My answer changes, depending upon whether I'm responding to men or to women.

I tell women that one of the most important things you can do is own your life. Most women have been socialized to be caretakers. Women are far more likely to define themselves by those they take care of. It may be a husband, children, or even career. The difficulty is, your husband may die before you or divorce you. Your children will grow up and leave. You could lose your career tomorrow. The only constant in your life is *you.* Owning your life means spending time taking care of yourself. It means simply what it says: You own it your life Your husband doesn't own it. Your children don't own it. Your employer doesn't own it. It's your life and you make your own choices. One of those choices needs to be developing your own interests, hobbies, and identity. Most women who are able to do this can avoid the advanced stages of the Zelda Complex.

The second thing I suggest to women: Never be exclusively "Mrs. Anybody." To subvert your own talents, as Katie did, will ultimately lead to dysfunction. It may take twenty or thirty years, but problems will always arise. Actually, I suggest this to men and women alike. Avoid defining yourself by children, spouse, or family. You are separate from your children. You are something other than your spouse's partner. You are separate and distinct from your biology. Defining yourself only through those things not only limits your opportunity, it squelches your development. It didn't work for Zelda, and it won't work for you.

Another suggestion is to avoid dependent relationships. Sometimes this means saying no to the trust fund mentality. If someone offers to take care of you, it's best to say, No thanks. Dependency will always lead to hostility, which is something you can live without. It's important to pursue your own goals. There is nothing wrong with taking the back seat for a while. But don't subjugate your own goals or dreams your entire life. There was nothing wrong with Katie working while Gary was in law school, for example, as long as he kept his end of the bargain later. This is possible in any partnership as long as the terms are clear. Delaying gratification while helping someone else is noble. Delaying gratification forever is self-destructive.

I also suggest that there is no fantasy. And this one's very important. There is no "happily ever after." There is no perfect relationship. Any relationship is going to have trade-offs. There will never be anyone who can meet all your needs. You simply can't have everything. Katie didn't want to give up her lifestyle. She was more addicted to her lifestyle than she was to Gary. As I later told her, you can't have both a $50,000 car and a $50,000 marriage. You can have a $50,000 car and a $5 marriage. Or you can have a $50,000 marriage and a $5 car. But to expect both is unrealistic. A man who can give you a $50,000 car, and pay cash for it, cannot spend the time to be a $50,000 husband. He has to work too hard! On the other hand, a man who can be a $50,000 husband cannot give you a $50,000 car. A good marriage requires tremendous work, and, frankly, you can't divide your time that drastically. You can't have everything. You have to decide what's most important.

If you're waiting for Prince Charming to whisk you away so the two of you can live happily ever after, you are headed for disaster. In fact, if this fantasy of someone giving you everything is strong, it may be best to enter therapy and adjust your thinking. Women in general, and many men as well, need to remember to differentiate, individuate, and separate. Your identity is yours. Remain an individual. Define yourself as unique and separate. The word *separate* does not mean move out. It means you are different than other people; you are not enmeshed as one. The more you differentiate and individuate, the more truly independent and confident you can become.

The next two tips I give to women are best said briefly. First of all, any time you fall obsessively in love, you are probably headed for trouble. Run. If you feel overwhelmingly, viscerally, attracted to a person, he's probably the wrong one. Someone a little boring is probably safer. Similarly, it's important to realize that good sex does not constitute a good relationship. In some cases, sex can be wonderful and the relationship can still be tremendously lacking. Good sex will not make a good relationship. Sometimes, however, the reverse is true.

When I tell men how to avoid the Zelda Complex, my advice is a bit different than that I give to women. However, to one degree or another, the suggestions apply to both genders. Men today find themselves in a paradox. The biggest struggle they face is simply being men. All things traditionally described as male have become ambiguous. What it means to be a man is unclear. Commitments to marriage and family have grown cloudy. The role of men in the workplace has become confusing. And probably most troubling of all is men's sexual relationships with women.

Scott Fitzgerald began his struggle with these roles in the 1920s. Today the male role is being redefined even more dramatically. The changes can be attributed to a variety of things. Among them: the emphasis on materialism and the change in traditional gender roles. The rise of women in the workplace and the entire feminist movement have further impacted these changes from the outside. In addition, the fragmented nature of male-to-male relationships, accompanied by the large number of homophobic reactions, has made it far more difficult for men to define themselves.

During Scott Fitzgerald's and Ernest Hemingway's time, men were able to distinguish between their career and personal relationships. Men were able to plan for their future career and rely on spending their entire lives with one company, if they so chose. A tradition began of men's primary commitment being to the workplace. That is no longer true. Men usually fail to make commitments in their personal relationships because they fear the loss of control. That same fear now applies in their careers. They feel they have nothing to rely on. Fears of abandonment and inferiority are paramount with men today. This often results in men going from one relationship to another, continuously trying to prove their worth. But because they haven't proven themselves internally, they never succeed. And they never experience a lack of intimacy.

Intimacy begins with *you*. Before you can make a commitment to someone else you must make one to yourself. You need to feel inwardly secure.

This begins by getting to know yourself. Before you can emotionally commit to someone else you must first learn to recognize your own feelings. Then you can learn to discuss and resolve them openly.

Most men have difficulty accepting feedback given from a relative or friend. When somebody asks, "How are you?" men need to be able to say something other than "Fine." Once you are aware of your feelings, you can grow more comfortable communicating honestly with others. As I discussed in chapter 1, my office staff confronted me about my own Zelda Complex. Later, so did my children. Initially, I didn't want to listen. It was too painful. I had an impulsive, internal reaction and wanted to defend myself. But the more I listened, the more I was able to agree with them. It was not necessarily an easy thing to hear, yet I knew they were right. There was simply nothing to defend.

The first step, then, is to become aware of your own inner feelings. Rather than fear them, write about them; discuss them. Embrace them. Get to know your strengths and weaknesses. After you have done your own self-analysis, seek feedback from others whom you trust. That way, you will learn to appreciate it when someone who knows and cares about you gives you constructive feedback. Learn to answer honestly if someone asks, "Is there something wrong?" And most of all, listen when someone says, "You never listen anymore." Once we men realize that we can improve our lives far more by listening to and caring for ourselves and others, we will probably stop competing unnecessarily. It may just mean an end to warfare as we know it.

You will live your life secure in that you are no longer manipulated by what other people want you to do and be, and directed by your own inner desires.
—H. Stanley Judd

Odds are, you have been or will be in the midst of a Zelda Complex at some point in your life. What are you going to do? First of all, decide what you really want. There is no *one* right answer to that question. Your answer will be influenced by the stage you're in, combined with the complexities and length of the relationship. Frankly, at the advanced stages, the safest thing may be to exit the relationship, at least temporarily.

Distance and time away from the Zelda Complex do not cure it. However, they do give the relationship a needed reprieve. Unfortunately, people who find themselves in the advanced stages often have difficulty remaining away from each other. Zelda attained distance by hospitalizing herself. As a result, Scott was forced to take time away from her. The letters Scott and Zelda exchanged during the latter years are very insightful. There was a calm between them that never existed before. Yet they were separated for more than twelve years. Some time away is almost a requirement to heal from a Zelda Complex. It sounds almost paradoxical, but the truth is: to stay together, you must get away from one another! This is especially true if you are a woman in a relationship with a domineering male.

The traditional male has difficulty when his partner says, "We need to be away from each other." He cannot be in control if his partner is a hundred miles away. Unfortunately, many men interpret such distancing as a first step toward divorce. Occasionally they overreact because they see it as a threat. In the Zelda Complexes I've worked with, an honest letter describing what you are doing, and why, will often allay this fear of abandonment. If the separation is framed as an act of love, and a way to salvage the relationship, a hostile overreaction can usually be avoided. This assurance is best done in writing, even if a verbal explanation is given. A description of the motive—you are doing this to improve the relationship—will usually help. But it must be reinforced continually.

Jack and Sandra separated as a way of beginning to renegotiate their contract. Although the ultimate reconciliations did not lead to bliss, Jack and Sandra did reach an agreement on how to define their relationship. They eventually achieved a manageable level of closeness and proceeded with their lives together. Walt and David had long periods of separation. Some were simply a result of David's trips as a sales manager. Others resulted from recommendations made by their father. He intuitively thought it best that they distance occasionally.

Katie and Gary also went through several periods of separation. These resulted from Katie's hospitalizations, which were indirectly forced by Gary. This is not the kind of separation I encourage, however. In fact, I discouraged hospitalization. I am strongly against such separations because they imply "fault" and quickly become win-lose transactions. By agreeing to hospitalization, Katie indirectly identified herself as the problem in their marriage. She sacrificed her equity each time it occurred. I suggest that separations be of the no-fault variety, as a way of helping the relationship. If separation occurs because one partner is blaming the other, it will most likely be resented and ultimately rejected. Seen as a therapeutic intervention to help the relationship, however, separation will usually be respected.

Debbie, Sam, and Bob never separated, though I suggested it on multiple occasions. Debbie agreed to it. Sam agreed to it. Bob continually refused to cooperate. At one point when Sam attempted to distance herself from Bob, he hired several private investigators to find her. When they located her, Bob surprised her with a visit that led to yet another physical altercation. Once again, police were involved. Since this didn't occur in a local community, the reaction was different. Predictably, when the police began to manhandle Bob, Sam attacked them. As a result, both were arrested. They ultimately spent time in jail, and thousands of dollars in attorney fees. A simple period of separation would have been far less complex, and a lot less expensive.

To heal from the advanced stages of the Zelda Complex, distance is usually necessary. During the separation, examine your expectations and adjust them if necessary. It's also important to understand the contract you made at the beginning of the relationship. Changes have likely occurred since then that have not been incorporated into your current agreement. You may need to negotiate a new contract that is mutually agreeable to both partners. This agreement does not need to be acceptable to your parents, your therapist, or anyone else. It does not have to make sense to anyone else. It's *your* contract with *your* partner. The needs are yours. The relationship is yours. You and your partner are the ones who decide whether or not it's successful. If it meets your needs, it's successful.

Several years ago, I spoke at a conference attended by several hundred married couples. My topic was sexual relationships. The question I was asked most frequently was, "How often should couples have sexual intercourse?" My response was that it really didn't matter. Whether three times a day, three times a month, or three times a lifetime, frequency was not the issue. I suggested that the real question was what satisfied the people involved. As long as both were happy, nothing else mattered.

After my session, I remained in the auditorium to answer questions. One couple stood at the edge of the group shuffling their feet restlessly and looking in my direction. They never approached closely enough to speak, and I assumed they were waiting for a private moment. I made eye contact with them periodically, as an assurance that I wouldn't leave until we had spoken. Eventually, as the crowd thinned, they moved closer.

The husband was built like a six-foot-tall football. His small, almost pointed head was completely without hair. His thin, round shoulders sloped continuously to an apex at his belt line. There, his convex curve began to recede again, sloping gradually to uncommonly small feet. His head and feet were approximately the same size. His pale blue shirt was tucked tightly into gray high-water trousers. As he shuffled forward, his head kept rhythm with his pistonlike feet, moving in short, jerky, rapid-fire, movements.

His wife was frail in comparison. Her long brown hair was pulled behind her head and tucked into a small bun. She wore a long, sleeveless, navy blue dress, and black running shoes with short, white bobby socks rolled onto her ankles. As he waddled up to me, he held up three, short, stubby fingers of his left hand and smiled. I smiled back and held up three fingers of my own, nodding as if I understood what it meant.

"It's what you said," he grinned. "You were right."

I grinned back and swallowed uncomfortably. "Good. Great." I nodded my head while shaking his hand. "Which part did you agree with most?"

"All of it," he snorted. "You were absolutely right." He winked. "You know what I mean?"

"Sure." I nodded my head, not having a clue. "But I really don't know what you mean about this number three." I held up my three fingers.

"Sure you do, you snake." He punched me in the arm while chuckling. "You know about us. Somebody told you, didn't they?"

I smiled while shaking my head. "No, no. Nobody told me anything at all about you."

The man snorted while he interrupted me again. "It really don't matter if they did. The truth is . . . " He leaned over and jabbed me with his short, stubby finger. "We're as happy as two pigs in slop and we only had sex three times in thirty years, just like you said." He smiled while shaking his head and finally laughed out loud.

I gazed past him at his wife who was standing several steps behind and off to one side. She smiled shyly while crossing her arms and nodding in agreement. We made eye contact for a few seconds before I asked the inevitable question.

"Three kids?"

Without blinking or showing any emotion, she responded. "Two. The third time we just got carried away."

I looked back and forth at both of them, not knowing how to respond.

"And you're . . . um . . . you're . . . happy?" I asked. They both nodded affirmatively. "Okay," I nodded. "That's the real test."

> *So they were married—to be the more together—*
> *And found they were never again so much together.*
> *Divided by the morning tea,*
> *By the evening paper,*
> *By children and tradesmen's bills.*
>
> —Louis MacNeice, "Les Sylphides"

Jack and Sandra had proceeded with renegotiating their marital agreement. They had remained together, but were redefining their expectations. Walt and David had cooperated with their father's plan, though not necessarily respecting it. I had consulted with them on ten occasions at this point. They were confidently managing their relationship, but were not necessarily moving toward intimacy. Katie and Gary were deteriorating. The relationship was in precarious condition and seemed stuck. By this time, as he lost more and more control, Gary had resorted to violence on three occasions. They alternated between Stages Three and Four of the Zelda Complex. Katie appeared to be growing more awake and in control of her life, and it threatened Gary immensely.

The Bob/Debbie/Sam triangle was speeding out of control, beyond Stage Four. There seemed to be very little peace in this relationship. I had attempted on several occasions to help them negotiate a resolution. Tragically, they were incapable of doing so. Actually, all of these relationships are tragic. None of them reached anything near their potential.

As philosophers and writers have indicated throughout time, we all are at our best in a meaningful relationship. One philosopher said, "A good friendship is like a temporary state of grace." It promises happiness, excitement, and, at times, even nirvana. It forgives early mistakes. It keeps people together through difficult times. As a result, the soul is fed a magical elixir that actually promises more than it's able to deliver. There is a feeling of unity. Boundaries are lowered. Apathy disappears. One views the other as somehow special, or magical. Deep down inside, we all know that magic doesn't exist. But for a short time, we allow ourselves to be deluded.

The changes that follow are immeasurable. We begin to have imaginary conversations when our partners aren't present. We see them through our mind's eye and smile warmly. We become fixated with their special traits or the way they look. We grow anxious awaiting the next opportunity to embrace them, gaze into their eyes, or brush their hair away from their face. We begin to blend together at this point. We become one. Our energies become the same.

As seductive and refreshing as this state of grace may be, however, it's also frightening. We run from it. We dodge it. We sabotage it. For with this transient state there is the proportionate risk of lowering our defenses and letting our partners see us as we really are. And the most frightening possibility of all is, they may reject us.

This fuels the pattern that ultimately results in the Zelda Complex. Most of the work I've done in marital psychotherapy over the years is an attempt to understand these self-defeating patterns. They cause us to elude intimacy, slamming the door before we even begin to step through it. But the price of the pain, as well as the inherent risk, is worth the potential reward. For the alternative can be psychological and physical death.

In April 1995, 165 people died from the combustible mixture of fertilizer and diesel fuel. In 1940, F. Scott Fitzgerald died at the age of forty-four as the result of a similar mixture. Eight years later, Zelda died from the same cause. So have many others. On many occasions, they could have gotten out, but decided not to. Getting out would have been a better alternative. Many people in Stage Four need to get out of these relationships, unless they're willing to die for them.

To her credit, my own Zelda got out of the relationship without taking another step. It was to her benefit. We were both hurt deeply, but in the long run, dissolution benefited everyone. Fascinatingly enough, the last time I spoke to her she lied to me again. This time I laughed rather than winced. I had changed my expectations, and stepped outside the Zelda Complex.

CHECKLIST

Instructions: Grade your relationship in each of the following areas. Remember, grade yourself as a couple by averaging your individual grades together. For example, if you rate an A in one area and your partner rates a C, the overall grade would be a B.

Your Relationship GPA

_____ Self-confidence
_____ Communication
_____ Commitment
_____ Equity
_____ Investment
_____ Couple identity
_____ Self-esteem
_____ Conflict resolution
_____ Affection
_____ Compatibility

Zelda Complex GPA

For these factors that characterize the Zelda Complex, grade yourself again, using the same averaging method described above. These grades reflect your identification with each series of factors. The lower the grade, the more problems you (as a couple) experience with that set of factors. The higher the grade, the fewer problems experienced.

_____ Family background
_____ Achievement level
_____ Role playing
_____ Unrealistic expectations
_____ High risk

Scoring: For each A give yourself four points; for each B, three points; for each C, two points; for each D, one point; for each F, zero points. Total your points and divide by the amount listed. The grade your answer is closest to is your overall GPA. For example, if the total (after dividing) is 1.2, your overall GPA is a D; if the total is 1.7, your overall GPA is a C.

Your Relationship GPA

Number of As _____ x 4 = _____
Number of Bs _____ x 3 = _____
Number of Cs _____ x 2 = _____
Number of Ds _____ x 1 = _____
Number of Fs _____ x 0 = <u> 0 </u>
                    Total= _____ ÷ 10 = _____
                    Overall GPA= _____

Zelda Complex GPA

Number of As _____ x 4 = _____
Number of Bs _____ x 3 = _____
Number of Cs _____ x 2 = _____
Number of Ds _____ x 1 = _____
Number of Fs _____ x 0 = <u> 0 </u>
                    Total= _____ ÷ 5 = _____
                    Overall GPA=_____

JOURNAL SESSION

1. Examine your grades in both lists. List the areas that need work.

2. For those areas listed, write a definition beside each one. For example, what does "Commitment" mean to you? Examine your definition to see if it's realistic. If not, adjust it to fit your circumstances.

3. Determine what needs to be done to bring your relationship in line with your definition. At this point, it's usually helpful to discuss this material with your partner. From his or her point of view, you may already be moving toward the ideal you've defined. For example, is your relationship closer to your ideal now than it was at this time last year? If so, perhaps it is already improving and you simply need to speed up the process.

4. Brainstorm possible ways to improve your scores in the areas that need improvement. At first, list all solutions, no matter how bizarre they may seem. Later you can narrow them down to workable answers that fit your situation.

5. If, after brainstorming together, you find no workable solution for the present time, it may be better to move on to areas where more alternatives exist. Regardless, the understanding should be that when the situation can be improved, it will be.

Epilogue
THE ZELDA DESTINY

So Close
Yet so far away
We're living in a dream world, Girl
We're so close yet so far away.
— Daryl Hall and George Green "So Close"

In a 1936 magazine article, Scott Fitzgerald described himself as "a cracked pot." Scott said he was not good enough to be brought out for company, "but would do to hold crackers late at night or go into the ice box with leftovers." Scott vastly underestimated what he had contributed to society. Unfortunately, he also failed to predict what he still could have accomplished. Upon his death, he left an estate of only $10,000 to Zelda and their daughter. Princeton University declined to purchase his collective papers for $3,750, explaining they "had no obligation to squander money supporting the penniless widow of a second-rate, midwestern hack." Obviously, his position with the academic world in 1940 left much to be desired. Ultimately, however, his papers did arrive at Princeton and are now valued in a vastly different light.

At the time of his death, Scott had written nine books. Hundreds of copies were wasting away in Scribner's warehouse. None of his books were republished until a second printing of *The Last Tycoon* in 1945. That same year, Edmund Wilson edited and published *Crack-Up Essays*, and *The Great Gatsby* and *The Portable F. Scott Fitzgerald* came out in paperback. By 1951, virtually all of his titles had been republished. In 1953, Zelda's novel *Save Me the Waltz* was reissued. Penguin Books eventually republished *The Great Gatsby* in French, German, and Swedish. Since 1950 it has been translated into thirty-three languages, including Bengali, Hindi, Macedonian, Croatian, and Slovak. Additionally, there have been more than forty books and several thousand magazine articles written about Scott since 1950. Zelda's novel *Save Me The Waltz* has been translated into several languages as well. In 1991, Little, Brown and Company published Zelda's collected writings. And her life has been the subject of a movie as well as a biographical study.

F. Scott Fitzgerald's death was chronicled around the world. He died of a heart attack in Hollywood at the age of forty-four. He was described as "the voice of the lost generation." The lost generation did not include a large number of people. Yet his work described the lifestyles of a few people who experienced something from which we all can learn. Scott and others like him felt cheated, just as many Generation Xers feel cheated. They drank. They partied. They practiced free sex. And when they awoke they were prepared to do very little. A reporter once asked Scott what had become of the generation he wrote about in *This Side of Paradise*. His answer: was, "Some became brokers and threw themselves out of windows. Others became bankers and shot themselves. Still others became newspaper reporters, and a few became successful authors."

Scott had become a successful author. Though at his death he still had doubts. Scott still had not answered questions that plagued him throughout his lifetime. In many ways, he was to his generation what Kurt Cobain was to the generation lost today. Scott Fitzgerald made himself the voice of youth. It was the voice crying out in the darkness. During his own life, some people listened and then forgot. At his death, he didn't know whether his life had made the slightest impact. Scott was a product of his time in the same manner Kurt Cobain was a product of his. The turbulent twenties following World War I taught people they weren't as secure as they perhaps thought. Scott spoke with a brilliant and at times profound voice. It's not so much that he taught people with his writing, as it was that he encouraged them to think. That itself was an accomplishment.

We can easily speculate that Scott's late years were unhappy. Separation from Zelda, the sometimes estranged relationship with Scottie, and an unsuccessful tryst with Hollywood marked this period in his life. From all appearances, it would seem he was still in pursuit of other Zeldas. Zelda herself was sequestered somewhere between Montgomery, Alabama, and Highland Hospital. She simply refused to waltz any longer. Her withdrawal was so radical that it became her insanity, and ultimately her death.

The place is nothing, not even space, unless at its heart a figure stands.
—Amy Lowell

I have introduced many people during the course of this book. Obviously, the tales of the Fitzgeralds came from a variety of sources. The other people I have mentioned are equally real. Their identities have been altered to protect their privacy. But their lives and stories are as painfully real as mine. And probably yours.

One of the first people I introduced, and probably one of the first few people in whom I actually recognized the Zelda Complex, was the paramedic mentioned in chapter 1. As of this writing, he remains divorced from his own Zelda, but she attempted on several occasions to reenter his life. His last offer to assist her in getting psychological help was snubbed. He suggested that she enter psychotherapy and volunteered to pay for it. She responded that it was his problem and that he was the one who needed to see the shrink.

Unfortunately, he didn't accept her advice. He has now returned to and is living with his Zelda. At this point, it is difficult to understand whether his attraction is to her, or to the Zelda personality itself. This is something we are currently in the process of investigating. In all honesty, there simply are people attracted to the "rush" that accompanies the Zelda Complex. He may be one of them.

I introduced Jack and Sandra in chapter 3. We are fairly close friends, though I don't talk to them on a frequent basis. Both are absorbed in their careers. Jack is still very active in his business. Sandra is busy teaching school and active in several volunteer organizations. They have few visible difficulties at this time. They did renegotiate their misunderstandings and have modified their expectations of the relationship. To an outsider, it may seem bizarre. They have a great friendship, but in most ways lead lives of intimate emptiness.

Sandra still has a relationship with Charles. It's a fascinating relationship, and one I'm not sure how to describe. They are very involved emotionally, yet are not lovers in the physical sense. It is possible for paraplegics and quadriplegics to use injections to arouse and maintain an erection, yet this does not seem to be an interest for either of them. In many ways, their relationship fits the description Sandra offered to Jack. Charles is similar to one of her regular girlfriends. The relationship is safe for everyone.

I am convinced she and Jack will remain together, primarily because they have negotiated their expectations properly. As far as I can tell, Sandra has been honest about every aspect of her life. Jack has been at least consistent with what he has told Sandra and me. Yet factually, I know he has lied to each of us. At one time, he was actively involved in a sexual relationship with one of his employees. Sandra was quite aware of this relationship and had grown to accept it. It was not something they have mutually acknowledged, however.

During the course of therapy, I grew to realize that Sandra had an asexual nature. They adopted children, rather than have any of their own. Jack and Sandra's sex life had been so sporadic at times that it was almost nonexistent. The relationship she chose to have outside the marriage was asexual as well. Jack, on the other hand, did have a high sex drive. But it was repressed. It's my opinion that he channeled this energy into the compulsive work pattern that still preoccupies his life. Since they remained in Stage One, we were able to discuss most of these ideas openly. Jack acknowledged that he would like to have more of a sex life with Sandra, but was willing to accept the status quo. This became part of their new contract, and, furthermore, part of their waltz.

I have openly described the barracuda waltz as being an integral part of their relationship. We laugh about it at times. Jack even purchased a large painted portrait of a barracuda and placed it in their den. Sandra bought a 1971 Plymouth Barracuda. She fixed it up, painted it bright orange, and gave it to Jack for his fiftieth birthday. They have adopted the barracuda concept into the vocabulary of their lives. Once again, they have intellectualized their problems. This is the way they cope. If they made the changes we had discussed, they probably could have been a lot happier. But there were risks associated with those changes. What they do works for them. It continues to work because they've made their decisions consciously. They certainly have more control of their relationship. Jack and Sandra will likely remain in Stage One their entire lives. Because they have contracted and adjusted their expectations, they will not proceed into the advanced stages.

If you have it, you don't need to have anything else,
and if you don't have it, it doesn't much matter what else you have.
—Sir James M. Barrie

There are many men who, like Scott Fitzgerald, are attracted to Zeldas. Scott was seeking stimulation from his relationships, alcohol use, and lifestyle. His entire life was a search for proof that his existence transcended itself. His escapades as a child, the aborted attempts to prove himself in World War I, his writing—all were an attempt to prove his worth. Taming Zelda was a similar exercise. Unfortunately, it too ended in failure.

Zelda, on the other hand, provided stimulation. She searched for some calming reassurance and thought perhaps she had found it in Scott. This was ultimately the attraction that led her to marriage. All the men she had dated before were like herself. They were bold and brazen, often careless, and always carefree. Life was a risky venture for Zelda, and for anyone who loved her. The young pilots who crashed their planes on her behalf are indicative of that. The French pilot who risked his life for Zelda's love is evidence as well. And for Scott, the proof of risk was in his premature death.

Zelda was most capable in many ways. But she was least capable in the most important ones. Zelda truly didn't like Zelda. She never got to know herself, and this lack of awareness later resulted in mental illness. Her actual biological death occurred in 1948, but her psychological death occurred many years earlier. When her other attempts to be rescued failed, Zelda gave up. My own Zelda followed a similar pattern. When she finally believed that she could not control me, it was over. Within the brief period we were together, she left on five different occasions. But to her, leaving was simply one more part of the pattern. It was still part of the game.

In the Oklahoma City disaster, three elements led to the explosion. The first was fertilizer. The second was diesel fuel. The third was the trigger reaction from dynamite. All explosions have a simple interaction in common. The same is true with the Zelda Complex. With Zelda, the interactions were just individual components in the ultimately violent combustible response. To some mildly disturbed people, the sport of relationships is like a contest. But to members of the Zelda Complex it's not sport at all. It's an all-consuming obsessive-compulsive disorder. The reaction they are looking for is an explosion. The greater the explosion, the more they're satisfied. During our tryst, my Zelda was like a heroin addict looking for a fix. At times, the intensity was almost overwhelming. When she left for the last time, she went through a detox period. She had relapses and appeared at my door on multiple occasions, usually in an emotional frenzy. In one case, she had tantrums at my front door, thinking perhaps if she screamed loud and long enough, I would relent.

Regardless, she ultimately made it through detoxification and survived the withdrawal pains. Today, when we do have the occasion to speak, her emotions are flat. I think that she is fearful to relax with me at times. It's almost as if enjoying the most perfunctory of interactions could lead her to the compulsion again. I understand the process on an intellectual level. I cannot identify with it, but I do understand. Unfortunately, I think, the opposite is true for her and all Zeldas. They live it, but they don't understand it.

After all, when you come right down to it, how many people speak the same language even when they speak the same language?

—Russell Hoban

While preparing for this epilogue, I arranged a discussion with Walt and David's father. I explained what I was doing and asked him to assess how the brothers were getting along. I also asked him how the business had progressed. He told me the company was running about like he expected it to. It was profitable. They had been achieving all their goals. Productivity and quality were both climbing, and turmoil among employees was down. He gave a good assessment of corporate conditions, but a rather mundane one for his sons.

"They seem to get along on the outside," he suggested. "I guess they do give the appearance of cooperating. But I don't think there has been much change on the inside.

"I think it really is what you told me a long time ago. The boys are in a contest to see who I am going to favor. As you know, that's not something I ever wanted. I realize my mistakes as a parent. Truth is, I spent all my time building this company. I thought I was doing the right thing. Of course, their mother was just about as busy as I was. I never thought the boys would resent it. We figured we'd do the best we could to give them a future and secure them financially, and they'd grow up and be grateful.

We tried to make sure they wouldn't have to work seven days a week like we did. But honestly, if I had to do it again, there are some things I'd do differently.

"There is probably a happy medium somewhere. But I never could have lived with myself if I was a great father but a poor provider. So going to the other extreme wouldn't have solved the problem. If I could do it over again, I think I would've spent more time with them. I would've made an effort to let them both know that I did love them and that they had my approval.

"But I tell you what. If we hadn't done something we would have been in some deep mud today. Those boys were just about to wipe us all out. It's one thing to destroy your own life. But it's another to destroy your family, the business, and hundreds of other people. That's a little too much! It's like Samson who brought down the whole damn building just because he was pissed off at a few Philistines. Or that idiot who blew up the federal building in Oklahoma City because he had a bone to pick with ATF. That's what my boys were getting ready to do. Thank goodness it's nothing like that now!

"So, in answer to your question, they are a whole lot better in that respect. I'd like to see a lot more change, though. I hope that we can do that." Later in that conversation, he agreed to enter family counseling with Walt and David. This is something he had refused to do earlier.

I spoke to Walt and David individually as well. They each agreed with their father's assessment. The problems they have within the company are greatly diminished. They consider their working relationship the major problem at this point. The biggest conflict they have professionally is the presidency remaining on a rotating basis. I consulted with their father about the possibility of changing that, but had no success. He suggested that he would offer me the position on an honorary and gratuitous basis. I respectfully declined. Walt and David both got a good laugh out of the suggestion.

I also had a discussion with Walt and David about their personal relationship. It was something they didn't want to pursue. They felt, probably correctly, that if they reconciled with their father, their own relationship would improve as well. They felt their corporate relationship was manageable and their needs had been met.

Another couple mentioned in this book is the late Dan Broderick and his wife Betty. Betty's case has received national publicity on multiple occasions. It has also been the basis of several made-for-TV movies. The story of Dan and Betty is fodder for talk shows even to this day. The merits of the case have been, and will continue to be, debated. Betty is currently in prison. She has telephone contact with her children. Obviously, the money she received from Dan has been depleted. The financial legacy he left is exhausted. Dan and his wife lost their lives, and Betty lost her freedom. This seems a high price to pay for the Zelda Complex. Unfortunately, it will continue. There will be others.

> *Heav'n has no rage, like love to hatred turn'd*
> *Nor Hell a fury, like a woman scorn'd.*
> —William Congreve, *The Mourning Bride*

One of Zelda's responses to Scott was threatening to leave. After an argument she would pack an entire steamer trunk full of clothing, drag it out to the sidewalk, sit on it, and wait. The spot in which she would choose to wait was not on the bus line. She would not call a cab. No one would come riding on a stallion to rescue her. She just sat on the trunk and waited. After awhile, when she was sleepy or bored, she would return inside and go on with her life. Sara Murphy, a longtime friend of the Fitzgeralds, described, "One always knew when the Fitzgeralds had rowed; the trunk marked the night." Zelda's life was full of gestures like this. Usually, they would not be discussed afterwards.

Scott's early experience reflected a similar pattern. The first time he ever ate a family meal with the Sayres, a similar episode occurred. Zelda had been teasing Judge Sayre for quite some time. Finally, in exasperation, he grabbed a butcher knife and chased her around the table for ten minutes. Scott reported that no one looked up or even acted like anything extraordinary was occurring. After they tired, both she and her father sat down and the incident was never discussed.

Apparently, nor was Zelda's fascination with fire ever discussed. We know that Zelda set three fires. The fourth occasion occurred with the firemen when she was nine years old. The fifth time she died. No one can claim with factual certainty that Zelda set the fire that killed her. Yet this series of events cannot be coincidence. It is my belief that Zelda indirectly that took her own life.

But Zelda's behavior was not about fire, or suicide. It was about being rescued, and escaping the perceived pressures of her life. I don't believe that last, fatal fire was an overt suicide attempt. Although she did apparently have some premonition of death when she left Montgomery for the last time: She told her mother that she was not afraid to die. Zelda's mental condition was such that she probably could not have consciously chosen to end her life. She was still a little girl on the rooftop. She was still the young, gorgeous damsel hauling the trunk to the sidewalk. Zelda still fantasized that a knight, dressed as a fireman or pilot, would save her. She was the southern belle awaiting her rightful place on the plantation. She was still herself, and she was waiting to be rescued. Zelda had neither the strength nor the will to get out of the relationship with Scott and save her life. Apparently, neither did Betty Broderick. But other people have.

Since I began writing this epilogue, Katie has filed for divorce. The timing of this action was probably not coincidental. Her oldest child is now in college. Her second child is a senior in high school. Her sixteen-year-old son is very close to his father and would probably choose to live with him anyway. Gary does have temporary custody of the sixteen-year-old, but he visits Katie on a weekly basis. The last time we spoke, Katie told me she would not challenge for custody of her son.

Gary has not returned my phone calls. Katie says he blames me, the psychiatric hospitals, and her friends for the divorce. He is not accepting any responsibility himself, but that does not surprise either of us. She describes her life as not being easy since the separation. Gary has attempted to destroy her financially, but she doesn't regret her decision. She describes herself as beginning life anew. Her parents are puzzled, but supportive. Many of her friends think she has gone off the deep end. She says most people within the community treat her like a leper. Yet she remains committed to the divorce. At this point, negotiations are continuing. She hired an attorney from an entirely different county to represent her in the legal action. The case will not be heard in the county where Gary was elected district attorney. She understands that the financial settlement will likely be unfair, but says that her mental health is more important than money. During our last conversation, Katie suggested that even a large financial loss would be a small price to pay.

It will not be an easy journey for Katie. Since college, she has had virtually no life outside of marriage. There will be many lonely and desperate moments, but thus far, she has few doubts about her decision. It may be that Katie is making her own decision for the very first time in her life.

Any divorce is tragic. They are all painful. In some cases, however, one must choose between   marriage or health. At others, the decision is between a relationship or death.

Scott and Zelda stayed in their relationship and died as a result. Betty and Dan Broderick got out of their relationship, but never got over it. As a result, Dan gave up his life. Betty gave up her freedom. Their children gave up their parents, and their financial future. Sometimes getting out of a Zelda Complex is not enough. It must be gotten over as well. The consequences of holding on to negative feelings can be immense psychological pain. The consequences of holding on to the Zelda Complex can be fatal.

Katie is getting out of her marriage to Gary, and she feels it's the correct decision. At the same time, she is getting over the pain that accompanies such a relationship. Obviously, I don't know whether Gary is or not. Either way, getting out of the relationship, and getting over it, is vital for Katie. If you should decide to walk away from your Zelda Complex, it will be necessary for you to do the same.

After working with people such as Gary and Katie, I always ask myself if there was any way their relationship could have been saved. I believe the possibility always existed for them. But Gary invested his energy in making sure things remained as they were. His goal was that the status quo be perpetuated. Whatever his pain, it was manageable to him. Katie, on the other hand, was experiencing pain she considered impossible to endure any longer. As a result, her goal was to improve her life. As long as Gary and Katie remained stuck, each fixed on a different solution, there was no possibility of negotiating compromise. A negotiated dissolution seemed the wisest, although unfortunate, alternative. Apparently, Gary was unwilling to carry that out in a peaceful way. As a result, the court will be used to negotiate the end of their relationship. That, as well, is unfortunate. I doubt it was necessary.

Katie was never prone to the dramatic gestures of Zelda Fitzgerald. Though her lifestyle mirrored Zelda's in many ways, she was not one to pack her trunk and sit on the sidewalk. Fascinatingly enough, there was well-founded speculation that Gary had become involved with a trunk-packing Zelda after Katie filed for divorce. Because of the impending divorce procedures, he had attempted to keep it under the covers. Apparently, she was a friend both he and Katie knew socially. As the story goes, Gary and his Zelda became involved in a heated argument after a date.

His new Zelda responded to the disagreement by going to Gary's houseboat where they had been meeting and burning their nuptial bed, plus some of Gary's clothing. Immediately after starting the blaze, she called 911 to report the fire and then called Gary and Katie individually. They arrived at the scene shortly after the firemen to find Gary's new Zelda supervising the firemen as they put out the blaze. Apparently, she was arguing with one of the firemen about which chemical to spray on which part of the houseboat to extinguish the blaze. To hear about it was pretty amusing. But the reality is the tragedy of the whole situation. It would have been a much healthier course for Gary to negotiate his differences with Katie, and learn how to avoid Zelda relationships in the future.

> *The mystery of our existence is the connection*
> *between our faults and our misfortunes.*
>
> —Germaine de Stael

Sam was also prone to some of the dramatic gestures of Zelda Fitzgerald. I had been attempting to negotiate a new contract between her, Bob, and Debbie. At times we would make progress, and then someone, usually Sam, would sabotage it. On one occasion, it appeared we had made a breakthrough of some significance. After that particular session, I was feeling quite satisfied with myself, thinking perhaps we had deflated what could have been a problem of disastrous consequences. When I checked my voice mail several hours later, there was a revealing message left by Sam.

"Dr. Baucom," she began. I recognized her voice. "This is Sam Walters. I just want you to know you haven't won. I understand what you are trying to do and I want to assure you, sir, that you have not, and will not, win."

For the very first time, I realized that for Sam, and probably for Bob as well, this entire process was one big game. When I got the message off the recorder I turned to LA, and cursed.

"What's wrong?" she asked.

"I just can't believe it!" I exclaimed. "She thinks this is a contest. She actually thinks someone will win! To her, its like some stupid rehearsal for a little theater production. She just doesn't understand that this is real life. This is not a dress rehearsal!"

"Okay," LA began cautiously. "What's going on? What happened?"

"It just burns me up!" I responded sternly. "You know this whole case I've been working on with Sam and Bob and Debbie. It's been really tough. It's potentially a very explosive situation. I work like crazy to help these folks, and Sam acts like its a dress rehearsal for a play. She's got to have her hour of glory. And she thinks this is drama. She can't separate the theatrics from real life. But this is real. This is the only life she's got. This is the only relationship she's got. And its a mess! It's a big mess! But she's acting like if it doesn't work out right in rehearsal, she can go for another take. She just can't seem to get the idea that this is reality. And there is a big, big difference. Life is not a dress rehearsal. It's the only one you've got. Everything you do has consequences. Maybe Sam never figured that out. At least it appears that way. I'm not sure if Bob has figured it out either."

Up to this point, to the best of my knowledge, everything I've described is accurate. I can only speculate about what follows. I do know the events and their results, though not the precise order. I have spoken to various people, including police, emergency medical personnel, and family members. The information I have is fairly accurate, but I can only speculate in some instances.

I lost contact for several months with Bob and Sam. Sam was apparently in the fourth month of pregnancy when they decided to take a trip to Las Vegas. I heard through the grapevine, which included Debbie, that there had been physical altercations between the three of them. Sam had apparently gotten into a shouting match with a client who she thought was making a pass at Bob. Others speculated that Bob was already having an affair with the other woman when the cat fight occurred. Regardless, Bob and Sam decided to take a trip to Las Vegas.

They had apparently been at the new MGM Grand Hotel for two nights, gambling, drinking, and generally carousing. There is no way of knowing the actual details. Several people have speculated. They were leaving Caesar's Palace one evening, headed back to the Grand. They had rented a car and were driving down Las Vegas Boulevard. Bob was highly intoxicated, but not driving. The fight had begun at a blackjack table. The shouting and screaming had continued into the parking lot, as documented by Caesar's Palace employees and security personnel. They were escorted out of the casino and to their car. Speculation is that the argument continued in the car. Apparently, Bob reached over and grabbed the steering wheel, trying to take control of the car from Sam. They crossed into the oncoming lane and were struck by two other cars, and ended up colliding into a third. Neither of them were wearing seat belts. Sam was thrown from the car and run over by an oncoming vehicle. Her chest and skull were crushed and she was killed instantly. She was rushed to a nearby emergency room. They were unable to save her, or the unborn child.

Bob literally stumbled away from the accident. He was totally inebriated, but unscratched. Passengers in the other two cars were seriously injured and subsequently hospitalized. Bob escorted Sam's body home and she was buried with an elaborate funeral ceremony. He ended up facing criminal charges in Las Vegas, and civil suits from the other drivers and their insurance companies.

Bob began drinking excessively. After returning home from Las Vegas, he began complaining of back pain. It was a legitimate complaint, even though he was unscratched by the accident. A physician friend prescribed some painkillers. Certainly Bob suffered some physical trauma. Yet the worst trauma he suffered was the emotional trauma of losing Sam. It was also suggested by a mutual friend that he was excessively worried about the liability he faced back in Las Vegas. This same friend told me that Bob didn't know what he would do with the business in Sam's absence. He felt inadequate to run it alone, and felt she could not possibly be replaced by any other single person. That was probably quite accurate. I had called Bob on three occasions, but he didn't return my calls. I saw him at Sam's funeral, but he was in a daze.

It's one of those things that could be analyzed forever, and no one would understand it. Two weeks, to the day, after Sam's funeral, Bob didn't open the office. Instead, he stayed home drinking. That afternoon, he ended up at the cemetery. The coroner said he died from an overdose of painkillers mixed with alcohol. He left no note. He left no will. He left no instructions. He died on Samantha's grave. His body was found by a jogger the next morning. To me, it wasn't death by an overdose. It was death by the Zelda Complex. And I'm sure it won't be the last.

> *The long habit of living indisposeth us for dying.*
> —Thomas Browne, *Urn Burial*

If carried to its logical extreme, the Zelda Complex always results in death. The Brodericks demonstrated it. Zelda and Scott demonstrated it.

Now, Bob and Samantha have demonstrated it as well. Generally, if you don't get out of the Zelda Complex, death is the only conclusion at Stage Four. A better alternative, though it can be a sad one, is to step outside of the relationship and survive.

As I was working on the epilogue, I received a call on my nightly radio talk show. A female caller described her husband pulling a gun on her while he was intoxicated. She had left the relationship temporarily, but was considering going back. We discussed her case in detail. She's a very emotional young lady and was responding to the emotional pull of a recent letter that begged her return. This particular call received a variety of responses from my audience, including a moving reaction from a truck driver passing through town. You could tell by the sound of an idling truck engine in the background that he had pulled over to a pay phone to call in to the show.

"I used to do stuff like that to a woman I dated," he explained. "It's hard to describe what you feel as a man when you do something like that. You feel power. You can get kind of high off it. It ain't really a good feeling." He continued, "But I don't do stuff like that anymore. Once he loves you enough, he'll stop. But he has to *decide* he loves you enough to stop. That's the real thing."

Several calls later, a woman called in, encouraging the previous female to get out of the relationship. "I stayed in a marriage like that for twenty-eight years," she said. "I went through every kind of abuse you can imagine. He raped me. He beat me up. He cussed at me and hurt me every chance he got. Finally, I just gave up and attempted suicide. But, as if that wasn't bad enough, it took one more thing to wake me up. When I was in the hospital, he came to visit me. I was laying there, half dead. He came into the room and leaned over me. He pointed his finger and started cussing.

"'How could you do this to me? Do you realize what I've gone through since you've tried to kill yourself? How'm I supposed to eat? What am I supposed to cook?' He wasn't concerned about me one bit! All he cared about was what I could do for him. He was only worried about himself. Well, that did it! I finally decided to get out."

That same night, several men called in who had been at the receiving end of a toxic relationship. The Zelda Complex affects not only women; men suffer from it just as fiercely. So do children. In the advanced stages of the Zelda Complex, everyone becomes a victim. It always starts out benignly. People usually begin with good intentions. Yet ultimately, everyone suffers. My children suffered as a result of my own Zelda Complex. In fact, they still react emotionally to the thought of my Zelda. The mere mention of her name torments them.

My Zelda's favorite color was purple. Most of her clothes were in one shade or another of that color. One evening, my children came to me and explained a recent discovery. They had each experienced nightmares of a purple witch that lived downstairs in our house. In their dreams, the witch had attacked them and threatened to cut them up and eat them. They had these dreams independently of each other, and at different times. This eventually surfaced when one was talking about his nightmare and the other began finishing it. They had virtually the same dream. I let them discuss the dream without interruption and we later discussed some of its implications.

The dream was about my Zelda Complex. Though in their dream the purple witch didn't look like my Zelda, it did represent her. They still discuss the nightmare, but rarely initiate any conversation about my Zelda. More seriously, each of them told me that if she ever returned they would go live with their mother. This is the only time they have ever taken such an extreme stand, on any subject. It's probably a good thing they have. In spite of the pain my Zelda and I have both suffered, there were times I was tempted to try it again. That is the seductive power of the Complex. Today, my children are recovering well. They have full lives and I am very proud of them.

Financially, I am still paying for my Zelda Complex. Each time I realize that, I still feel a little bit of pain. As I explained to Sam countless times, there are always consequences for your behavior. Every action has consequences. And it all began with good intentions. Deep down, I know my own Zelda really did love me. But it was more than love. As with Zelda and Scott, and all the others I've described, it was far more than love, or even simple addiction. My Zelda Complex occurred because she became attached to someone she wanted to become. Then, when I began to succeed without her receiving the attention she wanted from the relationship, she simply could not handle it. She lost control and combustion resulted. It's likely that no one's life that is affected by such an experience will ever be the same. The implications continue long past the time the relationship ends.

If you do not tell the truth about yourself you cannot tell it about other people.

—Virginia Woolf

In the years since my own Zelda left, I have attempted to gain more understanding and clarity about the relationship. While working on this epilogue, I had a brief discussion with her. She was in a rare, insightful mood, and seemed willing to discuss the relationship honestly. I had asked if she was ever in love with me, or if she was just obsessed.

"I'm not sure I was in love," she replied, calmly. "I know I was addicted."

"What were you addicted to?" I asked sincerely.

"Oh, I don't know. You can be addicted to a lot of things." She attempted to skirt the issue. "I guess I was just addicted to being a recovering emotional freak. Maybe I was addicted to the uproar, the pain, and the craziness. Maybe I couldn't handle being normal. I don't think an addiction has to be to alcohol or drugs. It's nothing to brag about to say, 'I don't use alcohol or drugs.' Probably everyone has some addiction," she continued circuitously.

I finally tried to find out if I was following her. "It sounded like you had an addiction to affliction. Is that it?"

She laughed and nodded her head. "Maybe. It's still so hard for me to talk about it. I've got to go. I have to get back." She turned and walked up the stairs to her apartment. I turned around to walk away, then followed her retreat with my eyes.

"Hey," I called, "wait a minute. I want to ask you one more thing." I ran toward the stairwell. As she looked back I noticed she had tears in her eyes. "I'm sorry," I apologized. "I'm not trying to make this rough on you or anything. I've just got to know. Do you think you would have gone crazy if you hadn't left? Do you think you would have ended up institutionalized?"

"Take off your sunglasses," she said, attempting to smile. "You always complained I never looked at you when I talked to you. Now when I do, all I see is my reflection." I took off my sunglasses and smiled.

"I don't *think* I would have gone crazy." She hesitated and crossed her arms. "I was already on the way. I knew I was losing it. I knew I had to get out, but I didn't want to. And I wasn't sure when I left that I wouldn't try to come back. But I had to leave. And now I have to go."

She turned around and continued up the stairs. I chuckled, but sadly. I wondered if her new apartment was perfect. But I turned and walked away without asking or looking. One of Scott Fitzgerald's essay collections was called *The Note Books*. In it, he said, "There never was a good biography of a novelist. There couldn't be. He's too many people if he's any good." Scott and Zelda both were many people. They were extremely complicated and both made an impact on America that will never be lost. No one writer will ever again make the impact on society that F. Scott Fitzgerald did in his time. In a similar way, I can't think of any relationship that could ever replace that of the Fitzgeralds. The contributions they have made to literature will probably never be surmounted. My hope is that, as a result of the study of the Zelda Complex, the contributions they have made to humanity will be equally profound.

INDEX

243

destructive, 8, 39, 84, 86, 88, 94, 99-100, 115, 118, 151

divorce, 1, 6, 9, 11, 32-33, 38, 54, 74-76, 81-83, 89, 99, 116, 120, 128-29, 143-44, 157, 176, 179, 188, 194-195, 204, 213, 217, 233-34

do/do argument, 87-88, 92

double O, 86-87, 92

entitlement, 13-14, 29, 121, 161, 165, 167, 173

entrapment, 88, 99

equitability, 210-211

escape, 28-29, 31, 34, 45, 67, 74, 157, 180, 184-85, 198, 200

expectations, 13, 17, 32-33, 57, 68-69, 121, 127, 148, 157, 160-81, 186-87, 192, 196, 204, 211-12, 218, 220-22, 227-28

family background, 13, 192, 211-12, 222

friend, 2, 4-5, 35, 65, 70, 77, 82-83, 110, 122, 139, 161, 165-166, 169, 173-74, 177-78, 190, 216, 232, 234, 237

games, 35, 73, 83-84, 88, 104, 129, 144, 158-60, 183

high risk, 18, 211-12, 222

intellectualization, 84

intimacy, 10, 18, 51, 53-71, 76, 84, 115, 147, 158, 167, 181, 185, 208, 215, 220-21

investment, 51, 158, 189-90, 207, 209-11, 222

jealousy, 7, 14-15, 38, 69, 116, 118, 124-25, 134

marriage, 1-3, 6-7, 9-10, 14, 17, 27, 33, 37-38, 45, 56, 58, 63, 65, 67, 73, 77, 82, 84, 89-90, 93-94, 96, 99, 107, 115, 124, 129-30, 137, 139, 143-45, 148, 159, 164-68, 173-176, 179-81, 183-89, 191, 193-96, 199, 203, 205-6, 208, 214-15, 217, 228-29, 233-34, 238

mind reading, 85, 92

obsessive-compulsive, 53, 133-35, 137, 143, 146-49, 152, 205, 229

psychiatrist, 46, 85, 92, 96, 157, 166

psychotherapy, 9, 39, 51-52, 55, 64, 75-76, 78, 82, 107, 109, 122, 128, 137, 181-83, 192-93, 221, 227

role playing, 16, 212, 222

romance, 57, 179

Fitzgerald, F. Scott and Zelda, 4-5, 7-11, 13, 18, 20, 27-28, 30-32, 34-41, 45-47, 56-58, 60-62, 65-67, 69, 73, 75, 80, 86, 89, 93-96, 102, 104, 109, 113-17, 121, 123, 128, 130, 133-135, 140-141, 144, 148-49, 151, 157-58, 164, 166, 169, 180-82, 189-90, 203, 209, 211, 215, 217, 221, 225-26, 229, 232-34, 237, 239, 241